Herlands

Herlands

*Lessons From Societies Where
Women Make the Rules*

MEGHA MOHAN

1 3 5 7 9 10 8 6 4 2

Harvill, an imprint of Vintage, is part of the
Penguin Random House group of companies

Vintage, Penguin Random House UK, One Embassy Gardens,
8 Viaduct Gardens, London SW11 7BW

penguin.co.uk/vintage
global.penguinrandomhouse.com

First published by Harvill in 2026

Copyright © Megha Mohan 2026

The moral right of the author has been asserted

Penguin Random House values and supports copyright. Copyright fuels creativity, encourages diverse voices, promotes freedom of expression and supports a vibrant culture. Thank you for purchasing an authorised edition of this book and for respecting intellectual property laws by not reproducing, scanning or distributing any part of it by any means without permission. You are supporting authors and enabling Penguin Random House to continue to publish books for everyone. No part of this book may be used or reproduced in any manner for the purpose of training artificial intelligence technologies or systems. In accordance with Article 4(3) of the DSM Directive 2019/790, Penguin Random House expressly reserves this work from the text and data mining exception.

Set in 13.4/16pt Garamond MT Pro
Typeset by Six Red Marbles UK, Thetford, Norfolk
Printed and bound in Great Britain by Clays Ltd, Elcograf S.p.A.

The authorised representative in the EEA is Penguin Random House
Ireland, Morrison Chambers, 32 Nassau Street, Dublin D02 YH68

A CIP catalogue record for this book is available from the British Library

HB ISBN 9781787304772
TPB ISBN 9781787304789

Penguin Random House is committed to a sustainable future
for our business, our readers and our planet. This book is made
from Forest Stewardship Council® certified paper.

For the bridge-builders, the peacemakers
and the architects of community.

Contents

Author's Note		ix
Introduction		1
1	Herstory	17
	Australia, 30,000 BCE; Greece, 8th century BCE; China, 19th century	
2	The Queen and her Wives	49
	South Africa, 1800	
3	House of women	77
	Rio de Janeiro, Brazil, 1940	
4	The Evolution of Womyn's Lands	107
	United States, 1970s	
5	Oasis of Forgiveness	143
	El-Samaha, Egypt, 1998	
6	Villages for Single Women	173
	Kenya, 1990	
7	Girlboss Island – and a Club for Africa's Elite	193
	Fjärdskär, Finland, 2017; Lagos, Nigeria, 2021	
8	The Troll Feminism of Megalia	215
	South Korea, 2015	
9	The Babayagas and New Ground: Co-living in elderhood	249
	Paris, France, 2012; London, UK, 2016	

CONTENTS

10 The Nair Tharavad: Four Corners for Women   281
   India, 1800s

11 Lessons of Herlands   307

Acknowledgements   329
Notes   333

Author's Note

This book is the product of several years and hundreds of hours of research, interviews, writing and rewriting. The stories and descriptions of women-led societies in *Herlands* come from me personally visiting locations and/or speaking with multiple people who have and had direct access to them, sharing their stories as they remembered them. As much as possible, I've used direct quotes from recorded interviews, emails and texts. Every effort has been made to preserve the original language, tone and intent of the speakers. In some instances, quotations have been minimally edited for clarity without compromising their meaning. Throughout the book, I've aimed to standardise the spellings of non-English words, though many have multiple variations and readers from those regions may be more familiar with different versions.

All people interviewed have given their informed consent to be in this book, although some names and details have been changed to protect their identities, especially those who still live in private women-led spaces. The changed names are indicated by an asterisk (*).

To tell the stories of historical women's societies, I've used archival material, news clippings and secondary testimonies.

My goal is to share stories with balance that reflect the dignity and autonomy of people, as well as addressing the traumas they've experienced. There are some descriptions of physical and emotional abuse that readers may find upsetting.

AUTHOR'S NOTE

Australian First Nations people should be aware that Chapter 1 may contain knowledge passed on by deceased persons. I have attempted to convey some ancient First Nations laws, while trying to avoid the use of deceased people's names, due to the belief that it may disturb their spirits. I have also asked journalists I know from corresponding regions and identities to read and advise on sections of the book where I write about cultures that are not my own. While individual voices matter, no single person can speak for the full range of experiences that women live through. I hope readers come away from *Herlands* with a sense of the diversity and range of collective stories and narratives.

Introduction

Over a hundred years ago, my great-grandmother lived in a women's space – a community that centred women. She wasn't a radical, nor was she living in an experimental, alternative commune. This was just how her centuries-old matrilineal society functioned; it had been shaped by and for women, and sustained across generations.

I only learned about my ancestral women-led living space in southern India through a chance conversation with a distant family member, and I found myself wondering why this part of my family's history was spoken of so little. In trying to better understand my great-grandmother's life, I also began a search for current-day women-led spaces and societies around the world.

Yet when I told friends about my research, some were cautious.

What could such a space possibly teach a person who wants to live in an inclusive world? Today, not everyone needs the silos of women's spaces, some of my friends insisted. They didn't, nor did they know anyone who did.

It struck me then that a lot of people haven't been invited to think deeply about women's spaces, let alone know that they can experience them.

I began listening to the women who created and care for these communities, some of which have existed for several hundred years. I listened to the women who invited me into their private spaces and explained how they function and why they came to fruition.

What I found inside was powerful: across continents and civilisations, women-led communities have reshaped culture, reimagined economies, driven political change and fostered peace. They've provided refuge, resilience, and deeper connections to the land. However, they are by no means perfect societies. Not all of them offer women freedom or autonomy.

The more I explored, the more I became convinced that there was an urgent and layered story to be told about women-led spaces and societies. A story not just for women, but for anyone willing to learn from them.

So I asked new questions. Why are women's spaces so often overlooked? What knowledge and what wisdom are we missing out on when we choose to devalue and dismiss them?

A place for women

When you picture a women's space, what comes to mind?

Is it an imaginary place, like Themyscira, Wonder Woman's island? Or historic, like a suffragette meeting? A gathering where men are still somewhere on the periphery, like a girls' night out? A sports team?

I picture the world of *Herland*, a novel published in 1915 by the American writer Charlotte Perkins Gilman.[1]

The story starts with three unlikeable American men who hear rumours of a women-only country high in the mountains, hidden within an unnamed continent. They decide to go in search of it – explorers looking to 'discover' a society where people already live, like many discoverers before and after them. The men are all arrogant and tiresome, although you're definitely supposed to dislike Terry the most. He jokes about becoming the King of Ladyland, a less than subtle nod to his innate desire to dominate, evidenced later when he tries to rape one of the women. When the three men reach the settlement hidden within a plateau, they find a 2,000-year-old advanced social structure, free from fear and violence.

The country in *Herland* is meticulously organised: clean, efficient and harmonious. Forests are cared for, food is abundant and waste is managed sustainably. Even the 'jail' is a cosy room. Each woman may become a mother only once, via an asexual process, to prevent overpopulation.

Still, no woman is overburdened. Child-rearing is shared, spaces are designed for safety. There is no money, crime or worship of tradition.

I found the novel so fascinating that I encouraged two of my closest male friends to read it too. Alvaro and Alex were as interested in it as I was, and we found ourselves discussing whether a real-world version of the fictional Herland, a collaborative and functional country built by women, could ever take root in reality. Then I caught myself. There was a glaring omission that I was missing as a reader. Herlandian women were capable, athletic, strong and fearless. They were also all white.

Left out of the story

Herland may be a trailblazing imagining of what a country created by women could be, but it also offers an important accidental lesson. Advanced feminist ideals do not automatically include all women, and do not always align with anti-racist values.

In the novel, Gilman describes Indigenous people as 'savages'. In her academic life she went even further, arguing that white people were inherently superior.[2] While she believed in the capabilities and liberation of (white) women, she didn't feel this for other ethnicities. Her biographer writes that Gilman gave preference to racial hierarchy, stating, 'I am an Anglo-Saxon before everything.'[3] Like many who speak of equality, Gilman's feminism was selective and exclusionary, and there is no ambiguity that she held racist and supremacist views.

Acknowledging this makes the experience of reading *Herland* complicated. Still, I found the novel, in itself, thrilling. Generations of readers like myself have grappled with the complexity of dividing the message from the messenger, or the art from the artist. Could a reader admire writing as visionary as *Herland* while being repulsed by the racist views of its creator, I asked myself.

Then I had a video call with my cousin Tushanka – an educator for girls in India and an avid reader. As I was explaining the plot of *Herland*, Tushanka interrupted me.

'Sounds a lot like "Sultana's Dream",' she said, going on to describe a short story written by Bengali feminist Rokeya Sakhawat Hossain. 'Sultana's Dream' was published in 1905, a decade before *Herland*.

Tushanka and I smiled at each other. This was a topic we'd discussed a lot together: an idea seemingly originating from a woman of colour later appearing in a piece of work by someone from the global north, without proper acknowledgement or citation.

There's little way of confirming if Gilman knew of or had read 'Sultana's Dream' (which had been printed in an English-speaking magazine in India in 1905) and decided to borrow certain themes for a Western audience. But the parallels between 'Sultana's Dream' and her own *Herland* are there and they are evident.

'Sultana's Dream' imagines a women-led country called Ladyland (which is what Terry calls the unnamed women-led country in *Herland*). In 'Sultana's Dream', women move freely and men are hidden away behind murdahs – a reversal of the gender-seclusion practice of purdah. Ladyland is peaceful, clean, and powered by solar energy – a fringe concept in the early 1900s.

The women of 'Sultana's Dream' and *Herland* are engineers, teachers, farmers and scientists who keep their societies functional and free of combat. They are confident and free from the timidness that comes from fearing a predator. The message is clear: when women are undistracted by war and division, they innovate. Yet 'Sultana's Dream' wasn't embraced for its futuristic feminism at the time of publication, nor celebrated for the fact it was written by a woman living not only under patriarchal structures but also under British colonial rule. It was ahead of its time. Perhaps even ahead of our time.

These worlds, imagined by writers, offer us an escape from the male-centred power structures that dominate our lives.

In our world, no country has been built with women's security and comfort at the forefront. More than thirty countries have no laws addressing domestic abuse. Globally, a woman or girl is killed by someone in her own family every eleven minutes.[4] In the US, 81 per cent of women have experienced street harassment,[5] with transgender women experiencing disproportionate levels of abuse when outside.[6] The yanking away of women's rights in the country was especially in focus in 2017, when Donald Trump's first presidency gave employers the option to opt out of providing free birth control to millions of employees. Then access to abortion was removed at the federal level in 2022, when the US Supreme Court, with three judges handpicked by President Trump, overturned *Roe v. Wade*, the landmark decision which had protected national abortion rights since 1973. This shook many women, across all strata.

I learned this first-hand when an interview took an unpredictable turn. In November 2023, a year before the US election where Donald Trump would win a second term, I was filming a documentary about child marriage in Malawi with the former first lady Michelle Obama. I asked her if she thought that an issue like child marriage was something people watching our TV interview or seeing it on their social feeds would identify with. She gave me an answer that I wasn't expecting.

Taking a deep breath, she paused and said that she feared the rights of girls and women around the world were clearly under threat. Unprompted, she pointed to the rescindment of *Roe v. Wade*, adding, 'In the United States, we are dealing with a rollback in reproductive rights, things that people thought they could take for granted, things that my girls thought that they could take for granted – that they would have the choice over – their own reproductive health. That has been rolled back and a lot of it is because of the devaluation of women, the belief that women don't have choice and power over their own being.'[7]

Our exclusive interview was taking place in South Africa, following a field trip where the filmmaker Yousef Eldin and I had accompanied Obama – along with the philanthropist Melinda French Gates and international human rights lawyer Amal Clooney – to visit projects that explored the abuse of underage girls in Malawi. Obama, Clooney and French Gates had decided to join forces to amplify the rights of girls through a shared partnership. These were three influential and powerful women who were pooling their skill sets and resources to magnify attention on a cause. The top line issue was how to eradicate child marriage, but in reality that involved tackling multiple other challenges affecting girls and women.

What we saw in Malawi and South Africa was a range of social, economic and political barriers that actively blocked girls and women from progressing – issues including cultural expectation, poverty, gender-based violence and ageism. Addressing these challenges demanded a multifaceted approach, Obama, French Gates and Clooney told us – one that called for bold and creative legal, educational and health-based solutions. Equality was a long way away.

We are nowhere near the United Nations Sustainable Development Goal of achieving gender equality by 2030, and if we're going at the current rate, it will take more than 135 years for women to be represented equally in positions of leadership in the workplace. The World Economic Forum predicted that global gender parity could be achieved around the year 2158.[8] Others are even less optimistic, predicting we may not have equality for all women until around 2308.[9] Given these depressing statistics piled up against women, women's spaces have become essential lifeboats in choppy waters. A women-centred approach, modelled by women-led communities, is possibly the only way to accelerate equality.

In a world that is so hostile to us, it's unsurprising that women have created pockets for ourselves where we feel understood and safe. Places, both physical and online, where we can be vulnerable and feel the support of friendship and encouragement from other women who say, 'Yep, I know exactly what that feels like.'

Scratch the surface and you'll see that women's spaces exist all around us, anywhere in the world – often on the periphery of our lives. Some are obvious, transient gendered spaces; others are permanent, built to foster sustainable community. They've always been there. Their existence reveals the shortcomings of our society. Yet many still deny they are needed.

Ask around and you'll hear of worlds where women have always congregated without men. I learned that a friend of a friend had grown up in an Irish Traveller women-only squat that banned entry to all men, including male cats. In almost every place I have visited, there has been at least one women-only corner. I've met lesbian women in Burundi who built a home where they gather to love and have sex, away from their husbands. I've stretched my legs in a fenced-off garden near a tea plantation in Malawi, where girls meet for a 'radio club' and plot how to avoid early arranged marriage and to stay in school. I've spoken with women who are trying to set up a 'mommune' in the US, where young and single mothers share accommodation to alleviate financial pressures.

These parallel worlds, quietly healing the failures of the mainstream, are everywhere – the shadow governments cementing the potholes of societies that have let them down.

Worlds without men

I was interested in women's spaces long before I heard that they existed in my own ancestral home. The seed was planted when I was nineteen years old, in my second year of university and living as the only woman in a houseshare with five men, when I first read about much more desirable lodgings that had existed almost a thousand years earlier. I was transported to the 1200s, a time when Northern European women had two choices of submission: marriage or the convent. However,

INTRODUCTION

many pioneered a third way. They chose to live together in a beguinage.

A beguinage was a walled compound for financially independent women from all social backgrounds. These were the women who did not want a husband and did not want to be nuns – the ones who actively resisted the script of motherhood, wifehood and state-controlled worship. By the 1300s, hundreds of beguinages existed across Northern Europe.

The beguinage was a society that strictly excluded men, an almost thousand-year-old community that upended the expectations placed on women by our masculine societies. I felt bubbles of excitement, and so began my voyage to places where women thrive without men. It was the start of a curiosity that has lasted decades, and taken me around the world.

I stayed for hours at the Senate House and Maughan libraries in London, obsessively researching. I became fixated with the beguines, the women who lived in these communities. Their homes – the beguinages – ranged in size from fewer than a dozen women to several hundred. They sprang up in France, Belgium, Germany and the Netherlands. While they did have their lodgings donated to them by wealthy churchgoing families, they were not presided over or instructed by men from a church in the same way as nuns. The beguines were referred to by writers as the 'sœurs grises' (grey sisters), because of their humble grey tunics and head coverings.[10]

Unlike nuns, though, these women had to earn a living. Their jobs were diverse, ranging from weaving to childcare and even brewing beer. In the evenings, they were free to return to their all-women haven – behind the high walls and a lockable gate – and they could leave this lifestyle any time they chose.

The beguinages were leaderless, with no founder and no formal way of life.[11] They were urban single-sex phenomena, which produced writers like Mechthild of Magdeburg, Hadewijch, and Marguerite Porete – women who were accused of heresy and strongly criticised by wider society's patriarchal leaders.

I convinced my friend Rachael that we needed to catch a train from London to Bruges in Belgium and see a beguinage in person. I was sure that we were going to visit an ancient but advanced women-only civilisation – some kind of Pompeii of matrilineal preservation.

When Rachael and I entered the beguinage, we were both disappointed. We'd loved walking from the historic centre of Bruges, over the arched Wijngaard Bridge and through the gatehouse and into the beguinage, which had existed since 1245. It was beautiful, but not revolutionary. I didn't feel we had entered an alternative matriarchal dimension, a sci-fi alterworld, a Disneyland of historic feminism. Instead we found cobbled streets under pale steep-gabled A-frame houses around a central courtyard of lime and poplar trees. The collection of houses had separate sleeping quarters but communal indoor gathering, shared gardens and a church.

It was pretty and peaceful and dull. We couldn't visualise the sœurs grises who once lived in self-sufficient simplicity – as single women who had chosen a life away from marriage – in this women-only compound.

'Would you have lived here in the 1200s?' teenage-me asked teenage-Rachael as we sat on a bench to eat ice cream.

'Definitely not,' I recall teenage-Rachael replying. 'I went to an all-girls school. I absolutely would not spend the rest of my life in a beguinage.'

We left to find a bar.

That afternoon, we weren't curious about the mechanics of a beguinage. We didn't speak about it again that day. We didn't wonder how this women-only community had differed from societies that were set up and designed by men. We didn't talk about how the grey sisters had organised their money. (They shared their earnings.) Did this complex for women have a unique architectural design? (Yes – beguinages were arranged to prioritise communal space over private quarters.)[12] Were there other live-in communities consisting of just women? (Yes.) Did they exist in the present? (Yes.)

Although we didn't ask these questions over beer in Bruges, I began thinking about women's spaces more and more. Over the years, after dozens of women I knew sought shelter and strength in women-only communities – and after needing them myself – the topic was pushed to the front of my mind.

I mentally ran through all the gender-separate spaces I had visited as a tourist in my personal and professional life – from sleepovers to sports clubs and religious ceremonies to safe-houses. I questioned what point they had served, and still did serve, in my life as a woman. I started asking women around me about places they went to without men.

Stories started emerging from the shadows.

Architects from the margins

Over the past few years, there has been a recognisable uptick in the creation of spaces for women. Women-only hotels have popped up all over the world, including in Japan, Morocco, and Spain.[13] Google searches showed a 69 per cent increase in queries about women-only gyms between 2023 and 2024.[14] *Architecture Australia* magazine reported in 2023 that they were receiving more design briefs with requests to incorporate yarning circles into corporate buildings around the country.[15]

Yarning circles are often divided by gender, respecting traditional cultural protocols that honour the distinct roles, experiences, and ways of sharing held by men and women in First Nations communities. Often, women-only circles use a 'no language' method, inviting participants to share thoughts with few interruptions or questions asked. A woman is allowed to arrive at her own conclusions in her own time. Meanwhile, women-only scream clubs, where women meet in parks late at night to howl and release their frustrations, have popped up in Ireland and Australia.[16]

In this book, we will travel to women-only spaces – some centuries old, others more recent. We will explore villages, satellite clubs, secret societies, and women-led rituals that ban men. We will ask why they were created in the first place, and listen to the answers: the stories from the women around us, often side-lined in the margins.

We will travel across six continents. We will go to a rural hundred-acre womyn's land on fertile soil tucked behind sweetgum trees, where a community of lesbians live together, their identities unknown to some of their neighbours. We will learn how women tend to and care for the land, treating it like another living person in their community. We will visit an urban residence for older women, named in homage to a mythic witch who existed for her own pleasure. We will enter the sacred realm of a regal women's rainmaking ceremony. We will explore the rise and fall and reconfiguration of certain women-only spaces, from an island in the Baltic Sea to an explosive and controversial anonymous community in South Korea. We will learn from women peacekeepers who have often been left out of stories that favour war and violence. We will learn about the unique approaches of female governance, and how women have physically built and cultivated homes, community hubs, refuges and safe havens against a backdrop of danger.

This journey will also take us to my family's own women-led past — to a special place where my great-grandmother spent her childhood in South India in the early 1900s. Her unique community was led by women who didn't worry about marriage or union with a man to guarantee their security. It was a place where single and widowed women were protected by other women.

Matriliny is different to matriarchy. The latter is a social order where women have authority and power over a society. Matriliny, the system of inheritance where property is passed down from mother to daughter, is a form of security. A stable home is the foundation from which a woman can fully participate and thrive in society. It is an insurance policy designed by great-grandmothers to protect their descendants' futures. We will learn how centuries-old systems devised to protect women were undone by male-focused laws.

A new story

As a woman of colour, born in the global south,[17] mine is still not a face you often see as an authority in reportage, despite what some talk-show hosts may insist. A 2022 Pew Research Center report found that 76 per cent of US journalists are white,[18] a higher proportion than in the US workforce overall. It is worse in the UK, with the 2024 NCTJ *Diversity in Journalism* report showing that 88 per cent of journalists are white — again, a proportion not reflected by the country's labour force. The number of women journalists (41 per cent) is lower than the proportion of women working across the economy (48 per cent).[19]

It's a statistical truth that people do not want to hear from women. Analysis of data from over seventy-five countries by the United Nations Development Programme stated that, despite decades of progress, almost 90 per cent of men and women hold some sort of bias against women.[20] A large faction of people around the world still think that men make better leaders and men are better analysts. All genders are more likely to criticise, question and undermine a woman.

The news stories you see, therefore, are often filtered through a particular set of eyes, through people without the lived experience of the communities they are hoping to explain in the two and a half minutes of a TV report. If storytellers are homogenous, it's perhaps not surprising that the typical consumer of news is an older, educated man. Research from the Reuters Institute for the Study of Journalism and Harvard's Nieman Journalism Lab indicates that university-educated men, higher-educated individuals, and those with a strong political interest are more likely to actively engage with the news.[21]

Other audiences are more likely to disengage from the news, describing it as overwhelming, relentless and exhausting.[22] Women, especially, identify themselves as news avoiders. According to researchers, this behaviour often stems from a desire to conserve emotional energy and time, enabling them to better manage responsibilities at home and the caregiving expected of them.[23]

Is it possible to regain the trust of avoidant audiences with new kinds of storytellers?

In 2018, I became the BBC's first global gender and identity correspondent, with the brief to tell stories and elevate voices from gender-diverse and women-led communities and cultures who had been underserved by traditional Western media. It was a time when trust in traditional news organisations was already fragile, and social media was compounding these issues. This new role was a great opportunity to boost the voices of people who didn't feel represented in the news. A voice is nothing if it's not amplified.

I spoke with people who were actively working to elevate the voices of women and gender minorities. I went to women-led workshops and women's shelters. I met with transgender, non-binary and intersex people. I asked them how the traditional media was failing them and how a gender correspondent could best serve issues affecting their communities. The people I interviewed often told me that they were used to storytellers who were looking for soundbites to slot into news packages. They were tired of it.

A community is a curious concept. It's a word used by politicians, activists and storytellers to assign common values that a set of people may share – but in reality, a community of shared values isn't a magic bullet.

As we travel for this book, we will see that women's groups are nuanced. Women-led societies are not free of tension. They are not perfect and they are not inhabited by flawless people; they have their own challenges, conflicts and frustrations.

Many have confided in me that they worry about the harsh scrutiny so often directed at women – the tendency to dismiss or diminish women's stories and perspectives. Too often, women's experiences are picked apart rather than honoured. It's something I regularly discuss with other women storytellers. My friend the journalist Aina J. Khan and I have often spoken about how under-represented communities need an open, unjudging ear in order to tell their untold experiences.

Aina shared this quote with me by the poet Mary Rose O'Reilley:

Attention: deep listening. People are dying in spirit for lack of it. In academic culture most listening is critical listening. We tend to pay attention only long enough to develop a counterargument; we critique the student's or the colleague's ideas; we mentally grade and pigeonhole each other. In society at large, people often listen with an agenda, to sell or petition or seduce. Seldom is there a deep, openhearted, un-judging reception of the other. And so we all talk louder and more stridently and with a terrible desperation. By contrast, if someone truly listens to me, my spirit begins to expand.[24]

I invite you to read these stories of women-led societies with a spirit of openness and a willingness to listen. These are not just stories, but lived experiences. They have unfolded slowly, through dozens of hours of conversations, long drives, shared meals, emails, texts, video calls, walks and quiet companionship.

I hope the company of these women will offer you new ways to look at your own communities. I hope their experiences bring fresh perspectives on relationships, economic security, the nature of leadership, and what it means to care for the world and for one another. I hope these stories echo questions you've asked yourself or reveal insights you may not have yet considered.

Each community of women in this book has surprised me. I've found their experiences complex and nuanced. I've found myself empowered by their strength, angered by the injustices they have faced, energised by their imagination, challenged by preconceptions I had about them, and comforted by their resilience. I hope their stories resonate with you too.

I

Herstory

*Australia, 30,000 BCE; Greece,
8th century BCE; China, 19th century*

Our planet is a largely masculine programme. As of November 2025, only 28 countries have a woman serving as head of state and/or head of government. Meanwhile, 101 countries have never had a woman hold their highest executive leadership position.[1]

Before we travel together to current-day women-led societies around the world, let's first take a step back and look at the story of how earth has been designed for the comfort of men, and how women have always secretly gathered to resist this reality. In doing so, they have created their own forms of refuge, their own spiritual practices, their own governance and mediation, their own types of communication and economy. Let's look at history through a woman's perspective: what some feminists refer to as 'herstory'.

Since recorded time, in every part of the world, women have been denied the ability to gather without men or the ability to move freely. It even took centuries for women to be granted private and comfortable places to pee. While some argue that public restrooms, and who's allowed to be in men's and women's bathrooms, is an over-focused-on tinderbox of a subject, they are not a space women have always been allowed in at all.

In nineteenth-century Britain, for example, most public bathrooms were male-only, as it was accepted that only men needed to leave home for lengthy periods. Women had to plan shorter journeys or drink less water, all the time mindful of the limits of their bladders – their movements controlled by what some historians call the 'urinary leash'.[2] Working-class women, as always, were penalised further and had even less access to toilets than socially privileged women, who were sometimes permitted to use men's bathrooms in restaurants. In many ways, the urinary leash was a form of gender control. Women were tied to their homes; the outside world was an uncomfortable and hostile place.

At the same time, women weren't always free to seek comfort, nor vent, with each other. Women together, sharing knowledge and experience, were often seen as a threat. At one point, men were so suspicious about women-only gatherings that they banned them altogether. According to the Italian-American scholar Silvia Federici in her book *Witches, Witch-Hunting, and Women*, a proclamation was issued in 1547 England that prohibited women from meeting together 'to babble and talk' without men.[3] Women who ignored this were often accused of being a coven of witches, and punished by torture.

However, following the technological and economic growth of the Industrial Revolution, things changed in several countries. By the end of the nineteenth century and early twentieth century, formal spaces – women-only lodgings for factory workers, and hotels like the Martha Washington for middle-class female travellers – were common in cities across the US. They were still largely seen as a necessary compromise in a society that very much excluded women, and even as late as the 1960s several restaurants and bars hung signs reading 'No Unescorted Ladies Will Be Served', allowing women to eat only if accompanied by a man.[4] The Oak Room of the Plaza Hotel in New York City wouldn't allow women in during lunch hours so men could make business deals in peace. In 1969, feminist and writer Betty Friedan and fifteen of her female friends entered the Oak Room at lunchtime. *Time* magazine reported that they refused to move even when the waiters ignored them and removed the table. It was an act of defiance, and it worked. Within three months, the Oak Room changed its sixty-year-long men-only lunch policy.

But entry to the Oak Room was just the cherry on top. More important were the women-only spaces that started to appear as necessary places where women could go to escape harm. It was women who fought for and built safe spaces for other women, in a climate where violence against them was dismissed and largely ignored by the medical and legal sectors. There were versions of shelters in the 1960s in the US – including Rainbow Retreat in Phoenix, Arizona, and Haven House in Pasadena, California, helping battered women married to alcoholic men – as well as other informal versions in the global south, but it wasn't until 1971 that the world's first formal domestic violence shelter for women opened in England.

It started by accident, at Belmont Terrace in Chiswick, west London, when the feminist organisation Chiswick Women's Aid obtained a derelict house, with an outside toilet, from the council. They planned to use it as an office, a place to organise against rising food prices and Margaret Thatcher's plan to end free milk at school for children over seven years old.[5] It would be a space for administrative purposes – to arrange meetings and protests.[6] However, within days, a woman from an abusive home knocked on the door, seeking help, a place to escape. Co-founder Erin Pizzey did what was needed, and invited the woman to stay in the building until they could find her more permanent accommodation. According to the National Archives, word soon spread that there was a safe, women-only space in London. The office was quickly 'inundated' (according to a *Guardian* report from the time) with women and their children.[7]

After obtaining further grants, in 1973 the women moved to a fifteen-room, four-storey property with a garden. It was the start of a movement – a ray of light in the dark age story of domestic violence. Chiswick Women's Aid is now called Refuge and is one of the largest providers of women's shelters in the UK.

It's hard to overstate the radical achievement of creating a shelter for women at a time when marital rape was not criminalised in many parts of the world. In 1970 it was illegal only in a handful of countries – including Poland (which outlawed it in 1932) and Sweden (which outlawed it in 1965).

There was no standardised medical protocol for healthcare providers to spot patterns of abuse; a doctor would rarely enquire about a woman's bruises, and nor would a policeman. All fifty states in the US had a 'marital exemption' that allowed a husband to sexually assault his wife without fear of legal consequences, until the 1970s, after formal shelters were set up. The shift began in 1974, when Michigan and Delaware partially outlawed marital rape. In 1975 South Dakota and Nebraska implemented more comprehensive bans. Over the next two decades, other states followed suit. The nationwide criminalisation of marital rape was in place only by 1993. The legal precendent that criminalised marital rape in England and Wales was set in 1991. It was laid out explicitly under the Sexual Offences Act 2003.

Feminists battled to build spaces where they could ensure women could gather without the threat of male harassment, abuse or even opinion. In 2010, the Equality Act allowed UK women-only spaces to be enshrined into law, which in turn allowed service providers to run single-sex spaces like domestic violence shelters, fitness classes and changing rooms.[8] It could have been seen as a win for women, but there were deeply sensitive and painful conversations coming.

Look up current-day women-only spaces on English-speaking social media platforms and you'll be sucked into a haunted house of uneven corridors and broken mirrors that lead you directly to the front line of the so-called Gender Wars. The crux of the battle centres around the inclusion of transgender women – especially those who choose to self-identify without having gone through a medical transition – in women-only spaces like bathrooms, domestic violence shelters, sports teams and prisons.

Today, the wars have had gasoline poured on them by content creators, who often use sensitive conversations they have historically shown no interest in to rack up engagement and build their own brands. These creators almost always pose a seemingly simple proposition: if you want to talk about protected spaces for women, you must first define a woman. Yet any good-faith attempt at a definition seems to back almost everyone into a corner where a torrent of toxic tweets and abusive accusations are waiting to be flung at you.

The very question – 'what is a woman?' – inspires complex and emotional responses because the answer depends on whom you speak to.

One of the most nuanced discussions around this tripwire topic that I've seen was led by *Prospect* – a monthly magazine that focuses on current affairs, politics and general interest – in

2022.[9] The team took the question to a number of thinkers, including a biologist, a former Supreme Court judge, and a women's rights campaigner. The answers varied greatly.

Some argued that it came down to the dictionary definition, 'adult human female', and that womanhood has often meant a type of subjugation on the basis of sex, a reality that should not be ignored. Others insisted that a woman is anyone who defines themselves as an 'adult human female'.

The linguist Sarah Ogilvie pointed out that the definition of woman has been in flux for centuries, as culture has evolved. In Old English (spoken from around the year 450 to about 1100) a woman was a wifmann – a compound word where *wif* means 'woman' and *mann* means 'human'. *Wif/wyf* later evolved to the word 'wife' (a married woman).

Brenda Hale, a former president of the UK Supreme Court, pointed to the legal framework of womanhood as stated in the UK 2010 Equality Act – notably Section 11 and Section 212(1) – which protects men and women from discrimination on the basis of the protected characteristic of sex. A man is defined as a 'male of any age' and a woman as a 'female of any age'. Additionally, the UK 2004 Gender Recognition Act allowed adults to change their gender – with the clause Section 9(1) stating that a person's gender becomes their 'acquired gender' once they receive a full Gender Recognition Certificate. A person's legal sex therefore could change to match their acquired gender.

Then, in April 2025, the UK Supreme Court unanimously ruled in favour of the campaign group For Women Scotland in its legal challenge against the Scottish government. The group had contested the statutory guidance issued by Scottish ministers under the Gender Representation on Public Boards Act 2018. This guidance stated that a trans woman with a full

Gender Recognition Certificate (GRC) should be considered a woman for the purpose of achieving the 50 per cent gender representation target on public boards. For Women Scotland argued that this interpretation was unlawful. The Supreme Court agreed: the five justices concluded that sex-based protections should apply to individuals recorded as female at birth, and that holding a GRC alone does not guarantee trans women access to women-only spaces.[10] However, it remains uncertain how this decision will play out in practice, and how individual service providers across the UK will choose to implement the ruling.

The ruling added more eyes and internet clicks to a conversation that has lasted decades. Several academics and historians, including the American gender studies historian and professor Susan Stryker, have argued that it is reductive to narrow a woman to a definition based on her body – her biology – especially when Western feminism has historically excluded so many women, especially women of colour, because of their bodies.[11] African American women's rights leader Mary Church Terrell, for example, was said to have asked white feminists to ensure that the 19th Amendment, the right to vote, included all women. She was supposedly told in return that race was separate from women's rights, and they would not help. Black women in the US eventually got the vote in 1965, forty-five years after white American women.

And while questions over womanhood, biological sex and who is eligible to enter women's spaces have led to an endless cycle of debate in today's current online discourse, several communities have long welcomed gender-fluid individuals – including Two-Spirit individuals, a term used by some Indigenous North Americans – to women-led spaces. Although gender-fluid individuals have existed in Indigenous cultures for a long time, the term 'Two-Spirit' was only introduced in the 1990s, during the Third Annual Intertribal Native American, First Nations, Gay and Lesbian American Conference.

'The concept of Two-Spirit folks existed well before the arrival of European settlers on Turtle Island,' says Isabella Thurston on the Indigenous Foundation website. 'Indigenous individuals who identified as Two-Spirit folks were seen as gifted and honoured in their community because they carried two spirits with them, both male and female.'[12]

In 2020 I interviewed Geronimo, an Indigenous Two-Spirit individual who lives on a Navajo reservation in the US and uses he/him pronouns. He identifies as 'masculine-feminine', one of the Two-Spirit gender identities for his people (others include masculine-masculine, feminine-feminine and feminine-masculine). Geronimo told me that his Two-Spirit identity means that he is welcomed into Navajo sacred women's sites and women's ceremonies, something he is grateful for and doesn't ever take for granted. He explained that these sacred spaces are much more than places where women meet without men – they are spaces where women define the purpose of the wider community. But, aside from these details of his experience as a Two-Spirit person, Geronimo didn't want to speak on behalf of the women in his community.

The reality is that gender fluidity has been accepted in several cultures, especially in the global south, and over several centuries gender-fluid individuals and trans women have been quietly included in women's spaces.

Fa'afafine, which translates as 'in the manner of a woman', are people on the Pacific island of Samoa recorded male at birth who take on traditionally feminised roles within communities and families, including domestic and caregiving duties. Okule, which translates as 'like women', are transgender women in Lugbara of the Democratic Republic of Congo and Uganda. Okule have been included in sacred women's ceremonies and are valued for having a special connection to the spiritual realm. Similarly, the Zulu of South Africa have sangomas – healers (some who identify as transgender) who help with maternal healthcare.

Gatekeepers of history

We've all heard of the alpha wolf. Cultures everywhere often glorify a dominant male, fighting for control at the top of the pecking order and cementing the story of their ascent in the history books. Even the term 'alpha wolf' has become symbolic of masculine, authoritative leadership. In reality, though, there is rarely an alpha wolf in the wild. The term derives from the 1947 'Expressions Studies on Wolves' by Rudolph Schenkel, who looked at two packs of captive wolves that established a (male) alpha wolf and (female) bitch wolf. The hierarchy was then written about by American biologist David Mech in the 1970 bestseller *The Wolf: The Ecology and Behavior of an Endangered Species*. Wildlife biologists these days do not use the alpha term, and largely accept that wolves are community-based animals, where responsibility is divided amongst the adults.[13] Mech even started trying to convince his publisher to stop distributing the book – and they finally agreed in 2022. However, the term 'alpha wolf' has become common in everyday language, inviting an idea that in order to get things done you need a type of aggressive dominance. As humans, we seem to love the concept.

The more I spoke to women about women's spaces, and the more I learned about them, I kept coming back to one question. If sacred women's spaces have been integral to communities, why aren't they spoken about more in mainstream history?

There are two reasons for this. One, not many women from these communities have had a chance to write their stories, from their perspective, in textbooks. Stories often centre the actions of an aggressive alpha wolf and his army, from a very male-led point of view: destruction. This has been explored at length by the German academic and pioneer of matriarchal studies Heide Goettner-Abendroth, who says 'history always only begins with the establishment of classically patriarchal patterns: hierarchical social structures with dominant men at the top; a subordinate status for women and other population groups . . .'[14]

In her study *Matriarchal Societies of the Past and the Rise of Patriarchy*, Goettner-Abendroth argues that while egalitarian women-led societies have existed for centuries, they are rarely given significant attention by historians and writers. Community-building doesn't inspire the same excitement as community destruction. Community-building isn't as sexy to document as what she calls the 'Eternal War' – the concept that if we're not in a conflict, we're waiting to start one. Goettner-Abendroth says that the Eternal War dominates discourse.

A women's community, however, often organises around more society-centred values. An example is the matriarchal Khasi culture in India's north-eastern state of Meghalaya, where the clan mother is chosen for her ability to nurture and care for the people in her charge. Her skills in diplomacy and mediation play a key role in assessing her suitability to lead her community.

Similarly, Western reporting of the Tuareg people – nomadic groups that live in the vast space of the Sahara Desert – has often centred around drought and eruptions of intense violence between men. Less written about is that the Tuareg, who have existed since at least the fourth century CE, are a historic matrilineal community, traditionally organised according to a common female ancestor. Women didn't have their movements restricted, and chose to convene in the tents they weaved from goat hair. Lecturer and Tuareg expert Mustafa Bashir, from the University of Tripoli, told me that they were once called the 'mistresses of tents', and that historically these tents were mostly women-only spaces where women led discussions of the business concerning pastoral communities. Even today, the Tuareg drum on the tendé, an instrument exclusively played by women. The tendé is constructed of stretched goatskin and mortar, and the songs (which are generally lessons about leadership) are handed down from mother to daughter. Yet these are not stories that inspire as much attention.

Over the past decade, the growth of male armed militant groups in the Sahara has inflamed tensions amongst the pastoral communities, including the Tuareg. A news bulletin about the region will almost always focus its programming on this conflict – feeding into the Eternal War. But if they shifted the lens slightly, storytellers could just as easily give more prominence to the efforts made by women-centred communities to bring about peace in the region, just as the mistresses of tents did in the centuries before.

Women like Mouna Awata, a civil society leader from northern Mali, have made an effort to highlight these stories. In 2014, Mouna created a women-only building, the Case de la Paix (or Women's Peace Hut), in what UN Women told me is one of the most dangerous parts of northern Mali, at the southern edge of the Sahara. Using inspiration from the Tuareg women-led tents, around sixty women from different ethnic groups meet weekly to play Oware, a traditional and popular game in West Africa. At these games they discuss tensions in their communities, and the game breaks the ice as they talk through the daily stresses and pressures happening in their groups in a more informal manner. Mouna and her friends sometimes make arrangements to act as mediators between fighting male militants in their communities. The women of the peace hut act as a buffer between the men in their worlds, and the men generally seem to welcome this. These women are doing what they can to slowly change the dial in their troubled world.

The women of the Case de la Paix embody the Heide Goettner-Abendroth philosophy that women create spaces that do not romanticise violence. Destruction is not some distant filmic concept; it's an everyday reality. Instead of hiding from it, the women of the Case de la Paix have developed personal strategies to extinguish violence in their region and their communities, even as reportage focuses on the destruction.

The erasure of women's influence in society suggests a second possible reason we haven't heard of women-led spaces throughout history: we haven't been great at deciphering clues of their existence. In a society obsessed with the final say of Western researchers, we may be looking at history in all the wrong ways.

Genevieve von Petzinger is a paleoanthropologist with a TED Talk on mysterious ancient symbols that has more than 9 million views. She has spent more than 300 hours underground studying some of the oldest art in the world in caves across Europe. In her presentation, she shares how she encountered walls decorated with depictions of animals and genderless humans that are more than 10,000 years old. This cave art immediately got the attention of the media, but it was something else that intrigued von Petzinger. She found dozens of the same symbols on walls that were repeated across locations, countries and time periods. These included inverted triangles and circles, and some academics have wondered if they represent womanhood – an inverted triangle being a vulva and a circle a gathering of women. Genevieve von Petzinger won't commit to a definitive answer on this. 'It's interesting that it was predominantly male archaeologists doing this work early on, and there were a whole lot of vulvas being identified everywhere,' she told *New Scientist* in 2016, 'but then again, many cultures do place importance on fertility.'[15]

Other archaeologists have been more convinced that women were leaving us signs in early art. Professor emeritus of anthropology at Pennsylvania State University, Dean Snow, who studied caves containing artwork from the Stone Age, said that 75 per cent of the handprints were those of women. Women were documenting life, carving and drawing the communities around them.

In Australia too, First Nations people have imprinted their stories into their land in petroglyphs (rock engravings) and pictographs (drawings using pigment) at more than 100,000 sites. Fewer than 10 per cent of the sites have been opened to people outside First Nations communities, and they have long histories. Engravings found in the Olary region of South Australia are carbon-dated to be around 30,000 years old, although some First Nations women have told me there are other engravings that are even older.

Murujuga, at the Burrup Peninsula in Western Australia, is home to over a million petroglyphs. I've been told by the Murujuga Aboriginal Corporation that there are examples of rock art here that clearly show women gathering in groups. A traditional elder woman of Burrup confirmed that they will not allow the images of ancient women-only gatherings to be viewed or photographed by the general public. She did say, though, that I shouldn't just be looking for physical examples of women-spaces.

'Listen to the stories,' she said. 'Ours are letters from the past.'

A sacred place for women, Australia, 30,000 BCE

Australia's First Nations cultures have one of the earliest known traditions of women gathering without men. Speaking openly about these gatherings with outsiders is considered taboo, and I am deeply grateful to the First Nations women who, over the course of a year, entrusted me with their experiences in these sacred spaces.

First Nations communities have long upheld distinct gendered traditions, with separate spaces for sharing history, social practices, and ceremonies. These are known as Women's Business and Men's Business. The practices are unique, vary between regions and groups, and symbolise a sophisticated form of connection between people and their land. Communities call themselves 'mobs' and have their own teachings and oral stories – which they share on sacred ceremonial land. Men are not told what happens in Women's Business, and women do not enter men's sacred sites or partake in Men's Business.

The Arrernte people are one of more than 500 communities representing Australia's First Nations populations, and have been on the Australian continent for at least 30,000 years, making them one of the oldest civilisations in the world. They are said to have originated from the African continent over 75,000 years ago.

Women from the Arrernte mob, from the heart of Australia, spoke with me at length –the first time they had done so with a journalist outside their community – about the practice of how girls are introduced to women's space. I was especially grateful to speak with Arrernte woman Jody Kopp, of the Central Land Council – who is based in one of Australia's most remote and inaccessible areas, in the country's north-west heartland. Jody told me about the long history of Arrernte women and women's space, starting with the recent example of her granddaughter Oleiana's introduction to sacred land.

When Oleiana could no longer be called a baby, it was time for her to be introduced to the sacred women's place her Nana Jody and aunties call Country. They drove hours and hours inland into Bush – into Country – from their homes in the city. And then they reached it.

It's a place that is unmarked and unspoiled, unknown to Australia's wider, and white, population. A stranger may think it beautiful and rugged – a typical landscape in a country of beautiful, rugged landscapes – but that day, as ever, its magnificence made Oleiana's family shiver. This place is their Country, first introduced to them by their grandmothers, who were introduced to it by theirs, and theirs before. This is a place where Oleiana's female ancestors convened without men for thousands and thousands of years. They call the stories passed down in women's sacred sites 'Grandmother's

Law'. Women's Country is perhaps the oldest women-only space in our planet's history.

Australia's First Nations people are spiritually connected to their lands and waterways, or Country. So much more than a physical location, Country is a sophisticated and complex concept that links landscape to customs; spiritual and ancestral legacy to identity, family and gender. Country has sacred sites, which can be vast vistas and waterfalls or a singular rock or ancient tree, where people meet to exchange cultural knowledge passed on through the generations. These sites are said to be sacred as they are inhabited by the deceased spirits of direct ancestors.

Oleiana's family are custodians of lands in Mparntwe (known by Westerners as Alice Springs) in the Northern Territory. It was muggy and overcast the day Oleiana was introduced to the sacred space, but her grandmother Jody wasn't worried. Jody knew what was waiting for Oleiana. As they reached the large waterfall bordered by sand, the toddler became quiet, taking in her surroundings. Her grandmother could see that Country was already calling to her. Jody gently put Oleiana down on the sand and told her to introduce herself.

'I told her, "Pick up the sand and say, *I'm Oleiana*,"' Jody shared with me. As her granddaughter obeyed, Jody felt relieved. She had taken her first granddaughter through this rite of passage, one that generations of women in her family had observed. Oleiana had paid her respect to Country.

Country knows her, Jody thought.

Then something happened that Jody's daughter, Oleiana's aunt Armani, described as 'really freaky'.

'After Oleiana did that, the biggest gust of wind came right through and swept the whole land,' she told me. The sky cleared and the water glistened, as if it was acknowledging the new little spirit in the family. 'It was saying "come in for a swim". It was welcoming my brother's first daughter. Magic.'

Jody was not surprised. She knew Country would embrace Oleiana as it had her and her daughters before. 'Country knows that she belongs here and she belongs to all of us. It's Women's Business. Women's Business guides girls into womanhood and prepares them to play the same role for the next generation of young girls,' Jody added. 'One day Oleiana will do the same for her granddaughter.'

Jody Kopp and her daughter Armani Francois are part of the Message Sticks working group in Strong Women for Healthy Country, a network of over 300 Indigenous women from across the Northern Territory and beyond, who connect to discuss issues impacting First Nations women. They have committed to caring for the land and the community.

Message sticks are pieces of wood with ornate images that signify news of anything from peace and unity between communities to tension and environmental disaster. They are a traditional part of First Nations culture and were in effect early newspapers, carried by messengers over long distances to deliver news between different communities. These days, Jody and Armani meet with other First Nations women over a video call to share their news: part of their online Message Stick community.

An important topic is the preservation of sacred women's sites, where communities of women gather and discuss anything from fertility and health to land management. Often, discussions of everyday business develop into sharing ancient stories passed on through a line of ancestors across thousands of years, connecting women to their grandmothers.

One such story is that of the Seven Sisters, an epic tale that details the journey of a group of young women through the earth until they settled as a cluster of stars in the sky. The details differ depending on which First Nations language group you speak with, but the tale largely involves the sisters being chased by an overeager male suitor through the earth and sky. Jody was reluctant to tell me details and I didn't push her. But she did tell me that the story incorporates knowledge of geography, geology, biology and astronomy, and is fully known only by First Nations female elders. Many feel the story is a symbol of sisterhood, resilience and independence.

First Nations women can point to the Seven Sisters in the sky, and so can astronomers, who call the cluster Pleiades ('Seven Sisters' in Ancient Greek). But scientists rarely mention Australia's First Nations women when talking about these stars. Instead they attribute the story behind the stars to the Ancient Greeks, whose civilisation emerged tens of thousands of years after First Nations Australians – and is widely accepted as the cradle of the Western world.

The Greek story centres around the seven daughters of the Titan Atlas being pursued by the huntsman Orion. He followed the women through earth and eventually the heavens, where they now live as stars. The myth goes that Orion continues to chase the sisters across the night sky – a story almost identical to the one shared in Australia's women's circles. Of course, there's no research that confirms that the thinkers of Ancient Greece knew about the Seven Sisters story of First Nations Australia and deliberately avoided crediting them. Just like there's no evidence that the American writer Charlotte Perkins Gilman knew about Rokeya Sakhawat Hossain's Ladyland. Yet, what a coincidence.

The reputation of Spartan women, Ancient Greece, 8th century BCE

Southeast Europe from around the eighth century BCE (the time of the poet Homer) to around the fifth century CE (the decline of the Roman Empire) fascinates mainstream historians, and understandably so. The people of Ancient Greece gave us inventions like the alarm clock and plumbing, the theatre, the Olympics, and the mechanics of democracy – an organised political process. What they didn't give us, though, are women's rights.

The men of Athens could choose their leaders through a voting system, a democratic process. Women in the city had no citizenship and virtually no political say of any kind. Middle-class women were largely confined to the women-only quarters within their homes, in the gynaeceum. There was also the andron, the most grand room in the house, where all-male social gatherings called symposia were held. Any women allowed at symposia were generally hired by the men for entertainment.[16]

Pottery from that time period – now on display at galleries like the Louvre in Paris – depicts life inside a gynaeceum, featuring well-dressed Athenian women engaged in static domestic duties. They sit around, holding children or weaving. It wasn't this way everywhere though.

The women of Sparta, a warrior society in Ancient Greece, seem to have had much more independence, according to the limited sources from the time. The Greek philosopher Aristotle, accustomed to the women of Athens, criticised the confidence of Sparta's women in his thesis *Politics*, and said that their lack of deference to their husbands would be the downfall of their society. Spartan women were also allowed to own property and make business deals.

Spartan society was in some aspects divided by gender. For example, Spartan boys were sent away to study at the agoge (the educational system that trained them in the art of war). According to Professor Sarah B. Pomeroy, who wrote the book *Spartan Women*, girls remained at home but still received an education. They married later than Athenian women and a wife wouldn't live with her husband until he turned thirty, affording her more time to spend with women of her own age. The Spartan male poet Alcman wrote about Spartan women-only choirs and running races (where the crowd knew them by name), indicating that Spartan women thrived in society within their women-only spaces.[17]

While Sparta controlled over 800 square kilometres of territory, and its men and women would go on to enjoy a historical reputation for warrior dominance, it was women from another part of Ancient Greece who are better known for creating women-only communities. Lesbos, a small island in the eastern part of the Aegean Sea, is thought to have been home to some of the most famous all-women communities in Ancient Greece. It was also the birthplace of one of the best-known women of the time, the poet Sappho.

Sappho was born to an aristocratic family around 620 BCE, and her poems depict a clear, unambiguous longing for other women:

> I would much prefer to see the lovely
> way she walks and the radiant glance of her face
> than the war-chariots of the Lydians or
> their foot soldiers in arms.[18]

The poet has given us the current adjectives to depict woman-on-woman attraction with words like 'sapphic' and 'lesbian', a nod to Lesbos. Very little can be proved about Sappho outside her own writing, and academics argue over its meaning, but it is widely believed that she ran an artistic school for unmarried women that focused on them expressing their desires through poetry and literature.

Several lesbian communities have run with this theory and created their own Sappho-inspired women-only spaces. In the early 1900s, the openly lesbian writer Natalie Clifford Barney was so inspired by the idea of Sappho's women-only academy in Lesbos that she opened up a series of women-only intellectual gatherings at her home in Paris.

This was a time where women's rights were gaining steam in France. As literacy rates among women rose, magazines and journals aimed at female readers, known as the 'presse féminine', also grew in popularity. Women were writing their own stories, and Barney wanted to create a world where they could tell them. Her gatherings were a republic, with a constitution set by women. As scholar Dr H. J. E. Champion writes in her study 'Remembering Sappho': 'In a reappropriation of a traditional "nation", as one uniting citizens within a "common fatherland", emulations of Sappho united women writers under some form of "common motherland", with the poet as the "founding-mother".'

Barney called the women-only nation in her living room L'Académie des Femmes and the weekly gathering attracted influential writers like Gertrude Stein and Colette. (In an unconnected but interesting titbit, the latter is credited with personally casting the then-unknown actress Audrey Hepburn in a Broadway adaptation of her novella *Gigi*.)

These women-only Sappho-inspired spaces gave women

artists a community that would support their creative spirit: the ultimate form of rebellion in a world that did not want to hear what they had to say. And it was in another rebellion – one that wasn't born in Europe, but in rural nineteenth-century China, over 4,000 miles from Athens and 5,000 miles from Paris – that women had found an intriguing way to communicate without the knowledge of men.

Nüshu: a secret language for women, China, 19th century

More than 200 years ago, women in the landlocked Hunan Province of South Central China invented a language that men could not understand. They used it to communicate with each other in a society and time where they had little value – and they either destroyed their texts before they died or were buried with them. Back then, Chinese women were not permitted to read or write, and they followed the 'Three Obediences': to obey their fathers during childhood, their husbands during marriage, and their sons during widowhood. Women were also restricted physically – confined to the home with their toes curled and feet bound tightly by bandages in order to create a tiny three-inch lotus shape that men were said to find attractive.

It's not clear how or even when the secret of Nüshu (which translates as 'women's writing') was first discovered by men. Researchers say it was at the start of China's Cultural Revolution, in 1966, when the raid on an elderly woman's home revealed a vast amount of writing in a language no one could read. When the Chinese Communist Party decoded the text, they decided that the writing represented a past that China was trying to move on from, and the artefacts were destroyed.[19] The language became known as 'witches' script'.

Even without the discovery of the mysterious elderly woman's papers, the secret might have been revealed by a man named Zhou Shuoyi, who had been looking into the language since the 1950s after his aunt had mentioned it. In an interview with the *China Daily* newspaper in 2004, Zhou stated that he had been forced to burn his research during the Cultural Revolution and had been sent to a labour camp. In 2003, he authored the first Nüshu dictionary, and is widely credited for bringing a deeper understanding of the language to a mainstream audience.

It was in 1982 that Nüshu was finally pushed into the spotlight – when a young (male) Chinese academic named Gong Zhebin found a tranche of Nüshu writing in the village of Yao, in Jianghua County, the southernmost margin of China. The script was discreetly shared in the folds of handkerchiefs or handmade fans, the delicate, small text evading the wider gaze. The villagers told him that this was a language for women, rumoured to have been invented by a concubine to secretly talk with her sisters in another village. He was advised to head to Jiangyong, a remote county where he could find more.

Gong presented his findings to the Chinese scholastic community, and they received excited attention, quickly reaching international academic ears. Soon researchers from around the world were heading to the river valleys of Hunan – notably Jiangyong County, where most of the writing was found – in search of more texts that spoke of women's solidarity and community. According to UNESCO, one of the best-known Nüshu artefacts is a bronze coin dating to the mid-nineteenth century.[20] On it is inscribed, 'all the women in the world are members of the same family'.

While the majority of Nüshu writing found is from the nineteenth century, some experts believe it dates way back to the Song dynasty (960–1279 CE). During that time, mothers – illiterate in the standard Chinese that men were taught at school – were teaching their daughters a language invented by and for women. The daughters then gathered with their friends, in the rooms at the top of the house, away from men, and practised Nüshu with each other. The friends who created this bond and exchanged Nüshu were 'sworn sisters'.

Within the texts of Nüshu, in the form of letters and poems, the women spoke openly about their frustrations. One example is the verse embroidered on a blue cloth found by Gong Zhebin in 1982, now on display at the Women's Culture Museum of Shaanxi Normal University:

> Sitting alone in an empty room, I'm thinking of nothing
> But writing a piece to lament my misery
> I was born a female of withered fate
> Who had no father to take care of me from the age of three
> When I turned twenty
> It was my two brothers who presided over my marriage
> Five or six years after I married
> I had borne neither a daughter nor a son, a constant worry
> My parents-in-law worked out bringing in a second woman
> Having her company to rely on, I was happy
> For four years, our lives went well
> But someone must have said something to change her heart
> And she ran away
> Which made us, husband and wife, angry and dismayed[21]

In this Nüshu text, the writer shares not only her pain under patriarchal life, but the development of a surprising alliance with the woman having an affair with her husband (his concubine) – a bond in the most unlikely of places, between women who shared a man and the restrictions of womanhood. It's a common theme in Nüshu writing: despair and sorority.

'Nüshu was an underground sisterhood,' film-maker Violet Du Feng told me over a video call in 2024. 'It was this secret space where women shared their vulnerability, and then built a sense of strength, solidarity and survival. Now it's about something else. Profit.'

In 2022, Violet Du Feng and her cousin Qing Zhao co-directed a moving Peabody-nominated documentary called *Hidden Letters*, which follows the lives of two millennial women with a passion for Nüshu. These women still experience a form of gender-based discrimination that connects them with women who wrote the original Nüshu texts they love. There is a clear and vivid cord that unites the women whose feet were bound, in the rural valleys of Hunan Province, to these women living in modern cities, who have the freedom to choose their careers and partners but are still undermined by a society that doesn't see them as equal.

The documentary shows how, in present-day China, Nüshu has been commodified for the masses. It's on T-shirts and pens, apps and chopsticks. Vampiric marketeers are ready to exploit the script to sell products. In one scene, two men are keen to brand supermarket-sold potatoes with Nüshu script. A woman in the meeting pushes back, insisting that this is against the spirit of Nüshu, which was always meant to be a private expression between women. Her male colleague tells her to expand her mind and think outside the box. They are keen to jump on the commercial potential of Nüshu. The woman is silent.

It's an infuriating scene, and the viewer is left frustrated that this once sacred, necessary, women-only space is now contaminated by profit-driven exploitation.

And, if you are in any doubt that is what we're meant to conclude, we're told this fact directly by He Yanxin, a small woman with papery skin, short white hair pinned away from her face, and a rebellious, unimpressed expression. He Yanxin was born in 1939 in Hunan Province, where she still lives. She is one of the last Nüshu masters, but hid her ability to write perfect Nüshu for decades after its existence became known by the world in 1982. She later helped Zhou Shuoyi with the Nüshu dictionary in 2003. Since the release of *Hidden Letters* she has refused interviews. Her Nüshu is not for sale.

'Our letters to the sisters were meant to share our sufferings in secret,' she says in *Hidden Letters*, gently confirming that her women-only space isn't open for commercial gain. 'Now it's so public that everyone knows.'

Nüshu was a type of self-created rebellion for women who had little to no autonomy in society. Without Nüshu, their lives could have gone unnoticed in a wall of history written by men. Men, who were taught to write, could document their stories, their perspectives. Nüshu created a culture and a voice, without the looming presence of male dominance.

However, not all women-only spaces have been created by women in order to achieve this intentional separation from men. Some have been designed by male-led societies to further seclude and isolate women, giving them no choice.

A debated space for women

Historically, when groups of women were permitted to gather in spaces without men, this was largely for religious and ceremonial events. These often symbolised a shift in a woman's status from maiden to wife. They were also opportunities for women to offer advice and protection. Traditional women-only pre-wedding rituals in countries like Turkey, for example, involved members of the bride's community giving her gold. The practice is still seen in several countries in South Asia, especially India.

Gold is such a prevalent form of insurance that a 2023 report by the World Gold Council, an international trade association for the gold industry, suggested that Indian women collectively own around 24,000 tons of gold, which accounts for about 11 per cent of the world's total.[22] BBC reporter Perisha Kudhail (who did a deep dive into the report) could not verify the data of ownership according to gender, but she hypothesises that culturally it is mostly the women in Indian families who are the gatekeepers of gold.

While the gold appears merely decorative, it also gives the bride the financial means to leave a patriarchal marriage if needed. A gesture to give women a sense of autonomy when entering a marriage, in a largely patriarchal scheme where a woman's security is in the hands of her husband, who controls the household finances.

With the prevalence of male dominance in partnerships with women, we cannot gloss over the reality that women may not have always had a choice in their participation in single-gender spaces. Earlier we spoke about the murdah from the South Asian story 'Sultana's Dream' — a deliberate reversal of the gendered practice of purdah, where traditionally women were secluded from public life. These domestic spaces reserved for women have also been present in other parts of the world — referred to as 'harems' in many Muslim countries. Yet there has always been a question mark and animated debate on how much autonomy women actually had in these spaces. The conversation even went viral on Twitter shortly after Turkey's first lady, Emine Erdoğan, spoke at a conference in Ankara on 9 March 2016, the day after International Women's Day.

Mrs Erdoğan had just delivered a lecture titled 'Sultans' Mothers Who Have Left Traces on History', where she took aim at a widely debated, and internationally known, historic women-only space: the harem. The subject is a favourite of historians and artists, many of whom have depicted harems as exoticised jails where the wealthy wives and concubines of the household had their movements restricted. These women were watched over by eunuchs – enslaved men who had been castrated so they wouldn't pose a threat to the women they were meant to guard.

Mrs Erdoğan, however, described harems of the Ottoman era (1299–1922) as a wholly positive space for women, saying they were 'educational establishments that prepared women for life'. The negative depictions of harems, written about as places where women were trapped by men, were incorrect, she insisted. These portrayals had been deliberately skewed by Orientalism or Western scholars, who were presenting cultures they didn't completely understand through exoticised and sometimes racist perspectives.

Yet the notion that harems were secret universities was quickly dismissed by several journalists and historians on social media. Several insisted that Mrs Erdoğan herself was revising history. 'Rewriting male-created chambers that women couldn't leave as a good thing for women is crazy!' a user on Twitter posted. 'Talk about feeding the patriarchy!'

Others agreed, arguing that it was important to acknowledge the lack of autonomy women had in harems – that they were places where women were imprisoned behind heavy curtains and locked doors, according to historians such as Nabia Abbott, an American scholar of Islam. These harem women included enslaved concubines who had fewer rights than wives.

Other social media users, though, insisted that Mrs Erdoğan was right, and though formal education for women did not start until the mid-1800s, some women in certain harems seemed to have experienced private tutelage. This view was compounded by the studies of Professor Nadia Maria El Cheikh of the American University of Beirut, who argued that harems were not monoliths and varied greatly according to time period, location and family.

Mrs Erdoğan seemed to be echoing the findings of Professor El Cheikh, who wrote that some women were able to 'exercise social, economic and political power' by organising within the harem. These women enjoyed a great sense of power over the household – especially those who were the mothers of male leaders.

It's difficult to directly corroborate how much autonomy women in these women-only spaces truly had, as harems were phased out by the nineteenth and twentieth centuries. According to academics who have extensively researched them, including Dr Kate Fleet and Ebru Boyar, who edited *Ottoman Women in Public Space*, first-hand testimonies of women who had direct experience are noticeably absent in records compiled by men from the time.

A dangerous space for women

A purdah or harem may have been built according to the expectations of male-led societies, but there is no evidence that they were a dangerous space for women, unlike the current-day chhaupadi in Nepal or the punulu in West Africa. These huts, built on the outskirts of villages, are where women are forced to stay for the duration of their periods, due to the belief that women who are menstruating are impure bringers of misfortune. These period huts can be hideous, dark, bitterly cold and dangerous places. Girls and women are not given menstrual or washing supplies throughout the time they are cast out there, and several have been attacked by wild animals and bitten by snakes while in the shed. Nepal tried to officially ban the traditional practice in 2005, and criminalised it in 2017, but it continues in more rural areas. The women's rights NGO CARE International says that, over the course of her life, a woman in Nepal may spend up to eight years in the chhaupadi sheds. Several lose their lives there. In 2019, a twenty-one-year-old Nepali woman named Parwati Bogati died of suffocation in a windowless chhaupadi. She had lit a fire to keep herself warm, and died choking on the thick smoke. The belief that she was too impure to open the door and step outside and return back to her family home had outweighed her instinct to save her own life.

When you read this book, please keep women like Parwati Bogati in mind – women who were forced out of and cordoned off from a world that does not understand womanhood. Please also think of women like Afsoon*, a make-up artist in Afghanistan whom I interviewed in 2021, two weeks after the Taliban had stormed Kabul. Beauty salons, a woman-only space in the country, were immediately shut down, and the militants covered the faces of models on adverts in thick black paint. Afsoon, who owned a leading salon in the capital, spoke to me several times while in hiding, in the early days of the Taliban takeover. She was in a women-only safehouse hastily arranged by fellow Afghan feminists in her city for high-profile, outspoken women who were no longer welcome in society. As a beauty influencer, Afsoon was a target.

A few weeks after we spoke, my messages to her failed to deliver. I like to think that she left her phone and made her way to Jordan or Egypt, like some of her friends did, and started again. Maybe one day she'll pick up this book and read that I've been thinking of her and would love to hear from her, and she'll send me an email.

In September 2021, Afsoon described her salon as a tranquil space that was in cool contrast to the hot and sticky male-dominated streets of Kabul. She said multiple generations of women, reflecting the cream of Afghanistan's society, would gather at her salon: grandmothers, doctors, TV stars, brides and teenage girls giggling with their mothers. A cave of colour away from streets about to be covered with black paint.

'I will build it again,' she told me then. I believed her.

To honour Afsoon's vision and dreams, and those of generations of women spanning thousands of years, I want to spend the rest of this book exploring the lives and motivations of women who have chosen to build current-day women-only spaces away from men. Spaces created so that women can enjoy a sense of autonomy; spaces designed for their survival.

Yet even the most empowered women-led community is fragile within the wider masculine project. The survival of women-led projects needs the permission and support of the wider ecosystem. But not all ecosystems welcome change.

An ecosystem is used to its natural zone, a particular order. And disruption to that order can attract the attention of predators.

2

The Queen and her Wives

South Africa, 1800

Over 200 years ago, a woman, with the support of an inner sanctum of other women, was appointed queen over the warring Balobedu people of South Africa. Her reign ushered in an era of peace. Six women would go on to inherit the title – each becoming Queen Modjadji, the ruler of the day.

Traditionally, Queen Modjadji's council of women were called batanoni, which translates as 'wife' in the Khelobedu language. The queen lived with her wives within the lush forests among the mountains of Limpopo, the northernmost province of South Africa. More than attendants, the batanoni formed a sacred circle around the queen – and each woman played a vital role in upholding the traditions of both the Balobedu people and one of Africa's rare women-led monarchies.

Modjadji, and her wives, could connect with deceased female ancestors, the Limpopo elders say. They could control the clouds by performing ceremonies that would generate rain for those who loved Queen Modjadji, and drought for those who wronged her. Queen Modjadji commanded respect and inspired awe from neighbouring male leaders. It was a leadership that the brutal regime of apartheid couldn't undo, that the great Zulu king Shaka revered and that the male chiefs of neighbouring countries Botswana, Zimbabwe and Mozambique bowed down to.

The queenship of the house of Modjadji passed down from woman to woman, from mother to eldest daughter. Should a son be born first, the queen would try to conceive again. She would try with a male lover approved by the royal court, for Queen Modjadji was not permitted to marry a man. The community would pray that a union would bring a girl, a future queen. It was a daughter that mattered to the lineage.

History books say that England's late Queen Elizabeth II was officially South Africa's only queen, but the Balobedu disagree. Queen Modjadji has been their country's one, true, indigenous queen. For more than two centuries, hers was a leadership that followed its own rules – free of imperialised protocol, or Westernised language. For example, the Balobedu did not call the territory over which Queen Modjadji presided her kingdom, or even her queendom.

'The word "queendom" is too close to the word "kingdom",' Dr Mathole Motshekga, a former advisor to two former Rain Queens – and a guardian of a would-be third – told me. 'We prefer the word "queenship".'

As of 2024, there are more than 2 million Balobedu people who live around the Mopani and Vhembe regions of Limpopo, amongst the abundant blue-green Lobedu Mountains. This is the Rain Queen's realm – the lush and fructuous land that is a jewel in South Africa's drought-prone north-east regions. South African writer Liz McGregor described it in 2007 as an oasis, where 'trees hang heavy with paw paw, nectarines, mangoes and bananas. Crops flourish, irrigated by streams that seldom run dry.'[1] It was the same when I visited over a decade later. Fertile, cared for, like the garden-like forests in the country in *Herland*.

For the Balobedu people, though, their nation is green because of their monarch. They call themselves a nation, not a tribe. Each Queen Modjadji has ruled more than 150 villages, presiding over 200 square kilometres of rural land.

Until recently, the Rain Queen's rule symbolised unity, which was nowhere more evident than in the way she selected her wives.

Historically, each wife came from a separate community within the queen's territory, and each represented a part of the queenship. Their position granted all communities an ear in the royal court. The wives were, in a way, the parliamentarians of the day.

Then, in June 2005, the future of this unique centuries-old women-led regal lineage came under threat.

The sixth Rain Queen had ruled the Balobedu queenship for just over two years, and she had given birth to two children. The oldest was a boy, and he was loved, but there was particular joy when she gave birth to her second child in January 2005 – Princess Masalanabo Modjadji. With the birth of a girl, the royal lineage was secure, the court believed. The child who was destined to be the seventh Rain Queen had been born. Princess Masalanabo was primarily cared for by her aunt, the then twenty-year-old Motsatsi Mokoto. It was normal for the child-rearing to be carried out by the queen's women relatives, but Motsatsi said it was vital that this daughter was especially protected.

'I came to care for the baby because her mother had royal duties as the queen, but there was also another reason,' Motsatsi told me quietly via video call, sitting on Modjadji grounds in the hills of Limpopo. This was her first interview. She paused before adding, 'There were rumours people wanted to assassinate her mother.'

When the baby was just a few months old, her mother, the ruling Queen Modjadji VI, died after a short, sudden and mysterious illness. The news reached the international media, and the *New York Times* reported that she had suffered from chronic meningitis. Yet some Balobedu, including Chief Gabriel Rasebotsa, the spokesperson of the Balobedu Royal Council, believe the sixth queen was poisoned, assassinated. She was just twenty-seven years old.

The royal court was in a panic, divided. One side was adamant that the line should remain matrilineal and Princess Masalanabo should ascend to queenship when she turned eighteen, supported by a group of women. Another faction insisted the nation should evolve, and bestow the title on the queen's first-born, turning a queenship into a kingdom. Men had ruled the Balobedu for hundreds of years prior to the installation of a female queen, they argued. Men could rule again.

Amidst the unrest, the princess's primary carer, her aunt Motsatsi Mokoto, came to a decision. Princess Masalanabo Modjadji would have to be taken to safety and hidden away until she turned eighteen. When she came of age, the princess could reign as the region's seventh Rain Queen, surrounded by her own wives.

'I decided to run away with her to protect her from these threats,' Motsatsi said. So, one night, she took the five-month-old child and hurriedly left the royal kraal – a fenced village of huts – in the hills of Limpopo. She prayed that the queenship, with such a rich and long history, would survive.

The dawn of the reign

Most oral history shifts and moulds depending on the teller, and that is the case for the origin story of the first Rain Queen. I first heard a version in 2017. Following a short reporting assignment in South Africa, I decided to take a holiday and visit the Modjadji Nature Reserve, a five-hour drive from Johannesburg. Friends had told me of a vast mountain forest in Limpopo where cycads — a type of rare ancient tree that looks like a large pineapple — grow throughout the reserve.

My guide said that the reserve was on land presided over by a powerful and divine queen who was truly pan-African. She belonged to a once-tribal people that had moved from Sudan to DR Congo, then further south. This piece of oral history was later confirmed to me by Dr Motshekga, the guardian of Princess Masalanabo, the would-be seventh Rain Queen. He added that the line had turned majestic long ago when one of the women became pregnant without having physical contact with a man. She was said to have been impregnated by the female deity Ka, the Queen of Heaven. The Modjadji line was no longer historic, it was regal and divine, Dr Motshekga insisted.

The nation later migrated to Monomotapa, now the country of Zimbabwe, and continued to have male leaders until the 1500s, when the kingdom was rocked by an event that threatened the very survival of the crown. Dzugundini, the daughter of the king, fell pregnant following an incestuous relationship with her brother. In other versions of the story it was the king himself who impregnated his own daughter. Either way, it was a catastrophe. To avoid the destabilisation of the kingdom, the king banished his daughter from the region. Dzugundini headed south, eventually settling in Molototsi Valley, in the region of Limpopo, in what is now South Africa. But before she fled, Dzugundini's mother, a rainmaker, bestowed her with powerful tools – a sacred horn belonging to an unknown animal, as well as magic beads. Dzugundini was taught to use these tools in a sacred ceremony that would connect her with her deceased female relatives in the supernatural and ancestral realm. These ancestors would advise her on how to rule her people as well as conjure rain.

Dzugundini was a natural leader. She soon gained territory and status by forming ties with other tribes, creating the Balobedu nation. Yet her line was patrilineal: her sons and their sons led, and over the next couple of hundred years, the Balobedu rulers were all men. Under these male chiefs, the Balobedu people were divided by infighting between chiefs and rivalries between different families.

Then the last male Balobedu leader, Mugodo, had a prophetic vision that the realm should return to female leadership, ensuring a unifying and peaceful age. In 1800, Chief Mugudo's daughter Maselekwane was crowned the first Queen Modjadji. Her rule was immediately impressive. So consistent was her rainmaking ability that she quickly gained the trust and respect of the male leaders around her. According to the Modjadji Traditional Authority – a council of royal elders led by Princess Masalanabo's great-grandfather Mr Rodney Mokgwakgwe Modjadji – even the great Zulu king Shaka, who conquered most of the neighbouring tribes in the region during the first few decades of the 1800s, left the queenship of Modjadji untouched. He sent the first Queen Modjadji gifts of cattle, asking her to bless his region with rain.

The female dynasty had begun.

Gender roles within the Balobedu nation

Balobedu gender roles cannot be viewed through a European lens. As noted by Ifi Amadiume, a Nigerian anthropologist and poet, the different roles of sexes in pan-African tribal communities do not equate to sex discrimination as viewed by modern Eurocentric feminism. Amadiume argues that modern feminists often misrepresent and patronise women from rural areas and undermine the roles they possess in their communities. She notes that in pre-colonial times, women shared social statuses with men – but these were eroded by the introduction of colonialism and a capitalist economy.

Until the recent succession issues put a pause on the matrilineal line, Balobedu women outside the queen's court held influence over their communities and observed a certain degree of separation from men. This was especially true of child-rearing. Balobedu women gave birth in a motswede, a women-only hut, with the assistance of women (and transgender) birth attendants called sangomas. If the child was a boy, villagers would beat the father with a stick, indicating that the life of a man would be followed by violence and conflict. Men symbolised the destruction, the Eternal War. If the baby was a girl, villagers doused the father with water, signifying a much gentler future. Women were life-giving.

'The technical term for "woman" in Khelobedu is "rain",' Balobedu-born academic Tebogo George Mahashe told me. 'So a woman is rain. They make rain because women are rain.'

For a few months after the birth, the child – along with the mother and female attendants – stayed in the hut, venturing out only when the skies opened. The baby would then be taken outside to give thanks to the live-giving gift of rain.

Marriage was arranged between families and formalised when a husband gave his future wife's family a bride payment – gifts including cattle and maize. A wife held a revered position in Balobedu society, with a unique definition – unlike in other cultures in Africa, or indeed Europe and the Middle East. A Balobedu wife was not a subject under a man but a bridge between communities.

'Marriage is not between a man and a woman, but between two families,' added Mahashe. He was speaking to me via video call from his office at the University of Cape Town. 'The wife position is held by a person who's able to unify those two families, and more specifically, the person that's able to neutralise disagreements within that family.' In this way, the wife is a peacemaker. A crucial position in societies set up against the backdrop of conflict – the Eternal War.

In the Khelobedu language, the word *musade* loosely translates as both 'woman' and 'wife' – feminine and nurturing. Each person is part of a whole, both feminine and masculine, and connected to the ancestral realm. It's not a direct translation, because English cannot adequately hold the complex meaning of this type of gender duality. In many ways, Queen Modjadji was the wife of the Balobedu nation, its ultimate unifier.

Men too held positions of status and were generally appointed as the headmen and chiefs of their communities. However, having a male chief or headman did not necessarily mean the men ruled the village. Each adult in each household and hence village – woman or man – had influence, which they exercised.

'The Balobedu do not subscribe to gender roles in the way that we conceptualise it today,' Mahashe explained, recalling his own community in the Balobedu nation, where a council of female elders would meet to discuss and solve challenges that arose in the community. 'In my own family, there was my grandmother, there were my grandfather's sisters, there were my grandmother's cousins. These women made decisions for the family. Then the older male members of the family had their own structure.'

This gendered separation of elder decision-making councils was repeated in houses across the Balobedu nation. The queen herself had both her female wives and her all-male royal council whom she could turn to.

This followed a long-standing socialised tradition that while living in the earthly realm, men and women had distinct roles and could make decisions in a harmonious manner when apart. The Balobedu were not, though, a segregated society. They were ultimately unified by one woman: the Rain Queen.

Understanding the importance of having both influential women and men on her side, the first Queen Modjadji created a uniquely centralised rule. She formed strong ties with Balobedu's chiefs and headmen, and did not interfere with the running of the leshako — the village that each headman looked after. She would only get involved in giving advice if she was directly approached.

To express thanks for being given land to oversee, the queen would accept well-mannered young girls from these communities to serve in the royal house. These girls became the batanoni, or royal wives. They would go on to serve Queen Modjadji in a unique women's space. The queen also had vatlhanuni — women who assisted with day-to-day tasks. Unlike the batanoni, vatlhanuni did not have any advisory authority but they were still key to the life of the royal court.

Morongwa Modjadji served as a wife to the fourth and fifth Rain Queens, between 1974 and 2001. The daughter of a former Balobedu headman, Morongwa told me that the royal wives symbolised the union of the queen and her people. The wives were a crucial thread between the royal household and the people, and the first line of contact to the queen. Once a woman from outside her own family had been accepted by the queen as a royal wife, the royal tie between the queen and the village would be secured for generations. Each queen had dozens of wives but fewer than ten lived with her in her residence, which was initially a mud hut with a thatched roof and several rooms, although it was modernised over the decades to become an expansive palace.

While the Rain Queen held a unique status in Balobedu society, she was not the only woman to enter into same-sex unions; as in over forty other pre-colonial African societies, marriage among the Balobedu was not limited to pairings between men and women. They practised woman-marriage – a formal union between two women, although according to historian Paula Akpan in her book *When We Ruled: The Rise and Fall of Twelve African Queens and Warriors*, this was not a lesbian relationship.[2] Rather, one woman would take on the role of the 'female-husband', assuming the social and economic responsibilities typically held by a male head of household. Her wife would bear children, and therefore have sexual relationships with men. She would assume 'paternity' for any children who were born in the house.[3]

This tradition was also established between the Rain Queen and her wives. They were all allowed to have male lovers. Yet, in an inverse of gender roles, their children would call the queen 'father'. Most of the wives married close relations of the queen, such as her relatives and district headmen.

The first five Rain Queens did not marry men, but they did

take on male lovers and had children with them. Their wives cared for their heirs.

Batanoni – the queen's wives and diplomats

The members of the inner royal court of Balobedu's Rain Queens have rarely spoken to outsiders about life inside the gendered, women's spaces of the Modjadji royal household. Two former wives and three aunts of four Rain Queens spoke to me for this book, and I want to take a moment to thank those who made that possible: the brilliant Limpopo-based journalist Thembi Siaga, and my friend Malesela Maubane, who jokingly calls himself a non-practising journalist, having left the profession a few years ago to work in public relations. Thembi and Malesela also translated the interviews from Khelobedu, a language of the Balobedu, which is not yet official in South Africa.

Makgwekgwe Mampeule-Maake was a wife to the third and fourth Rain Queens between 1959 and 1981, and is now in her early eighties. She is a poet, which is evident in the slow and lyrical way she speaks.

Makgwekgwe was born in a village near the Modjadji royal compound, the kraal, in 1942, at a time when the queenship was thriving. This was during the reign of Khesethoane Modjadji, and as a child Makgwekgwe was enthralled by Balobedu's third Rain Queen. She would watch in awe as the queen, surrounded by a group of regal women, walked in procession to a soda-like stream to bathe. Queen Khesethoane Modjadji III would be preceded by two young girls, two guard dogs (called maarola) and her chief advisor. Behind her were her wives. Following the bathing ritual, the entourage would return to the royal compound in the same order.

If anyone in the village passed them on the road, they would do the lotsha, a form of kneeling to show respect to the women-led regal group. The queen and her wives, with their quiet dignity, commanded the respect of the Balobedu.

Makgwekgwe had always been fascinated by the collective of women that presided over her community. Before she began menstruating, long before she became a wife herself, she was given a unique job. As her family were closely related to the royal family, Makgwekgwe was invited to a secret girls-only place in the royal compound, the dihlofseng. This was a sacred area, where the powerful pots used for the rainmaking ceremony were kept. It was also an area said to be so blessed that it served as a middle ground between this world and the plane where the ancestors lived.

The Bantu tribes, who have close cultural links to the Balobedu, centre women in rainmaking for their biological symbolism. A woman's body, notably her womb, is seen as 'wet' and so pleases the rain-giving ancestors.[4] As a woman is a life-giver, she is called upon to ask for rain to ensure the survival of her people, plants and animals. In short, rain equals fertility on the grandest scale – and she is the creator. Spaces for rainmaking therefore remain for women.

The dihlofseng was the beginning of this women-led ceremonial cycle. Makgwekgwe, and a group of other young girls who would later go on to become royal wives, were allowed to enter the space barefoot and collect a pot. They would fill each pot with water from the royal well and hand them to the queen's royal wives. The wives would then head to the forest with the queen to begin the secret rainmaking ceremony.

Only girls who hadn't begun menstruation were allowed to draw from the royal well.

'They were seen as pure,' Makgwekgwe explained, highlighting a belief that prevails in several cultures and countries still – that monthly periods somehow indicate a woman is spiritually unclean.

After Makgwekgwe began her period, like all Balobedu girls, she was invited to go through the dikhopa initiation, which involved spending a week at a designated house where men were not allowed to enter. She told me that it was here that Balobedu's older women taught her what to expect in womanhood. This involved discussions on resilience, the emotional support of other women, sex education and grooming tips. Boys would also go to a separate initiation school, where they were often circumcised and taught how to care for women in the community.

When Makgwekgwe turned seventeen, she was told that she had been chosen to be a royal wife. She would be one of the regal women walking to the stream – just like the ones she had so admired in her childhood. The thought of this delighted her. She would soon be part of the sacred women-only spaces within the queen's court.

The official roles of the batanoni depend on which faction of Balobedu you speak with. Those who believe the queenship must remain matrilineal, within the rule of a woman, insist that her wives play a crucial advisory and political role in Balobedu.

Academic Tebogo George Mahashe refers to the queen's wives as a 'college of women'. 'This was a horizontal structure. The queen was the principal and her wives were the diplomats of the nation. The queen's wives were a school of highly specialised individuals, specialists in diplomacy.'

He explained to me that batanoni played essential roles in supporting the Rain Queen on matters concerning governance, spiritual rituals, traditions, and the welfare of the community. They were also responsible for passing down oral traditions and folklore. They were scientists, with extensive knowledge of weather patterns, medicinal plants and healing practices. They were the preservers of Balobedu culture and heritage, ensuring the transmission of knowledge from one generation to another.

This is a view backed by Dr Motshekga, who was a male advisor to the fifth and sixth Rain Queens and is now the guardian of Princess Masalanabo. 'Men within a royal council were the spokespeople for the queen, spreading her message,' he told me. 'However, it was the women, her aunts and wives, who were closest to her.'

Nevertheless, not all Balobedu agree that the wives enjoyed advisory powers.

Ronnie Moroatshehla, a spokesman for the Modjadji Royal Council who supports a change to male leadership, insists that the wives were more like ladies-in-waiting, and men were the primary advisors. Through him, I was introduced to two former wives, Morongwa and Makgwekgwe. The women say they support a change to male leadership. They were there to serve, they say, and the men advised. I wonder if the conversation would have been different if Ronnie Moroatshehla had not been present throughout their interviews.

Rainmaking as a women's space

When Morongwa and Makgwekgwe – former batanoni of the third, fourth and fifth Rain Queens – told me about a typical

THE QUEEN AND HER WIVES

day serving their queens, they laughed as they said it would begin early, at the crack of dawn. Their duties ranged from sweeping the yard and preparing breakfast to coordinating the queen's diary. They would speak to the all-male royal advisory council on what messages the queen wanted to communicate to her people, and the council would act as her spokesmen. But all access to the queen came through her wives, who knew her daily routine.

The wives were responsible for overseeing the dikhopa initiation for girls, and scouting for girls who could be potential future wives, future keepers and protectors of the crown. They would also perform women-only dances called the Kekapa for royal visitors.

The busiest time of year for the wives, though, was September – the start of the new year for the Balobedu, and the run-up to rainmaking.

The rainmaking process involved several stages over a number of weeks, and was led by the queen's wives. Morongwa and Makgwekgwe told me that the wives would begin by brewing a special traditional beer called mophapo. It was used to pay respect to the badimo, or ancestors, during the performance of rainmaking rituals. The brew was then fed to a cow, who would walk around one of the shrines, the thugula, amidst chanting, drumming and dancing. There would be great relief when the cow dropped its dung. It was a sign that the ancestors welcomed the start of the ceremony and were satisfied with the request for rain.

After prayers, another traditional beer called madumelo was shared amongst the villagers who gathered at the ceremony – a unifying and equalising experience between the royal household and the subjects. Then the secret part started. The dithokamamo, the girls who hadn't yet started their periods, took the rainmaking pots from the sacred storage place and filled them with water from the royal well. The Rain Queen performed rituals or ceremonies at the shrines and altars on sacred land, calling on the ancestral spirits.

Chosen men were also involved. Senior male elders and spiritual advisors, such as diviners, could participate in certain parts of the ritual, particularly those involving community matters, land, or spiritual intercession. However, the core ceremonial power and symbolism lay with the Rain Queen and her female circle.

The queen would make her way to the forest with her rainmaking beads, the sacred horn, and rainmaking pots containing herbs brewed by a rain-doctor. She would be accompanied by her wives and key female members of the royal family. This part of the ceremony has never been witnessed by anyone outside the queen's trusted women's circle.

Many details of the rituals have been kept secret, passed down orally through generations. Outsiders – including men – have not been privy to the full ceremony, especially the most sacred inner rites.

Even before 1800, when the region was ruled by men, roles were gendered. Women, according to the Balobedu, have a direct communication with their ancestors and the cycles of the earth. For an agricultural society like the Balobedu, the production of rain is central to survival. According to husband-and-wife anthropologists E. Jensen Krige and J. D. Krige, who spent several decades visiting the Balobedu, rainfall is a central pillar of the society's sense of security, and so a rainmaker holds a divine position as the guarantor of cyclic regularity and the prosperity of the people.

The fact that the ceremony has always belonged to

women reinforces the prophecy passed on by the ancestors to Balobedu's last male leader, Mugodo – that women leaders bring peace. A woman rainmaker, supported by other women, will ensure unity amongst the people. Women are unifiers and men are war-makers. The best way to avoid war therefore is to trust women to nourish the land. After all, according to Balobedu tradition, women are rain.

Of course, critics and scientific purists argue that ceremonies cannot possibly trigger rain. Rainmaking, they insist, is a superstition that holds no influence in patterns of meteorology. Yet the villages of the queenship, the ones I have seen myself, are visibly green and lush, even when neighbouring regions look stonier, more arid. At my guesthouse the first evening I visited Limpopo, I searched online for an explanation that would pacify my journalistic mind. One such rationalisation is that there tends to be more rain in hilly regions than in lower-lying areas because of the orographic effect – as air rises over mountains it cools, and the water vapour condenses. Some claim that the secret combination of herbs burned in the rainmaking ceremony somehow condenses water vapour and stimulates showers. But without witnessing the full ceremony, which has so far only been seen by chosen Balobedu, I can only guess.

Of course, rainmaking ceremonies do not guarantee rain. For the Balobedu, however, a lack of rain, or overpowering rain, has historically meant that the Rain Queen is distracted. According to Krige and Krige in their book *The Realm of a Rain Queen*, the region experienced drought between 1934 and 1935. Elders told the anthropologists that this was because the third Queen Modjadji was deeply unhappy and distracted by her daughter's relationship with a non-royal man. She couldn't make rain.

The queen and her people

The first and second Rain Queens were elusive and mysterious figures who lived in near isolation in their compound, hearing news of the community only through their wives. Both Rain Queens killed themselves in ritual suicide at the age of sixty by drinking poison, as this was when rainmaking ability was said to wane.

Ritual suicide has been criticised by human rights groups as a type of cultural coercion when an individual's (often a woman's) use in society has been seen to run its course, with these practices often interpreted as glorifying early death. This view may have been shared by the third Rain Queen, who refused to kill herself, resisting pressure from her all-male royal council. She also made herself more accessible to her community than her predecessors did.

'Queen Khesethoane, the third Rain Queen, was a kind person,' her wife Makgwekgwe told me. 'She would instruct the royal announcer, who was named Titi, to blow a phalafala – or trumpet – and shout "Batho ka moka mobidibiding!" All the villagers gather under the mobidibidi tree!'

Located in a sacred part of the royal compound, this mobidibidi tree (Nyala in English) was towering and evergreen with glossy, drooping, dark green leaves and clusters of scented flowers. On hearing the trumpet, the villagers – women and men, girls and boys – would sit barefoot under the tree. They enjoyed the sorghum beer brewed from maize, malt, yeast and water by the queen's royal wives. They shared stories and discussed local and national events.

During the reign of the third Rain Queen, there was a lot to discuss. In 1948, South Africa's ruling colonial National

Party gave a name to the widespread racial segregation and political discrimination against the non-white people of the country: apartheid. But while the white government attempted to break South Africa's tribal chieftains by imposing heavy tariffs, Queen Khesethoane Modjadji III remained steadfast. Two key Balobedu leaders told me that she refused to pay the tax to the apartheid government.

Rodney Mokgwakgwe Modjadji and Chief Gabriel Rasebotsa explained that at a time when many traditional South African leaders were being pressured into compliance, Modjadji III's refusal signalled both a political defiance and a commitment to protecting her people's autonomy. She would not use her people for personal gain.

'The Balobedu were not a people driven by profit and money during the rule of the queens,' Rodney Mokgwakgwe Modjadji told me. 'Produce was farmed, consumed and traded between people, rather than marketed and sold. The queen did not tax her own people and did not want to be a part of a governmental hierarchy of money.'

The third Rain Queen was one of the few South African rural leaders to take this stance, and it partly worked. South Africa's apartheid government did not attempt to force her to pay taxes, but they did refuse to recognise her regal status, demoting her to a chief. It didn't matter; the queen had the support of her people. Buoyed by Queen Khesethoane Modjadji III's example, the fourth and fifth Rain Queens also shunned the apartheid tax.

Queen Mokope Modjadji, the fifth Rain Queen, ruled during the end of apartheid in 1994. Her wife Morongwa described her to me as a 'strong character, a stickler for rules' who had a reputation for not making eye contact. The spokesperson for the Modjadji Traditional Authority recalled that

Queen Modjadji V turned down an initial request to meet Nelson Mandela, although at least two meetings did eventually take place.

There is archive footage from SABC News of their meeting on 25 May 1999, when President Mandela gifted the queen with a 4x4 car. 'To go to the palace, I know you have to negotiate a hill,' he said. 'When I visited the palace, it rained and my own 4x4 got stuck.'[5] He added that he hoped the car would help her conduct her royal duties in more comfort.

In the footage, Queen Modjadji V, who is standing next to him, looks ahead, unsmiling and silent. I was told by Balodedu elders that she was suspicious of any government – including Nelson Mandela's – wanting to assert authority over traditional and rural people. Nor did she want her authority to be dependent on their approval. But, wanted or not, the Modjadji queenship received the backing of the ruling African National Congress.

Mandela and Queen Modjadji V went on to communicate regularly through advisor Dr Mathole Motshekga. At the queen's request, President Mandela built an agricultural school in Limpopo. The government also arranged for the tarring of a road to the royal kraal. The queenship began to receive annual funding from the government, under the Traditional Leadership and Governance Framework Act, in 2003.

But by that same year, when the sixth Rain Queen came to office, the dynasty was changing. Unlike her predecessors, Queen Makobo Modjadji VI had received a formal education and completed high school. Unlike her predecessors, she wanted to modernise the court. And her first act was to have a gender-agnostic group of advisors.

While Queen Modjadji VI had female advisors as well

as male, she didn't have live-in wives. The centuries-old and peaceful tradition of female envoys of the community seemed to be coming to a close. The sixth queen did not limit her life to her royal compound, either. She went to discos, wore Western clothes like jeans, drove a car, and was said to enjoy watching soap operas on television.

Several people admired the young queen for modernising the throne. The Modjadji tradition had placed restrictive expectations on some of the queens, particularly regarding personal freedom and autonomy. Queen Makobo Modjadji VI was changing that. She didn't want to maintain a mystic distance from her people. She wanted to live amongst them, and she had the support of many Balobedu. However, a growing faction felt that the queen was no longer observing the traditions and values required for a regal figure. Rumours circulated that there was a credible threat to assassinate her and assert a male leadership. When Queen Makobo Modjadji VI died suddenly and unexpectedly in 2005, her inner circle didn't want to take any further risks with her daughter.

That was when a group of them vowed to protect Princess Masalanabo, and the queenship, from any potential threats.

A fight for the throne

After the five-month-old future queen was whisked away in secrecy by her aunt Motsatsi Mokoto from the royal kraal in the mountains near the Modjadji Nature Reserve, Princess Masalanabo was hidden in the homes of Balobedu families who lived several hundred miles away. At one point, the princess lived with her father, a non-royal anti-apartheid activist named David Mohale, who was convinced that his daughter's life was under threat.

Female members of her family taught her the sacred women's ceremonies, ensuring she understood her birthright. In their eyes she would restore the queenship and oversee the women-only ceremonial rituals. Perhaps she would take on wives – or, if not, then maybe chosen women would be her representatives within the Balobedu nation. This was the dream for Princess Masalanabo.

In 2014, when she turned nine years old, Randburg Children's Court in Johannesburg granted the former Rain Queen advisor and politician Dr Mathole Motshekga, as well as his wife Angie Motshekga – who served as South Africa's Minister of Education between 2009 and 2024 – full guardianship over Rain Queen-elect Princess Masalanabo. The princess moved into the Motshekga family home in Johannesburg. The family wondered if the princess would prefer private tutors and home-schooling, but the child was adamant that she wanted a mainstream education until it was time for her to ascend the Balobedu throne on her eighteenth birthday.

Meanwhile, matters within the Balobedu royal kraal were being overseen by the sixth Rain Queen's brother, Prince Mpapatla. There was an expectation that he was a placeholder until the rightful female leader was old enough to take on her role, which was further confirmed when President Jacob Zuma legally recognised the Modjadji queenship in 2016, officially restoring the regal status that had been nullified by the apartheid government.[6] The South African press declared that the teenage Princess Masalanabo would be crowned Queen Modjadji VII, the country's next Rain Queen, when she turned eighteen in 2023.

Yet an unexpected development dramatically altered the course of events.

The royal household, brimming with tension that had existed since the sudden death of the sixth Rain Queen in 2005, split into two royal councils. The Balobedu Royal Council believed that queenship should remain under the rule of women. The Modjadji Royal Council felt that it was time for the rule to return to men. The former queen's brother, installed in the royal kraal at the foot of an escarpment, sided with the Modjadji Royal Council. He supported a ceremony in 2022 to inaugurate Princess Masalanabo's older brother as king.

Prince Lekukela Modjadji had been under the care of the council, growing up near the royal kraal, when his sister Princess Masalanabo was taken away from the region. He was the eldest born of the late queen, the Modjadji Royal Council argued, so the crown should now be his. He has the support of the council's spokesman Ronnie Moroatshehla.

'The kingdom is not married to being under woman rule,' Moroatshehla told me. 'Ours is not all about who sits on the throne but our traditions, customs and ritual practices. Nothing will change under a Rain King.'

However, the Balobedu Royal Council spokesman Chief Gabriel Rasebotsa – who backs Princess Masalanabo – insisted to me that it is 'impossible that men can conjure rain. Impossible. The very idea of a king is an abomination.'

The question of who will continue to reign remains unknown. But South Africa's government seems to want to keep the rule female.

Formally, a certificate of recognition is needed from the South African government to install a monarch to preside over the Balobedu nation, and it was finally granted on 13

December 2024 to Princess Masalanabo. On the South African government's website, President Cyril Ramaphosa legally recognised Princess Masalanabo Modjadji as the seventh queen of the Balobedu queenship.[7]

In a statement, the president described Queen Modjadji VII's legal recognition as a 'new chapter' and a 'moment of great significance to the rich history of Balobedu Nation'. 'On behalf of Government, President Ramaphosa wishes Her Majesty a long and prosperous reign and looks forward to working with Her Majesty and the Royal Family in advancing socio-economic development of people living under the jurisdiction of Balobedu Queenship.'

Her advisors told me that she was preparing to move to Limpopo to take up her position amongst the Balobedu people. It is unknown whether the young and modern queen will reinstate the advisory wife tradition, spend the majority of her time with the Balobedu people and shun marriage to a man. Having grown up in cosmopolitan Johannesburg, it seems unlikely. Her mother, the sixth Rain Queen, was in a monogamous relationship with a man. Perhaps her daughter will be the same. Or perhaps she will reinstate tradition, and the nation will return to being led by a school of women.

What we do know for sure, though, is that a seventh Rain Queen will not reign without challenge. The first Rain Queen was put in a position to rule in order to unify the people. The rule of the seventh will no doubt cause further schisms.

Ronnie Moroatshehla, who favours a switch to male leadership, told me via WhatsApp that some of the royal family who oppose Princess Masalanabo as queen plan to legally challenge the government. The whole family had not been consulted about the government's decision, and the move shocked them. 'We are dismayed by the act of the president, and we are dispirited. Princess Masalanabo is our blood daughter but she has not lived amongst the Balobedu people. She has not shown interest in living with her people. We respect all here, but it is Prince Lekukela who is prepared for rule. The rule should not be bound to just men or just women. If the world doesn't determine leadership on gender, neither should the royal family.'

A cloudy future

Until a formal Rain Queen returns to the kraal and fully resumes her ceremonial role, the women-led Balobedu society is not as it once was. There is, however, one remaining regal women's space on a hill beyond a gravelly road lined with mango and peach trees. This sacred and private royal cemetery is where the six former Rain Queens are buried. Their bodies, according to Princess Masalanabo's great-grandfather Rodney Mokgwakgwe Modjadji, have been wrapped in cow skins and covered with earth – an ancient eco-burial practice to symbolise environmental stewardship. The queen's deep and fluid connection with nature means there is no casket to separate her from her land.

The singular story of the Rain Queen line serves as a lesson for societies everywhere. In some ways, it offers a vision for how a new world might emerge from one in crisis. The first Queen Modjadji managed to course-correct the threat her Balobedu nation faced from warring brothers. Her reign attracted the respect her people needed, and she was seen as a link between this world and the next. She was visited by chiefs and kings as they asked for her help with rain – the one guarantee of sustenance and peace. In this way she was able to cultivate a sense of communalism that her male predecessors could not.

'As a woman leader she was invested in cooperation, whereas in most cases, the chiefs and kings were not invested in cooperation,' Tebogo George Mahashe told me. 'The male leaders of the time were invested in expansion.' In conjunction with her batanoni, the queen was able to serve as a supreme diplomat and foster relationships with the chiefs.[8]

In many ways, the Rain Queens were similar to leaders like Kwame Nkrumah, the former Ghanaian president who led the country to independence and who believed in the power of a pan-African sense of communalism and humanism.[9] These are concepts discussed at length by writer Richard Bell in his 2002 guide to pre- and post-colonial leadership titled *Understanding African Philosophy*: 'African humanism ... is rooted in traditional values of mutual respect for one's fellow kinsman and a sense of position and place in the larger order of things: one's *social* order, *natural* order and the *cosmic* order. African humanism is rooted in *lived dependencies*.'[10]

This is especially so in the Balobedu culture as overseen by the Rain Queen, where competition and personal gain are less respected – and mutual benefit, including rain that nourishes everyone, is valued. All the Rain Queens, and their wives, were ultimately unifying figures, power-brokers who galvanised their people to stand against the most destructive regimes in South Africa. The six Rain Queens stood firm despite territory expansion from the Zulu king Shaka, the Boer War fought in 1899–1902 between the British and the Transvaal Boers, and the crushing brutality of apartheid. Post-apartheid leaders, perhaps recognising traditional leaders for their influence as repositories for votes, courted the queenship.

While cultivating gendered spaces, from the women's

schools in childhood to the elder women-only councils, the women of Balobedu have historically had spaces where they could talk away from men. Those shared spaces reinforced a sense of belonging through rituals, preserving core values and maintaining cultural roots.

Some critics question whether such a role is still viable in the twenty-first century. The ruling Queen Modjadji was expected to live in seclusion with her wives, abstain from romantic attachments, and devote herself entirely to spiritual responsibilities – like rainmaking. Is this a fair expectation? And in a world increasingly attuned to gender equity, should such a role be reserved only for a woman?

The future of the queenship remains uncertain. Will the next royal ruler draw strength from a circle of women? Will they sit under a mobidibidi tree, drinking a mug of mophapo beer, cultivating a communal identity and belonging, and calling to the wisdom of queens who came before – the women who stood defiantly as the lands around them were seized by male tribal leaders and colonisers?

Perhaps not, or at least not in the same way as before, but I feel that parts of this regal matriliny's values ring through every women-only community I have visited, in Herlands across the world. Women have the ability to cultivate a lush and peaceful oasis, in even the most dangerous and threatening of circumstances.

3
House of Women

Rio de Janeiro, Brazil, 1940

Dona Orosina Vieira decided that it wasn't time for her husband to die.

Mr Orosina Vieira's health had worsened in recent weeks. His clotted, bloody cough was now leaving stains on their thin mattress. The tuberculosis that had entered his lungs left him restless at night, rolling back and forth. Dona thought she could feel the fever radiating from his body even when they weren't touching. During the day he would sit up in bed, staring at the same spot on the wall. They lived in a boxy room in a boarding house behind Rio's Central Station, surrounded by a sea of smoke and soot.

Dona was a midwife; half of her days she was supporting women from low-income backgrounds through one of the most important seasons of their lives – their pregnancy, labour, and the time after they gave birth. The rest she spent tending to Mr Orosina Vieira.

She insisted that they go for long walks together, to get Mr Orosina Vieira out of the cramped room, to expand his lungs. The Orosina Vieiras would walk the streets of downtown Rio, past the street buskers and factory workers clinging onto the sides of the São Januário tram, and head for the coast, to open air. The beaches of Copacabana and Ipanema were beautiful, but they were filled with boisterous young people, so the two aimed for higher ground. When they reached it, they would sit for hours in silence, just holding hands and breathing.

The hills of Guanabara Bay had fewer visitors in those days. There was an archipelago of nine islands that had once been the home of Indigenous fishing communities, but Rio's newer inhabitants, the cariocas, were put off by the marshes and mangroves that had to be navigated to get to the drier ground there.

But not Dona. The journey was worth it for her. She loved the expanse of open space, the silence.

So did Mr Orosina Vieira. His laugh while they were up there reminded her of the boy she had fallen in love with all those decades ago, back home in Ubá, 200 kilometres from Rio. Ubá was a furniture hub, with a reputation for creating and exporting the country's most stylish and sturdy carpentry. Ubá people knew how to build.

The promise of work had pulled the Orosina Vieiras to Rio from their home in the south-east of the country. They enjoyed meeting other Afro-Brazilian workers who had gathered there from all over Brazil. They had a community, but cramped living conditions and terrible sanitation were taking a toll on them both.

Then one evening, on top of a hill, mesmerised by the rolling tides of Guanabara Bay, Dona had an idea. They would take advantage of the large pieces of wood washed in by the tides and build a house away from Rio's centre.

Local historians say Dona built it with her own hands: a shack on spindly stilts, with sanded-down slats of wood and tin and beautiful crescent tiles. It was in this house on top of the hill that she and Mr Orosina Vieira would live for many, many happy years after.

This is the story of the first house in the favelas of Maré, passed down through oral history. Built in 1940 by a fifty-year-old Black woman who decided that it wasn't time for her husband to die.

Over the next few years, Dona helped her friends build their homes there too, and a neighbourhood rose up in the wetlands. Then, in 1946, the construction of Avenida Brasil, a major road connecting the centre of Rio to its suburbs, brought in more neighbours – workers looking for homes.

Today, more than 140,000 people live in fifteen favelas of Maré, spanning four square kilometres, making it one of the largest clusters of low-income homes in Rio. Some visitors incorrectly think of 'favelas' as types of makeshift camps, undermining their sophistication. Favelas in Brazil are small ecosystems, containing most of the facilities you find in any middle-class neighbourhood, including running water and electricity. Several have well-paved roads, delicious restaurants, schools and churches, and beautiful art created by residents who have lobbied and fundraised.

The memory of Dona, the mother of Maré, is precious to the people of the favelas. Her belongings are kept in Maré's small, community-organised Museu da Maré, which was co-founded in the 1990s by a woman named Marilene Nunes. The museum's coordinators have dutifully and expertly collected and archived artifacts and testimony from the community, and are in the process of digitising it. One of the coordinators, Vera Marta Alves, better known in Maré as Aunt Vera, is Dona's great-niece.[1] On Maré's more volatile days, the museum reminds the residents of their rich history. They can gather under its centrepiece, a replica of the type of house Dona built.

Many in Maré know Dona Orosina's story, but it took a group of teenage girls to bring her to the attention of the world.

Maré, Rio de Janeiro, February 2020

'Elephant,' I say.

Rhian looks up from the viewfinder of the Nikon F6. She's facing me, the camera pointed towards me.

'Really? Elephant?' she asks. I'm not sure if she's squinting at me because the sun is behind me, or if she is frowning disapprovingly.

'Yeah. I think so.' Suddenly I'm not so sure. 'Maybe not. Maybe it's in my head.'

'No, no,' Rhian says, turning her head so that her eyes find the shade. 'I wasn't questioning you. Elephant. Okay. Let's go.'

Because of regular gun violence and police raids, Maré has been determined to be a 'high risk' deployment by our BBC bosses back in London. We've had to go through an extensive risk assessment, writing down imagined responses to possible dangers. What would we do if our car broke down? If someone threatened us? If one of us fainted? What would we do if someone threatened us after the car broke down and one of us fainted, all at the same time?

James, our security advisor, told us to agree on a safe word. If one of us wanted to swiftly exit a situation, we would say it and the team, including our translator and driver, would have to comply – no questions asked. James explained that people filming high-risk documentaries often agree to safe words in challenging and unpredictable environments that can turn dangerous at any second. It is easier to have one unambiguous word than embark on a negotiation that will probably leave everyone confused.

For some reason, I thought it would be funny if the safe word was 'elephant'. Obviously no one laughed, but Rhian – who was the producer/director for this report – and James agreed that it was weird enough that we'd all remember it and unusual enough that we wouldn't accidentally say it and trigger an evacuation.

Now, on this street in Maré, I turn to our translator, Jan, who is talking to two men sitting on their doorsteps on opposite sides of the road.

'Excuse me, Jan,' I say, and when he looks up, I repeat the safe word: 'Elephant.'

Jan nods and waves over to our driver Joquiçan, who is inside the car, leaning back in the driver's seat. Joquiçan smiles broadly and gives us a thumbs up before starting the engine.

We are soon on the Linha Vermelha motorway, leaving Rio's North Zone and heading back to our hotel, bossa nova music pumping out from Joquiçan's radio. Complexo da Maré is blocked from view behind a brightly coloured Perspex wall that the Brazilian government constructed in time for the 2014 World Cup.

To travel from Rio International Airport to more postcard-friendly parts of the city, you have to drive past Maré. This Perspex barrier shields an excited traveller, keen to savour the gobsmacking beauty of Rio's art deco architecture and urban rainforest, from the reality of low-income favela living.

At the time of construction, the government pitched the wall as an acoustic barrier, a surface that would absorb the sound of traffic. It would be, they insisted, a service for the residents of Maré. The residents were having none of it, however. They called it the Wall of Shame, erected to hide them from the world.

'Megha?' Rhian asks gently as we drive. 'Are you okay?'

'Yeah, sorry. I am okay,' I reply, and then a breathless

word-vomit follows. I tell her that when we got to the street to film the B-roll, I had a strange feeling. A very, very strange feeling.

'What kind of a feeling?' she asks.

'I think we were being watched,' I say.

'Well, yes, they know we're not from there. People look at TV crews.'

She thinks I'm paranoid, I think.

I wonder if I should tell her about the boys I saw on the roof, but decide it would make me sound even more paranoid. We're journalists; we deal in facts. This was a feeling.

I need to get myself together by tomorrow, I tell myself.

The next morning we get a call from our contact Maira. She tells us not to come to Maré.

The gunfire started shortly after we left.

On our flight to Rio from London, a month before the global pandemic was declared, Rhian and I, who wanted both leg room and conversation, sat in the same row with the aisle between us and gossiped for the entire journey. It was six years since our last journalism deployment together – 2014 to Zambia to cover access to HIV medication for rural communities. We had bonded quickly over buffet breakfasts in our chain hotel as producers and the youngest women on the crew – both supporting acts for programmes led by older men. On our last night in Lusaka, we promised each other that we would work together one day when we could be in charge: I'd be the reporter and she'd be the director. Then Rhian moved to Portugal to work as a freelance camerawoman. We made the easy transition from colleagues to friends and rarely talked about work, until I invited her to come with me to Maré.

As a feminist, I had been aware of Maré since 14 March 2018, when Marielle Franco, a high-profile human-rights-activist-turned-politician who had grown up in the favelas, was executed along with her driver. Franco was shot three times in the head and once in the neck after leaving a talk titled 'Young Black Women Moving Power Structures'.

Her murder inspired angry protests across Brazil, and nowhere louder than in the favelas. The rage that women had pushed under the surface suddenly sprang out and exploded, and for days thousands gathered in the streets of Rio and São Paulo chanting 'Marielle, presente!' (Marielle is here) and 'Mulheres de Maré resistem! Não vá nos calar!' (The women of Maré resist! Do not shut us up!).

Marielle was thirty-eight years old when she died, and in that same week she had publicly denounced widespread police and government corruption. The man suspected of killing her, notorious hitman Adriano da Nóbrega, was then shot dead by the police, leading to even more questions. Nóbrega may have pulled the trigger, but hardly anyone in Maré believed he was the mastermind behind Marielle's murder. This was a woman who had been permanently shut up for speaking out.

Days after her death, Marielle's fiancé Mônica Benício told me in a telephone interview that she believed Marielle was killed for everything she represented: she was a young, Black, bisexual woman from the favelas. A woman who refused to be silent. Marielle's killing had set a fire in women, Mônica said. It gave birth to thousands of favela feminists.

Maré had attracted some journalists before Marielle's killing. For decades, at least three armed groups (involved with trafficking cocaine and crack) had been fighting for control of its territory, with deadly consequences.[2] Violence, the Eternal

War, attracts a certain type of storyteller. It was fairly easy to arrange a supervised visit with Brazil's police to Maré, and have them condemn gang violence.

Less investigated, though – by foreign broadcast media, at least – was the behaviour of the heavily armed state police themselves, who were the instigators of much of the violence, according to multiple eyewitnesses and human rights groups. The police would, as several favela residents I've spoken to insist, use rumours of gang threats or drug trafficking as excuses to install checkpoints or conduct spontaneous raids that would wreck the homes of people with no connection to the gangs. Rio's police denied this to me, but reports from Humans Rights Watch confirm that more than 9,000 people have been killed by police in the favelas since 2010, and three-quarters were young Black men and women.[3] However, few international news reports focused on this angle, and fewer still on the women from the favelas, unless the story was about what the women had lost to gun violence or drugs.

A story of women building peace doesn't always make it to the top of a news bulletin. A well-known veteran journalist friend of mine once told me that it's easier to get current affairs stories about women published if they sit within the expected rubric of a 'women's story' – rape, periods or babies. So I wasn't confident that I could get a commission, when I received an email in 2019 from a friend who worked in international development, asking if I'd heard about a group of teenage girls from Maré who were embarking on a unique archive-gathering project in the favelas. They had been going door-to-door in one of the most dangerous communities in Brazil, gathering oral histories that would otherwise disappear, about the women who had built Maré.

The girls had documented the story of Dona Orosina, the

mother of Maré. They had written about 'Maria of the Hole', a woman who had moved to Rio to find work in the 1960s. Maria of the Hole got her nickname because she couldn't afford a house, so she dug a trench on a plot of land in Maré and would sleep inside it each night. She looked after homeless or orphaned children, allowing them to share the ditch, which she expanded with each child. While going door-to-door, the girls found more than forty people, now adults aged thirty and above, who had been adopted by Maria of the Hole.

My bosses loved the pitch. They agreed that a different type of story needed to be told about Maré. I had a woman boss, who had a woman boss, who had a woman boss, and they all insisted that this report could go on *My World*, a children's TV programme on the BBC World Service.

My World was being executive-produced by the actress Angelina Jolie, who had expressed that she wanted to see more counterintuitive and empowering stories by and for young women, told by a new type of storyteller. And by 'a new type of storyteller' she may or may not have been referencing the viral 2016 NCTJ report about British journalism, which found that the industry – then 94 per cent white, 55 per cent male and dominated by gatekeepers who had attended private school – did not represent the cross-section of the population it was meant to serve.[4] Industry experts such as former BBC editor Marcus Ryder were vocal about the lack of diversity amongst foreign correspondents that was evident whenever you turned on the TV, arguing that we were all literally seeing the world reported through a white lens.[5]

I was desperate to meet the girls in Maré.

So, I WhatsApped Rhian, who now spoke excellent Portuguese, to ask if she fancied coming along. She instantly agreed and, within a few weeks, we were flying to Rio.

It was dark when we were picked up from the airport by Joquiçan, who would be our driver for the whole deployment. When you go anywhere that is deemed high-risk during a journalism deployment, it's best to partner with people who live or work in the area – people who know how to exit quickly and who can help you navigate the region respectfully. Joquiçan had lived in Maré his whole life. His vehicle wouldn't trigger questions from people who weren't expecting us.

We passed Maré on the way to our hotel, Joquiçan pointing it out on the side of the road – but it was hard to see in the dark, or over the Wall of Shame.

The next morning at eight, Joquiçan picked us up outside our hotel. He'd brought along Jan, a translator who had worked with several foreign media crews. Jan had also worked in Maré, so he knew the risks involved – and crucially, he knew a lot of people from there.

We all headed off to Maré in Joquiçan's car, Rhian and I in the back with the camera equipment between us.

I texted the Brazil group chat that had been set up for the trip, which included my bosses in London and James, the high-risk advisor. They'd asked us to send a message every three hours.

It took us around twenty minutes driving on the Linha Vermelha to get to Maré. Apart from gushing as we drove past the Christ the Redeemer statue, outstretching his giant twenty-eight-metre-span arms to us from Mount Corcovado, Rhian and I spent the journey talking over the schedule for the day. We agreed that the first day should be spent on introductions so the girls felt comfortable with us.

We were meeting eight of the girls, and because they were between the ages of fifteen and eighteen, I had messaged each of their parents to ask if they would accompany them to our interviews. The parents had all said that they would be happy if we met with the girls in a women-only building under the supervision of women from Redes da Maré, a civic network led by women from the favelas.

When we reached the border of Maré, both Joquiçan and Jan said 'Here!' in unison. Maré translates as 'tide' in Portuguese, and the buildings rose around us in a complex of colour, tin and concrete.

There are over a thousand favelas in Rio alone, born out of necessity. The end of slavery in Brazil in 1888 resulted in widespread rural unemployment, and thousands of Afro-Brazilians and labourers began to migrate to larger cities to look for employment. The Orosinos were part of this move. The informal settlements such as the one they built were called favelas as a reference to Brazil's 1897 civil war, according to writer Euclides da Cunha in his book *Backlands*. Soldiers camped on a mount where the thorny favela plant grew, and so any impoverished areas with temporary housing were nicknamed after the 'favela hills'.

My initial impression of Maré was that it throbbed with life.

The first thing I noticed were the brightly painted, box-shaped, flat-roofed buildings with levels stacked on top of each other to make tall houses on either side of the uneven roads. All the buildings I saw were made from concrete, brick and reinforced steel, although many had the bricks installed vertically (which saves material and time). Old men and women sat out in the street playing cards on plastic tables with beers. Their front doors were surrounded by potted plants. Children blew bubbles from bowls of soapy water. Hundreds of wires hung messily between electricity poles. There were clothes shops, electrical stores, and eateries on the corner of almost every narrow street. We had heard that there were over 3,000 businesses in Maré.

It felt like every building was blasting out music. I heard funk, forró, dancehall, Bad Bunny and Rihanna competing for dominance as people hanging out of windows talked to each other across the street.

I fell in love with Maré.

We went to meet the girls at Casa das Mulheres (House of Women), a concretised space built in 2016 after decades of organising by local women.

Joquiçan pulled up outside the building just as around twenty women were making their way inside. They looked like they were in their thirties and forties, and they walked in together in groups of two or three, their arms interlocked, laughing. The building had rows of flamboyantly coloured square tiles stuck onto its wall with painted words: Allegria (joy), Raça (race), Liberdade (freedom), Igualdade (equality). Further up the wall, written in white paint on sea-blue tiles, was the name 'Casa das Mulheres da Maré' – the House of the Women of Maré.

Inside, the hallway was small and neutral, with two doors leading to a large kitchen. The doors had small circular windows like on a cruise ship. Through them you could see the women who had walked in earlier, now wearing hairnets, standing in front of a large cooking station while a teacher gave them instructions. In the hallway, three women sat on cosy white couches working on laptops, with piles of law books, printed Excel spreadsheets and Post-it notes surrounding them.

Casa das Mulheres is run by women from the favelas, *for* women in the favelas. Every day, women come to drink coffee with friends, learn self-defence, cook, laugh, dance, heal, talk.

Women lawyers work inside, ready to offer legal advice, especially if women need to leave abusive partners.

'You're here to meet the girls?' a woman with pale brown hair, tied back in a loose bun, asked in English. 'They're up on the roof! My name is Maira. I'll take you.'

Rhian, Jan and I followed Maira up the wide steps flanked by potted plants instead of a banister. Jan, a man, was okayed to enter the women-only Casa das Mulheres because he fitted the sweet spot of being well known and respected as a translator by both the BBC's Latin American bureau and Maré residents. He was there as a supporting actor, to help a women-led team of me and Rhian connect with the women-led team of the favelas. The women of Casa das Mulheres approved of this.

We climbed the stairs up to the roof, passing a blue tile bearing the word 'Amor'.

You could hear the giggles getting closer with every step.

We were thirty minutes early, but the eight girls were all there, sitting on stools and beaming, the sweeping vista of their densely built neighbourhood stretching out behind us. The rooftops were alive with people – a buzzing, floating second city. Each rooftop showed a different postcard of favela life: Women hanging up wet clothes. A young couple cradling a newborn taking turns biting into a shared apple and kissing. A man sitting up in a shallow paddling pool smoking a cigarette, his eyes closed. Caged birds on a ledge chirping away as a group of shirtless boys looked down at the maze of streets below, drumming on the blue water tanks on their roofs and whistling whenever they saw a girl walk past.

The girls introduced themselves – Lorena, Julie, Thalita, their names overlapping, Thamires, Rayanne, laughing as they spoke, Stefany, Caroline, Ana Clara . . . I asked them to speak one at a time and slowly enough for Jan to translate.

Eighteen-year-old Lorena, who was wearing a red and white-spotted Rosie the Riveter headscarf, started talking first.

The girls had known each other since they were children, she explained, meeting at school and church, but they had only become close when the international women's festival, Women of the World, came to Rio in 2018. Eliana Sousa, the head of the Redes da Maré civic network, had seen this as an opportunity to showcase a different side to favela life. The Women of the World festival was a chance for women to tell their own stories, the way they wanted them to be told. Eliana had a vast network she could pull from and she asked the brightest women from Maré, of all ages, to brainstorm ideas.

The girls were influencers within Maré, with large Instagram followings – each of them displaying their unique talents. Stefany made beautiful clothes; Lorena cared about the environment and posted sustainability tips; Rayanna was a poet. The girls were the soul of Maré. Eliana had asked them to think of ideas for the festival.

When the girls met, they first considered an exhibition that could spotlight each of their skills, to demonstrate the richness and beauty within Maré. But after hours of discussion they came to a unanimous conclusion: the best way to share the story of Maré with the world would be to highlight the women who had come before. Favela women whose stories were not in the history books.

First, the girls mined the memories of their aunts and grandmothers, then women who lived next door, and a few doors beyond that. The girls asked them all the same question: Who were the women who built Maré? Through the answers they were given, they stumbled on stories about show dancers and midwives, teachers and healers, artists and activists.

These stories were displayed on posters at the Rio Museum of Art, which hosted the festival. It was such a success that the teenagers decided to stay together as a group. They gathered more oral histories and also started platforming their own skills – organising events and putting up stalls with their artwork around the streets of Maré.

During my first meeting with them on the rooftop, the girls spoke with such passion – reinforcing each other, stopping to hug each other, singing along when a song played from a neighbouring rooftop. I was surprised when Maira interrupted us to say that they would need the space back for a meeting. We had been talking for hours, none of it on tape, but it didn't matter. The girls were so charismatic and Maré so sparkling that I was confident that our report, a fresh look at the favelas, would tell itself.

As we hugged goodbye, we agreed to meet and film together the next day. The girls offered to take us to their homes to meet their families, eat at their favourite restaurant in Maré, go to a kickboxing class, and get a real sense of day-to-day favela life.

When we walked out of Casa das Mulheres, we asked if they knew somewhere we could get out our cameras and film some B-roll of the more lively parts of the favelas. We wanted footage of shops and restaurants, the kind of world-building vignettes you intersperse between scenes so the viewer is immersed in the community. Ana Clara said that she knew of a good spot; it was only a short walk away. Jan told Joquiçan to follow us in his car – he still had the camera equipment, as we had agreed that it wouldn't be wise to carry it while walking around the neighbourhood.

Ana Clara was seventeen, tall, with highlighted ringlets and large perfectly round glasses. She fell into step, linked arms with me, and began talking in rapid Portuguese.

'What's she saying?' I asked Jan, laughing with Ana Clara as she realised that she'd forgotten I did not speak Portuguese.

'She said it's nice to see a reporter who looks like her,' Jan said. 'She says if reporters come here they are always old white men. It's nice to see a girl who also has brown skin who likes the same things as her.'

'What kind of things does she think I like?' I asked.

Jan asked her and smiled at her answer. 'She says she saw you mouth along to songs playing in the background. You know all the words to Rihanna's "Pon de Replay".'

I laughed again, and with my free hand — the one not linked with hers — I leaned in to hug her from the side, clumsily pushing her into a shirtless boy who was walking past holding long metal piping. He lifted a palm as if to say 'don't worry' when I apologised, moving the piping onto his other arm, away from us, before walking off.

Except it wasn't piping. It was a machine gun.

After that, I saw guns everywhere.

The old men sitting outside houses playing cards had pistols clipped to their belts; young men sitting on the backs of vans held revolvers; middle-aged men leaned against walls with carbines. Then there was the evidence left by the guns: bullet holes on the front walls of dozens and dozens of the buildings we passed.

Ana Clara, her arm still linked with mine, had stayed in the same skippy mood after we ran into the boy with the gun. She waved at people she recognised, stopped to hug a younger-looking girl who was wearing low-slung sweatpants and a bikini top, and stayed with us when we filmed some street shots on a busy road near her home.

'Don't film without asking one of us if it's okay,' Ana Clara, our teenage bodyguard, said. 'Things turn quickly here.'

The following day, we filmed with eighteen-year-old Lorena at her bedsit. Outside her home, near a bank of grass, a group of young boys and girls were using a fallen tree as a climbing frame.

Lorena lived with her yappy dog, a pretty Brazilian terrier named Flora. Her room was immaculate, the smell a combination of bleach and cotton-scented candle. Lorena had painted her walls a seafoam blue and slept on a pink mattress that could be folded into a single seat. On the wall above her bed were shelves overflowing with books and a timetable of her schedule – night classes for college, and events she and the girls would be holding at Casa das Mulheres.

'Being a young woman who lives alone here, it is a political act,' she said in our interview. 'This is one of the most dangerous places in the world to be a feminist. We could be caught by a stray bullet, or we could be targeted if we speak up against the violence, like Marielle.'

Beside her bed, a well-thumbed book titled *Extraordinárias: Mulheres que Revoluticionaram o Brasil* (Extraordinary Women Who Revolutionised Brazil) lay open.

'I don't ever want to leave Maré,' Lorena continued. 'I am never alone. If I need anyone, I just message the girls' group chat and someone is here in minutes.'

After buying Lorena and her friend Kamilah lunch, Rhian said she wanted some B-roll of residential streets. But we didn't want to film outside the girls' houses or on the roads where they lived, as it would make them easy to locate. Joquiçan said he knew somewhere that was a few blocks away. We said goodbye to the girls and drove less than five minutes to our new spot.

There was no one on the road of squeezed houses when we pulled up. The gauzy curtains of the windows, which mostly had iron grills, were drawn, but you could hear the faint hum of a TV playing inside one of the houses closest to us.

I could see why this street would look good on film.

The houses were distinct and dramatic, each level a different colour with different types of bricks, as if they had been built in separate years, when people could afford the extension. Some jutted out into the road, boxing us in. Jan told us that once someone had lived in a space for five years, it legally became theirs, and while the buildings might not look uniform they were generally sturdy and crafted with great care.

When we exited Joquiçan's car, the sound of the TV suddenly stopped. A few moments later, the door to one of the houses opened. A tall and muscular man with leathery skin stood in the doorway, unsmiling. He watched Rhian fiddle with the lens of her camera, the narrow hallway behind him dark, cave-like and bare. Then, on the opposite of the road, another door opened and second man emerged. He too stood in his doorway, a dark cavern behind him, watching us.

Rhian was now crouched over, filming a close-up of a splatter of bullet holes on a white aluminium door – a reminder that, in 2019, there were 117 days of shootouts in different parts of Maré. The children in the area had missed twenty days of school because of the police raids that followed.[6]

Jan, who was standing next to me, followed my gaze and

spoke in rapid Portuguese to the men. I heard him say 'Eliana Sousa'.

Those were the magic words. Their faces relaxed. We asked them if it was okay if we filmed in their street, and they both nodded.

Rhian wanted to record me walking up and down the street as scene-setting footage to place me in Maré. She pointed her camera towards me and walked backwards as I went, a few steps ahead of me, with Jan acting as her back-watcher.

I thought about that saying 'Ginger Rogers did everything that her partner Fred Astaire did, but backwards and in high heels.' That's the same for the camera crew, doing everything you as a reporter do, but with the added pressure of making it look good – and without any of the praise.

'Look around you,' Rhian directed me. 'Look up!'

It was then that I saw the group of young men – no, boys – on one of the roofs, standing together silently and looking down on us from several storeys above ground. One was leaning on a ledge and three more were behind him. Two more appeared. I could only see them from the waist up. Then, from behind the ledge he was leaning on, the boy at the front lifted up an AK-47 and pointed it towards the sky. He smiled.

'Elephant,' I said.

The next day, while Rhian and I sit at the breakfast buffet of our hotel, Maira from Casa das Mulheres calls us at 7 a.m. to tell us not to come into the favelas.

Maira says she doesn't know who started the shooting the night before – whether it was between rival groups or initiated by the police – but it isn't over, and there is now crossfire and a raid by Brazil's heavily militarised police. No one is out in the streets, she tells us. Over a dozen schools have closed for the day and Maré's restaurants and shops have lowered their shutters. The girls are all safe, all accounted for, although fifteen-year-old Thalita's home has been raided, the furniture smashed or turned upside down. Her family are now washing the muddy footprints of police boots from their floors. Thalita is one of the few Afro-Brazilian girls in the group.

But will we still return to film? Maira asks. Will we now make the whole report about this violence?

We say 'Of course we will' and 'Of course we won't' – in that order.

In 2003, Eliana Sousa and her friend were eating dinner at a restaurant in Maré when the room suddenly fell quiet. People stood up and moved to the windows to look outside. An audience was gathering on both sides of the street. A group of excited teenage boys carrying large guns were pushing a wooden cart down the road. Inside it sat another young boy, his arms and feet restrained tightly by ropes. He looked terrified. They were the main attraction of this spontaneous parade.

Eliana's friend, who was not from Maré, looked confused. Was this some sort of theatre?

'The tied-up boy has probably stolen something or lied to drug dealers,' Eliana explained to her. 'They are taking him to be killed.'

Her friend's eyes widened and she stared at Eliana for several moments.

'How can you say that so casually, Eliana?' she asked her finally. 'That young boy is about to be murdered.'

It was then that Eliana saw the scene through her friend's eyes. The ritual that didn't shock Maré bystanders was deeply abnormal and horrifying, she realised. She had spent years advocating for access to basic rights such as clean water and education, but she hadn't thought much about the right to peace. She vowed to create more spaces for peace in Maré.

Eliana had been immersed in Maré community life since her parents moved there in the 1970s, when she was seven years old. As a child she helped out at her family's bodega, chatting with people from all over the favelas who came through to buy their daily groceries. She saw the police, who regularly patrol Maré's streets, target innocent young people, only for the media to incorrectly report the deaths as crossfire in gang violence.

Eliana was one of the first women from Maré to attend university, and at twenty-two she ran for neighbourhood president as part of the Pink Slate – an organising group that playfully leaned into the colour to embrace a women-centred approach. She successfully lobbied the city's council to bring refuse collection and running water into her community. She then fundraised for an office from which she could work, reaching out to private donors and feminist groups in Brazil, and paid cartographers to literally put Maré on maps. Soon, people in the favelas were getting mail delivered to them. In 1994, Maré was officially recognised as a bairro, or neighbourhood.

'Don't write about me as the only woman who is working for change. We are a community,' Eliana tells me when we meet after the shootout. 'Maré is a community built by many, many women. It is a community that is healed by many, many women.'

It was through a community brainstorm that they came up with the idea of holding night classes to help more young people from the favelas successfully prepare for university entrance exams. One of the girls who attended the night classes was Marielle Franco. Several of Maré's residents have told me that Marielle looked to Eliana as a mentor, but Eliana refuses to take sole credit.

'Marielle grew up in our environment of women's community activism,' she tells me. 'She saw that it was mostly women who were improving our environment, preserving our culture, creating art, cleaning up and patching up the community after violence. Marielle wanted to be part of that. Her way of advocating for change was to become a politician and represent us from the inside.'

The favelas were and are a dangerous place to live and work – all the nuance in storytelling cannot sugar-coat that reality. This is, especially, an added pressure on women. While men are killed at a higher rate in Brazil's favelas, women and girls are deeply affected by the gendered and racialised hierarchies. This vulnerability is evident in a myriad of terrifying statistics: in Brazil, a woman is raped every ten minutes,[7] and killed every six hours.[8] Black women are more likely to be the victims of violence. In 2021, Black women accounted for 67.4 per cent of all female homicide victims in Brazil, with a murder rate 79 per cent higher than that of non-Black women.[9] It's important to note these figures are based on reported cases, and under-reporting remains a significant issue.

But in Maré, few women admit that they are victims of violence. In a study conducted in Maré in 2017, 76 per cent of the women interviewed said they saw gendered violence against women in the favelas – but only 28 per cent said they had experienced it themselves.[10] The study leaders concluded that the women were either not openly admitting their own experiences, or they didn't recognise the abuse they had experienced as harmful, instead accepting it as the norm.

'It is because of all these pressures that we need a space for just women,' Eliana tells me. 'So they find the words to acknowledge their experiences by leaning on each other.'

For Eliana, it is essential to have these women-only spaces in favelas, which swarm with the hypermasculinity that gender experts from South America called 'machismo'. Machismo situates manliness with the expectation of dominance in community and family structures. This is often shown by the display of violence or the carrying of guns in masculine third places, which are community spaces separate from home and work. These include the ruas (streets), barzinhos (bars) and jogos de futebol (football games, especially in the neighbourhood).

If favela men have these male-only spaces, it's only right that women should too, Eliana adds. 'No one woman should be alone in her struggle, or her triumphs. Complete, unpolished, uninterrupted thoughts. We must share it all.'

Then she repeats a quote that is the mantra at Casa das Mulheres, underpinning the importance of community: 'Women are like water – they grow when they meet.'

Water – like the Balobedu in South Africa, who believe women are rain.

The day after the shootout ends, we return to meet the girls at a large warehouse. Casa das Mulheres has borrowed a number of spaces around the favelas to hold a series of listening sessions for the women of Maré.

The girls have said they want to continue filming.

'It's important that the world knows about us, how we live,' Lorena says.

No one knows how many people have been shot, but the girls know at least one boy they grew up with has been killed. Rio's police have said he died in the crossfire. Another 'stray bullet' ending the life of another young boy in the favelas.

The girls are struggling with his death, for complex reasons. The boy was not a friend. He had previously sexually attacked one of their friends. Yet they were devastated to hear of his death and feel guilty for mourning him.

We are told not to ask them about him.

'We don't want to add to the gossip,' says Pamela Carvalho with a smile, as she ushers us all to sit in a circle on the floor. 'Today we create!'

Pamela calls herself a cultural coordinator at Casa das Mulheres, and her specialism is a mixture of counselling with oral history and art.

She hands the girls sheets of white paper and places a tub of colouring pens in the middle. 'Write down, in large letters, "woman" at the centre of the page,' she instructs. '*Mulher.*'

They do.

'Now write down the best qualities of your favourite woman.'

As adjectives like 'strong', 'fun' and 'kind' are scribbled on the pages, Pamela moves her thick, long locs from her face and mops beads of sweat that are gathering on her forehead.

She turns on a fan. 'I hope it gets cooler before Carnival,' she says, looking over at the girls and winking. The largest street festival in the world, where 2 million people parade the streets of Rio, is three days away.

'You see, it's important that you remember on days like this that being a woman from Maré is a well from which you can draw,' she says. 'You have enough women from Maré who you can evoke. Ask them for help, they will come. Ask Dona Orosino to come.'

The girls continue to write on their sheets.

'Now write down the name of a woman you admire.'

Rather predictably, almost everyone scribbles 'my mother' and almost everyone also writes 'Marielle Franco'.

'When attacks happen, we are interrupted,' Pamela says. 'For young women like you, there is plenty of interruption.'

Pamela then walks slowly around the outside of the circle – around the girls.

'When you are interrupted, we, the older women of Maré, will pull you back to who you are. Then you will pull younger women back to who they are.'

Although I don't think this at the time, years later, when I reviewed the footage Rhian filmed of this session, I will wonder if this was a modern form of a women's circle, like the ones that First Nations Australian women take part in. A gathering to draw strength from women elders who have paved the way for your troubled community, and to commune in a physical space, with other women, on your own land. Perhaps it's similar to the gathering of the Rain Queen and her wives as they communed with their ancestors. A promise that there is more to life than the troubles we face in this world.

The girls are quiet for several moments before Pamela gets up and moves over to a radio on a table next to the fan. Classic, old-school Rihanna comes on. The girls, who were expressionless for the entirety of Pamela's speech, doodle on their pages.

Then Julie starts humming along and Rayanne joins in. Thalita asks if anyone wants to come to her house that evening for dinner. They have cleaned up now, she says, and the furniture has been put back to where it was before.

'Are you okay?' Caroline asks Thalita.

She looks up from her paper, nods and smiles, and goes

back to thickening the 'M' of the 'Mulher' written on her sheet of paper.

The police found a dog-eared piece of paper at the home of the hitman who shot Marielle Franco. A list of names. The Brazilian press called it a 'kill list'.

Eliana Sousa's name was on that list.

'We don't know who ordered Marielle's killing, but we know that they have their eyes on us,' she says as we sat in a garden near Casa das Mulheres, a mural for Marielle behind us.

Eliana is wearing a purple jumpsuit.

'The colour of women,' I say, referencing the branding adopted for International Women's Day to represent the feminist fight for gender parity.

'Deliberately,' Eliana replies. 'The colour of achievements gained and achievements still to come.'

I read about the kill list while back in London, but I wasn't sure how to broach it with Eliana. As it turns out, she speaks about it first. Besides her and Marielle, the list included several people working to improve the favelas of Rio – women and men speaking out against the oppression of the poor, against police and government brutality.

'Being a woman who refuses to be quiet, who doesn't just accept the lot she has been given in life, is a threat to a lot of people,' she says. 'For women, the threat is everywhere.'

The threat is, indeed, everywhere. During my hours of conversation with them over the years, several of the women – and girls – I meet in Maré will tell me about abuse they have experienced, domestic violence at home from fathers and brothers, and sexual violence from men around them. One tells me about being raped daily by a man whose house she cleaned, petrified to say anything in case she lost her income.

I have chosen (and choose) not to go into detail about this. Not because they asked me not to, but because the women are so much more than the worst things done to them by men. To allow them a platform to speak about their work, they have been made to trade graphic details of this violence by many male and many Western reporters.

When the coronavirus outbreak was declared a pandemic by the World Health Organization on 11 March 2020, the women of the favelas organised at the Casa das Mulheres kitchen to make food to distribute in Maré. Over WhatsApp, Eliana told me there was another reason for their community outreach. In the months that followed the WHO announcement, UN Women declared a 'shadow pandemic' – the alarming increase in gendered domestic violence as women were trapped at home with their abusers. In asking Maré women to help distribute food in the favelas, Eliana was also removing those who she suspected lived in potentially dangerous home environments for some of the day, under the guise of helping the community.

'It's a woman-only building, so these women could tell their husbands that no man is allowed while they worked,' Eliana said, 'and then we could advise them, and get them help.'

Some of the women who helped in the kitchens told me that Casa das Mulheres quite literally saved their lives.

The women of Maré had once again identified the problem and found the solution.

Casa das Mulheres is so much more than a four-storey, women-only building. It's a place born out of necessity.

'Help doesn't come to the favelas,' Eliana tells me. 'We have to help ourselves and each other. We need one space for just us. The most vulnerable of us can speak honestly if men are not allowed in this one space.'

At Casa das Mulheres, women organise for the good of the entire community. It's more than a shelter or a gathering place to learn and heal. It's an informal parliament, a city hall. The headquarters of a new way of living; a place that can organise food parcels for thousands of people while also allowing women to save each other. A place to have tea while seeking legal advice to end an abusive relationship. A place to sit with your friends on a rooftop while mourning the violent death of a neighbour. A place to organise a prayer or a protest. A place to come up with a business plan and learn self-defence. A place to just stop, drink coffee, eat cake and gossip with your friends.

A place away from the guns and away from the machismo of the streets outside. A model of what governance could look like when women decide they will build a world from a wetland.

The girls grow up, March 2023

The girls don't see each other every day any more.

Although she couldn't have imagined it in 2020, Lorena did leave the favelas. After university, she joined a business that promotes sustainable living. The day she moved out of Maré, all the girls turned up to her bedsit with cardboard boxes to help her pack up.

'I have left my address in Maré, but I haven't left the girls,' she said when we spoke over a video call years later. 'We are a community. That doesn't change if your address changes.'

Stefany now runs a thrift shop in Maré, featuring the

designs of artists from the favelas. Theramis is married and starting a family. Thalita works for a project supported by Malala Yousafzai, which aims to amplify the voices of young women from under-represented communities around the world. Ana Clara and Rayanne work for Casa das Mulheres, acting as supervisors for younger favela women who come through the doors looking for sisterhood.

The girls' group chat still pings daily, packed with news of individual triumphs, memes, songs and struggles. Their group chat is an online outpost of Casa das Mulheres – a digital women-only group where they share their complete, unpolished, uninterrupted thoughts. An enclave where they can work through their differences and take comfort in a shared identity.

4

The Evolution of Womyn's Lands

United States, 1970s

I won't be able to tell you exactly where I am, but I am on womyn's land – one of the last ones left in North America.

It takes me twenty hours, two flights and a two-hour drive to reach here from London. This is a permanent live-in women-only community. I wonder if it is similar to the beguinage in Belgium, or Umoja village in Kenya (more on that later). Unlike either of those places, this one is not advertised and it doesn't invite tourists, but the women here have invited me. I heard about them through a lesbian land directory. After I had spoken with them on several video calls, the women on the land agreed that I could visit and see how they live and how their community without men works, as long as I don't name their location. It's less to do with a fear for their safety and more a concern for privacy. The women do not want their land to turn into a spectacle that attracts people from outside their community.

I've mostly been speaking to Lynn, the first woman to move onto the land. She warned me that it would be challenging to find a taxi to agree to take me from their nearest domestic US airport to their land. She offered to pick me up, but I told her not to worry about me; I'd find my own way.

'You're an independent one,' she replied. 'A good quality in a woman.'

I had assumed it would take less effort to get to here, but six airport Uber drivers cancelled my request. Had I known how long it would take to find a driver to take me to this small highway town, where there are no restaurants that deliver food and a very patchy phone signal, I might have been less independent and taken up Lynn's offer.

It is the beginning of spring, and the first pops of chlorophyll have started to creep through the wintery tree limbs. Every now and then, redbud shrubs, with their twisting trunks and arresting lavender-pink flowers, demand attention. They seem to be multiplying in frequency as we drive closer to Lynn. But as we leave the freeway from the airport and head inland, into the rural American South, I keep wondering where the people are. No one is walking on the country lanes that thread out from our empty two-lane road. I can't see anyone on the farmlands on either side, and no one is pottering outside on the front lawns of the single-storey, ranch-style houses. Could a place this sparsely populated, in a part of America known for its conservative values, really be home to an intentional community of lesbians?

There are lots of American flags on poles, lots of hand-drawn 'Jesus Loves You' signs planted on sweeping fields where black Angus cows graze on gentle knolls. A hundred years ago there were more than 200 dairy farms in this county, and today there are fewer than ten. We're quite a way south of the Mason–Dixon Line that served as the division point of the North and the South during the American Civil War (1861–1865). States north of the line fought against the practice of slavery, while southern states, where I am now, were staunch supporters of the practice.

THE EVOLUTION OF WOMYN'S LANDS

When we reach the blinking red stoplight next to the small 1950s-style gas station, I sit up in my seat. We're close.

As my Uber turns into the gravelly private road, acres of flat land, sown through with blueberry bushes and daffodils, open up before us. Ahead, I can see a group of one-storey homes built metres from each other. They are each painted a different shade of pale pastel and have slanted gable roofs. Two have large porches where a number of rocking chairs with cushions and rainbow-coloured throws are grouped together, facing the land. A chicken coop housing four hens is cordoned off with electric wire. Peeking through clusters of bushes are two other homes, set a little back from the lane. There are more homes I can't see.

This open space is bordered by a line of towering pine trees, beyond which the woods are waiting. I've been told about the walking trails and ponds, and the hundred-year-old farrowing huts that once housed farm pigs.

My driver edges us up the lane, towards the group of pastel-coloured homes. We pass an old, abandoned wood cabin, one storey with an attic, its slats weathered and hugged by tendrils of poison ivy. Perhaps it was once a sharecropper's cabin – a home for an employee who worked the land. They were almost always Black people. Some still call these cabins 'slave houses', where farm owners previously kept enslaved people.

'You don't have to go far in the South before you see our painful history,' Lynn told me over a video call months earlier. 'It's in the buildings and sometimes it's in the people.'

Ahead of us I see a woman with short grey hair and large cat-eye-shaped glasses standing on a porch, her expression unreadable from the car. When she sees me waving from the back seat she waves back and walks down the steps, smiling.

She's the first person I've seen, aside from the Uber driver, in over forty-five minutes.

'Welcome, welcome.' Lynn hugs me and takes my suitcase, ignoring my protests that I can carry it myself. This is the first time a woman – a person – in their seventies has carried anything for me.

Lynn was born in the 1940s, in another part of the South, to parents who had been farmers but lost everything in the Great Depression. She was a child at a time when the United States was strictly divided along racial lines, and Lynn saw the poison of exclusion first-hand. There were Ku Klux Klan rallies where she grew up. Her mother used to say, 'Black people, they aren't like us.' It repulsed Lynn, and by her early twenties she had moved to New York, and later Massachusetts, throwing herself into anti-racism and women's rights activism.

She realised she was a lesbian then, and even though it was easier to be so in a city, she wanted to live in rural America and grow the food she ate. She also wanted community.

When Lynn and her girlfriend Yahoo bought the land that we are on, in 1988, they imagined a group of women, a lesbian community, sharing the farmhouse as a communal area and having small individual living spaces. The women would sometimes eat together and make a living from cottage farming, growing crops on the land and selling them at local markets. All profits would be shared in a joint fund for the women living on the land. That was the dream.

But by the early 2000s Lynn, now alone, needed to rethink her vision. Her friend Doreen encouraged her to consider dividing up the land and selling it to women. Women would feel more incentivised to move there if they could own their part of the land.

'I didn't want that at first,' Lynn says. 'I didn't like the idea of private property, of splitting up the land and turning it into a neighbourhood. I wanted a more intensive lesbian community.'

But she yielded, and today fifty acres are split between seven private lots and the other fifty acres are woods, which are placed in a land trust and available to all the women who live on the land. Covenants agreed by the women state that the lots cannot be subdivided and the woods cannot be built on. Other agreements include no commercial pesticides, no visible guns, the division of expenses for a tractor, the upkeep of the shared drive, and letting each other know if there's a visitor to the land. And men? Are they allowed on the land?

'Even the strictest separatist womyn's land communities allowed men on sometimes, friends and family, and also to do labour,' says Lynn. 'But they can't own property here.'

Fifteen women are part of the land community – although they're rarely all there at one time. Some regularly travel, and some use their houses here as holiday homes. The oldest women are in their late seventies, and the two youngest were born in the 2000s. Joni*, who is eighteen when I first speak to her in 2023, has jokingly nicknamed it Lesbian Lane.

The beginning of womyn's lands

To understand why North American lesbian lands emerged, we need to search the archives of the 1960s and 1970s. This was a particularly hostile time for women in the US. An unmarried woman couldn't always get a credit card, and a married woman often needed a co-signature from her husband. Universities like Yale and Princeton didn't accept women until 1969; Harvard waited until 1977. This was also a time when more and more women were entering the salaried workplace – only to find it an environment of steep pay discrepancy. John F. Kennedy's President's Commission on the Status of Women produced a report in 1963 stating that women earned fifty-nine cents for every dollar made by a man. Similarly, a 1976 survey by US women's magazine *Redbook* revealed that 80 per cent of women respondents in the US had encountered sexual harassment in the office.[1]

And these setbacks were for middle-class heterosexual white women. The vista was even more bleak, even more hostile, for women of colour, and lesbians. It is well documented that homosexuality was classified as a mental illness in the *Diagnostic and Statistical Manual of Mental Disorders* until 1973.

Lynn was in her twenties then, when a number of movements including second-wave feminism, civil rights and gay rights were beginning to overlap to form a surprising offshoot microculture: the women's 'back to the land' movement. Groups were moving to rural locations with the hope of dismantling patriarchal structures and building a new world together.

Dozens of womyn's lands sprang up throughout the US, Australia and parts of Western Europe, including France, England and Scotland. These women built houses and began to farm, with each group creating its own set of laws and covenants. The lands were intentional communities that methodically and deliberately erased a patriarchal notion from their identity. They were for 'womyn' or 'wommon' or 'wimmin' – words that defiantly removed the mention of 'men' in 'women'.

The women of womyn's lands in the US, who were mostly lesbian and bisexual, referred to themselves as 'landykes'. Their focus was social and economic freedom in agrarian societies. Many grew their own food and lived without running water and electricity. Some bathed in the surrounding lakes and pooped in buckets in the woods. All were keen to form a society that operated at a different pace, not only from heteronormative America but also the rhythm of the urban gay scene, dominated as it was by city-focused people.

'There was an exciting idea in the air, that a different world was possible for women and for lesbians,' Julie Enszer, editor of the US lesbian literary journal *Sinister Wisdom*, told me. 'As well as women's liberation and gay liberation, the landyke movement was also influenced by the hippie era of the 1960s.'

In the mid-twentieth century, North American women, of all races, were mostly confined to strict gender roles that centred around domestic labour and supporting their wage-earning husbands. According to the National Center for Family & Marriage Research, the proportion of women who were married was highest in 1960, at approximately 65 per cent.[2] (The US marriage rate hit a fifty-year low in 2020, when there were 28.1 marriages per 1,000 unmarried women.[3])

The promoted image of the married American woman was a political one.

'Embedded in the propaganda of the time was the idea that the nuclear family was what made Americans superior to the Communists,' says the PBS article 'Mrs. America: Women's Roles in the 1950s'. 'American propaganda showed the horrors of Communism in the lives of Russian women. They were shown dressed in gunnysacks, as they toiled in drab factories while their children were placed in cold, anonymous day care centres. In contrast to the "evils" of Communism, an image was promoted of American women, with their feminine hairdos and delicate dresses, tending to the hearth and home as they enjoyed the fruits of capitalism, democracy, and freedom.'⁴

By the 1960s, a counterculture movement had emerged, backed by women beat writers like Joyce Johnson and popstars like Joan Baez. This group publicly rejected social norms that forced women to care for husbands and homes and children. The possibility of freedom was in the air.

The Civil Rights Movement demanded equality for African Americans and other people of colour. It was a century since slavery had been abolished, but there was still widespread discrimination against Black people, with Jim Crow laws preventing people from accessing every part of society, from certain schools to bathrooms. The Civil Rights Act of 1964, which prohibited discrimination on the basis of race, gave a glimpse of a new way.

The marches and acts of civil disobedience had worked, inspiring other marginalised groups, including LGBT people, to consider how they too could demand to be seen and heard. The 1969 Stonewall riots – where police raided and targeted gay men at a gay club located in Greenwich Village in New York City – triggered violent protests and were a stimulus for the mainstream discussion of gay rights within the United States and around the world.

Feminism was also emerging from the fringes into mainstream discourse. A network of publications, presses, magazines and periodicals started up that were discussing women's rights; it was known as the Women in Print movement. Betty Friedan's 1963 book *The Feminine Mystique* made clear that not all women were satisfied with housework, marriage and child-rearing. Although she certainly wasn't the first feminist to write this, the book punched through to the mainstream, bringing feminist thinking to the attention of an everyday audience, including suburban mothers and housewives. But Friedan, like many feminist activists of the time, was famously exclusionary towards lesbians. She referred to them as a 'lavender menace', telling the National Organization for Women (NOW) in 1969 that their inclusion would be a threat to the feminist movement, making feminists look like man-haters who could not be accepted as respected members of conventional society. Several NOW members resigned, stating that Friedan was demonstrating a clear lack of understanding of the additional discrimination lesbians had to contend with.

'The exclusion from heterosexist feminism struck a deep and painful chord with lesbian and queer women,' says writer Bethany Kaylor in her long read 'Who Wants to Live on Women's Land?' 'Straight women like Friedan didn't have to worry about losing their family, or being thrown into a psych ward, or fired from their jobs, or denied a line of credit, or violently attacked, all because "homosexuality" was considered deviant and, in certain states, illegal.'[5]

Eventually, years later, at a women's conference in 1977, Friedan pledged her support for lesbians and admitted her error.

Negotiating a new way of living that embraced equality meant rethinking the old system entirely, especially for lesbians. The nuclear heteronormative family, headed by a man, was obviously unappealing. Feminism that didn't include lesbians, even more so. A desire to break with convention saw the rise in communal living for all genders, according to writers like Professor Timothy Miller, author of *The 60s Communes: Hippies and Beyond*, who says that hundreds of thousands of young people around the world set out to live in alternative communities.

The back-to-the-land movement emerged, and as many

as a million young Americans left the suburbs and cities and moved to rural parts of the country, with the goal of disrupting a corporate-growth, American dream mindset. They wanted to grow their own food and rely on their own personal labour. According to a *New York Times* clipping from 1975, one of the back-to-the-land mottos was 'Make Do with Less' – 'less machinery, less technology, less everything that comes from and depends on big business'.[6] This was appealing to women who had spent the past few years demanding a shake-up of the system. Lesbians especially were feeling revolutionary, and the idea of a true separation from the patriarchal order suddenly seemed possible.

'There was now the possibility to reimagine every aspect of life, from where they were living, how they were living, who they were living with, how work could be divided in households, how intimate relationships could be organised, how families could be organised,' Julie Enszer explained to me. 'All that prompted a group of women to say we could have an independent agrarian kind of lifestyle in land communities that reflected hippie values, values of feminism, that reflected values of lesbian liberation. And they went off and said, "How could we build this?"'

Julie recommended that I speak to author and academic Rose Norman – who co-founded the Southern Lesbian Feminist Activist Herstory Project and has interviewed over a hundred women from womyn's lands in North America. Rose responded within days to my email and was generous with sharing her expertise. As a journalist it's wonderful when people share their resources and knowledge with one another, instead of gatekeeping. I've been lucky that women have been generous this way with me, throughout my career.

Rose told me that the first lesbian womyn's land group in

the US was most likely started by writer Corky Culver. Corky had been part of a consciousness-raising (commonly referred to as 'CR') activist group in the late 1960s. Lesbian women, who often felt unwelcome in heterosexual feminist and male-led gay spaces, had begun CR groups in order to galvanise their place within activism, and Corky Culver's was believed to have been one of America's first CR spaces. Corky, along with around a dozen friends, bought forty acres of land outside Melrose in Florida. They started a residential lesbian land community called the North Forty in 1972, and it is still active as a community today. Soon after, the women's community We'moon opened to around ten women who lived in homes on fifty-two acres of forests and fields in Oregon.

Southern Oregon became a popular destination for back-to-the-landers. This was mainly due to its 'fertile soil, cheap land, and close proximity to northern California, where hippie and counterculture communities had already established themselves', wrote Heather Jo Burmeister in her essay 'Rural Revolution: Documenting the Lesbian Land Communities of Southern Oregon'.[7] It's believed that hundreds of individuals, families and groups – including lesbians – moved to the region. By the 1980s, there were over two dozen womyn's lands that were publicly and privately operational in the area. The 160-kilometre stretch of land between Grants Pass and Roseburg is nicknamed 'Amazon Country' because the hills resemble breasts, says writer Bethany Kaylor.

Each community had its own culture. Rules on the use of drugs, eating of meat, inclusion of boy children and owning private property varied greatly depending on the community. There was only one shared value: that men were not allowed to permanently live there.

'Residents at OWL Farm shared meals and a bank account,

while those at Rainbow's End lived more autonomously, each in their own cabins. Fly Away Home sat atop a mountain and Cabbage Lane in a wide ravine,' writes Sasha Archibald in her essay 'On Wimmin's Land'. 'WomanShare was nicknamed "fat city" because it had electricity and hot water.'[8]

One of the first women to chronicle the stories of women-only land communities was writer Joyce Cheney, who published a collection of interviews, essays and photos in the book *Lesbian Land* in 1985. *Lesbian Land* became a cult favourite and inspired retired University of Louisiana professor Jean Boudreaux, known in lesbian communities as Shewolf. She travelled across North America in her little camper van (nicknamed Casita) and compiled a directory of womyn's land communities (at least, ones who were willing to be listed) in *Shewolf's Directory of Wimmin's Lands and Lesbian Communities*.

Writer Cedar Heartwood, who lived in one of the communities Shewolf visited, described her as 'our troubadour, carrying the news from one place to the next, singing the praises of what each community was accomplishing. Our lands were so remote, and often we didn't know the other women who lived remotely too. She knew us all, and she sat in on all the meetings and we let her because she was trustworthy. She was careful not to spill the beans, not to gossip or tear down any of the communities she visited. She was as likely to say, "Why, what did you hear?" To seemingly agree without adding to the controversy. Her role was to bring women together on the land, to invite and connect.'[9]

Shewolf's first directory was published in 1993, and she kept up her networking through to the sixth edition in 2016, listing dozens of collectives.[10] She died in 2020, at the age of eighty-eight.

Some have claimed that, at their height in the 1970s,

thousands of womyn's lands were operating in North America, Australia and Western Europe. Having spoken to over a dozen lesbians who have visited several womyn's land communities in the US, Scotland, Wales and Australia, I'd say this is highly unlikely.

'I was trying to figure out if there was any way to analytically deduce the number of womyn's lands,' Rose Norman told me, adding that *Lesbian Land* author Joyce Cheney corresponded with ninety womyn's land groups and visited around thirty in the 1980s. And then lesbian country magazine *Maize* names about a hundred, although some that are listed are no longer active.

I shared that, during my research, several women had repeated a fact – that there had been many womyn's lands around the world. Maybe thousands, all homing lesbians who didn't want to be found. Women who wanted to stay out of reach.

Rose shrugged, as if to say *there's no way of knowing for sure*.

'I agree that there is a strand of the womyn's land communities that do not want to interface with the outside world, that don't want to be counted,' she conceded. 'But thousands? I doubt it.'

A dream without detail

By the 1970s, within the vibrant New York activism scene, Lynn knew that she was a lesbian. She edged towards women-only organising communities, which were fighting for the creation of domestic violence shelters and rape crisis centres.

'When you see the threat men can pose, you feel safer away

from them,' Lynn tells me. 'You know you'll be relaxed if you can live without that threat.'

Then there was an opportunity to live in Massachusetts, where Lynn became the director of the Women's Service Center – a specialist service for abused women. She loved the centre's farmhouse where the women could garden and spend their evenings sitting outside, breathing in clean air. She loved growing vegetables. But Massachusetts has extreme seasons, and the killer frost meant she couldn't always grow her vegetables. She soon learned carpentry and assisted another woman who restored old buildings.

Lynn had lived in cities, including in northern New York state, for over a decade in order to fully embrace her sexuality and be part of the civil and women's rights movements. But she missed the rural South, where she had been born – and where she could enjoy reasonable seasons and grow ripe tomatoes.

'If you were an out lesbian in the 1970s, you tended to live in a city where you could find more people like you,' she tells me. 'But I'm from the country. The South was calling me back.'

As she's speaking, I briefly recall Jody Kopp speaking about First Nations Australian women feeling the call and connection to land – the call of Country. I tune back in to Lynn, who is now telling me about feeling inspired by reading *Lesbian Land*, and discovering the different women forming intentional communities. After meeting Yahoo, she felt spurred on to create their own.

Lynn and Yahoo's idea was to have a community of women sharing resources and food. 'It was a dream without detail,' Lynn says now.

Yahoo shared Lynn's desire for nature and fellowship.

She'd been part of several new-age spiritual communities, with one of them responsible for the nickname Yahoo. 'It was well before the computer age, so nothing to do with the search engine.' Lynn laughs. 'Yahoo was a sound made during a spiritual celebration.'

Yahoo was an adventurous woman. Like Lynn, she embraced the outside world, tending to it, planting on it, climbing it, exploring it. The earth was a gift and they wanted to honour it – to lay roots as a couple.

The land we are on was available for $1,000 an acre. A bargain, but Lynn and Yahoo did wonder whether they would be welcomed in a small town like this, which sparsely fanned out from a singular crossroad. There were only a handful of neighbours and farmsteads. People were openly conservative. Houses proudly displayed the Confederate flag on their front lawns and many farms still had their abandoned sheds that may have housed enslaved people – the haunting slave houses. It was unclear if a lesbian couple would be accepted.

'When people get to know us and see we're hard-working,' Yahoo told Lynn, 'they'll be fine with us.'

Yahoo was right. The couple were welcomed into the fold. Over the next few years their neighbours waved when they saw the two planting tomatoes, chopping wood, trimming their redbuds or tending to their goats. The couple seemed to be looking ahead to a long and flourishing life together.

Then, in 1992, Yahoo died unexpectedly in a mountain-climbing accident. Lynn held a memorial ceremony for her outside their farmhouse, between the hundred-year-old magnolia and pecan trees. Hundreds of people came to mourn Yahoo's death – a lesbian who had bought land with her girlfriend at a time when gay marriage was illegal across the country and animosity to same-sex couples was peaking during the AIDS crisis. Some neighbours attended. Lynn wondered if they knew the two had been lovers.

Does the town know?

Lynn drops me off at the bed and breakfast that sits on a goat farm four kilometres away. It's owned by her long-time friends. They're goat farmers. Good people. I won't get to meet them as they're away for the weekend. There's no one else staying at the B&B either, but the farmhands will be around during the day. They'll be busy though, as it's kidding season. Lots of lovely baby goats will be born while I'm here. In the evenings, I'll be alone.

'I hope you don't get spooked out there, by yourself,' Lynn says as the kettle in the B&B kitchen starts whistling. 'Some city folk can't sleep out here.'

The B&B is a large two-storey farmhouse surrounded by a wide wraparound porch, and Clare, one of the farmhands, is waiting to take me to my room. Around us, the hundreds of acres of land are a portal to the South's rural past: there's a log hay barn and granary, a smokehouse dating to 1880, a tobacco barn from the 1940s. Three guinea hens toddle quietly across the garden in front of us, heading towards a cluster of sheds.

When Lynn leaves, Clare says that she's heard that I'm a journalist.

'Why are you here, though?' she asks. 'Nothing happens here.'

'I'm writing about women's communities,' I reply.

'Women's communities?' Clare repeats, her forehead creasing slightly. 'Like women farmers?'

I look at her and wonder if she knows that, only a few

kilometres away, there's land where men are not allowed to live.

The spirit of MichFest

Sometimes Lynn and the women who live on the land get messages from travelling lesbians, looking for camping space. The group almost always agrees.

Six of the women, and a friend visiting from Canada, have organised a pot-luck dinner. It's a clear March evening as we pile our plates with a wholesome vegetarian feast of bean stew, sauerkraut, devilled eggs and baked sweet potatoes, before heading for the porch.

I look out at the picture-postcard view. Three dogs, including Lynn's fifteen-year-old Labrador, Gabby, lie in the garden next to pockets of daffodils – in front of the sheep pen, where around half a dozen lambs were born a week earlier. There's a light breeze carrying a raft of red maple leaves, which spiral down, rotating like helicopter blades. This place would make a killing on Airbnb, I muse, before silently telling myself off for thinking in terms of transaction and profit.

I ask them about women's spaces generally, if they like being in spaces without men, and conversation soon turns to the Michigan Womyn's Music Festival. It's impossible to research the North American womyn's land movement without eventually stumbling onto stories from this festival, which was held for six days every August between 1976 and 2015 in Oceana County, Michigan. Set on 650 acres of land, over 6,000 women, who were mostly lesbian, would gather to listen to music and beat poetry, and camp out under the stars to the sounds of a constant beating of drums by makeshift fires. There were childcare facilities, a women of colour section and a sober section, and all access was disability-inclusive. Clothing was optional.

All the MichFest staff were women. At night, a crew of men came to clear out the portable toilets, discreetly disappearing before sunrise. It was a temporary women's microcosm set up and dismantled every year as a refuge from a world run by men.

But MichFest wasn't without controversy. In 1991, a transgender woman said she was asked to leave the festival, and the same year the organisers decided to take a public stance on the topic, releasing statements saying that the festival was for cisgendered women ('womyn-born womyn'). Trans rights activists camped outside the festival in protest, and LGBT journalists wrote op-eds criticising organisers for causing unrest in the community – especially as trans women had been present for several prior years at the festival with no reported disruption. With so much backlash, the organisers rolled back their stance, but a lot of damage had been done. The pressure-pot question of which women were permitted to attend had far-reaching consequences and the festival eventually closed – although many attendees say there were multiple reasons, involving organisation and funding, that meant it could not continue. Several women who attended went on to form their own get-togethers.

Two of the women in Lynn's community host an annual festivity for over a hundred of their friends on the land. They roast a large hog on a spit and light a bonfire, and some women from MichFest are usually in attendance. It's predominantly, but not exclusively, a women-only gathering.

THE EVOLUTION OF WOMYN'S LANDS

You can't force a community

Aside from Lynn, I've been Zooming with three of the fifteen women on the land for several months, but those three are not present for the pot-luck dinner.

One is eighteen-year-old Joni*, who is away at her east coast university studying for her undergraduate degree. Joni's mothers and little sister, who also live on the land, are visiting her when I arrive, but they will be there to see me before I leave. Joni texts to promise that one of her mothers, Ava*, and her little sister, Mia*, will take me for a walk on Sunday morning when they return to the land. Joni says she's sorry to miss me but that I will have fun; the land is special.

'Although don't forget, you're still in the South,' she adds over Zoom. 'It can be very white. It can be very racist. It can be spooky.'

Another woman, Themis (named after the Greek goddess of justice), texts to say she and her partner will show me around their farm later. Her partner doesn't enjoy socialising with the women on the land.

Themis, like several women on womyn's lands, grew up in alternative communal living. Her single mother, who had a deep distrust of authoritarian living, frequently moved. Sometimes they lived in isolated areas, including a desert in New Mexico. Themis often felt alone. They lived in rural areas across the country, and communes. These communities were mostly mixed-gender, and they were part of the 1970s counterculture movement. Each brought a new experience, with not all being positive. At an anarchist set-up in Texas, Themis was frightened by the public forms of masculine anger. It was an emotionally and physically hostile environment.

'It wasn't a great environment for a young girl,' she tells me.

There was shouting and destruction of property. I recall the machismo at Maré in Brazil, a form of aggression that the girls told me was unique to their favelas. Not so, I think now, sitting a few hundred miles away with Themis, on lesbian land in the US.

Themis was happier at a homestead community in Tennessee where she met Vietnam War veterans and women who had been part of womyn's lands, but even there, she was noticing a common thread. 'A lot of communities I've lived in were predominantly made up of white people,' she says, 'and womyn's lands especially were mostly white lesbians.'

This is the first time I've thought about race since I entered this womyn's land. There are no women of colour here. Themis says that lesbian women's communities centred white women just as second-wave feminism did.

Race and womyn's land in North America is a complex and emotive topic.

Although Black feminists like Blanche Jackson opened women-of-colour womyn's lands, other Black lesbians were vocally critical of lesbian women-only spaces, where progressive men were not invited. In 1977, the Black lesbian Combahee River Collective released a statement rejecting the concept of womyn's lands, saying they felt that white lesbians didn't appreciate the intersections of sexism and racism that required women of colour especially to include men of colour in their activism.

'Although we are feminists and Lesbians, we feel solidarity with progressive Black men and do not advocate the fractionalization that white women who are separatists demand,' read the statement. 'Our situation as Black people necessitates that we have solidarity around the fact of race, which white women of course do not need to have with white men, unless it is their negative solidarity as racial oppressors.'[11]

Themis, who is in her forties – three decades younger than Lynn – tells me that she believes there are cultural differences that come from being part of different generations of lesbians. Lynn didn't consider herself a lesbian until she was in her late twenties, when she had the vocabulary to know that her sexuality existed outside what was deemed acceptable by society. Her generation of lesbians led double lives, some closeted in heterosexual marriages. When they found their own community, it was natural that they would want to centre it in their existence. A younger generation in the US, Themis's generation, were less motivated to withdraw from a wider society that was largely accepting of them. Themis's desire to move to a womyn's land had little to do with her sexuality.

'When I bought the land from Lynn, I wasn't thinking of being part of a womyn's land or an intentional community,' she says. 'I'd seen so much conflict in different communities that I didn't really want communal living. I wasn't wanting a home where people drop by uninvited, or a group of people defining parameters on how everyone lives. You can't force a community.' She mentions travelling and living with Renaissance faires when she was in her late teens. Here communities often formed organically, through a shared interest.

Themis and her partner wanted to own land where they could grow food. They own a house on the land, with fourteen acres of their own, which they bought directly from Lynn. Land in the local area is now over $15,000 an acre, but Lynn offered them a lower rate.

I ask Themis if she plans on staying here.

'Well, we're planting crops that won't bloom for years,' she replies, smiling.

Their home is next to the woods, bordered by tall oak and pine trees. It sits slightly away from the other lots, with its own private drive. As Themis shows me round, she points to the sheet of silage tarp that is flattening a large section of earth. The sheet keeps out air in order to suffocate any weeds and create a soil that is ripe growing space for new crops. This technique bypasses the use of pesticides, which are banned as stated in the covenants agreed by the women. Ecological sustainability is a central tenet of most womyn's lands.

Around us is an abundance of edible plants: apple trees, fig trees, muscadine vines, tea plants, sweet peas, asparagus, onions, cabbage. There's a fragrant smell in the air – a mix of rosemary and lemon thyme. It reminds me of the country in *Herland*, where the forest looks like a manicured garden and every plant bears edible fruit – every plant has a function.

'Around 90 per cent of our fruit and vegetable consumption comes from our land,' Themis tells me. 'And we hope it'll be 100 per cent by 2030.'

Twenty-thirty, I think. The target year that the UN has stated for women's empowerment and gender equality. A date that no one, including the UN, believes is a realistic goal to achieve independence for women and girls around the world. But some women, in a small rural corner of the American South, are on track to securing a form of independence.

The Spooky Blondes

Back at the bed and breakfast, Clare, the farmhand, texts to say that a couple from Texas spontaneously checked themselves in late last night.

'Don't want you to be worried if you hear noises, it's almost

THE EVOLUTION OF WOMYN'S LANDS

definitely them,' she types. 'I know this place can spook city folk.'

I wonder exactly what could be spooking the city folk when they come out here. Everything has been wonderful. I've been sleeping peacefully. The women on the land have all been welcoming, and the farmhands at the bed and breakfast have been keeping me well fed on goat cheese and home-cooked southern grits, bacon and gravy. They even let me hand-milk a goat and bottle-feed an Alpine kid.

Even the three guinea hens, who diligently patrol the farmhouse, seem hospitable, toddling up and cordially sitting in front of me when I go on the porch for my morning coffee. But in the morning, when the Texan couple come down for breakfast, the guinea hens are restless. They are squawking loudly, running back and forth, guarding the farm from new visitors.

The couple make little eye contact as they sit down opposite me and start picking at the fruit and cheese. I'd guess that they're in their fifties – both bottle blonde with capped teeth and deep tans.

'What's it like being a reporter?' Mr Blonde* asks me, looking down at the farm-produced blue cheese he's spreading on a cracker.

I say it's a privilege to have the opportunity to meet people, especially those who have been traditionally marginalised from society, and have them allow me into their world.

'Right,' Mr Blonde replies, sounding bored. 'I'm a pilot. We flew here on our private plane.'

'We pick a different spot and fly there,' Mrs Blonde* says, adding they were just in Alaska. 'We're lucky.'

Unprompted, Mr Blonde tells me that they own thousands of acres of ranchland in Texas. It's beautiful, he says. The family have vast expanses of land which are split into smaller cattle towns – settlements of cow farms at the intersections of trails and railroads. Oak and mesquite trees surround the pastures, along with several ponds. A paradise. If it weren't for the unwelcome visitors.

'We have folk crossing over from Mexico.'

The guinea hens continue to screech outside.

'They can just walk on over,' he says, looking up for the first time to make eye contact with me. 'It's so easy for them to go wherever they want now. And do whatever they want.'

Mrs Blonde has been nodding along. She takes a noisy bite from her cracker.

'They kill,' she says. 'They behead people in bed. They're killers.'

This is wrong. There is no evidence to suggest that undocumented immigrants are responsible for more deaths in the US than those caused by citizens. In fact, immigrants are less likely to engage in criminality, says a 2020 study published in the peer-reviewed *Proceedings of the National Academy of Sciences*.[12]

According to Alex Nowrasteh, an immigration analyst at the libertarian Cato Institute who has studied undocumented immigrant crime in Texas, the state's homicide conviction rate between 2013 and 2022 was 2.2 per 100,000 for unauthorised immigrants, compared to 3.0 per 100,000 for native-born Americans. Nowrasteh concluded that, across the period where analysis was reviewed, non-documented immigrants 'were 26 percent less likely than native-born Americans to be convicted of homicide, and legal immigrants were 61 percent less likely.'[13]

This is not a conversation I want to have with strangers over breakfast, however.

THE EVOLUTION OF WOMYN'S LANDS

Mrs Blonde seems satisfied with my silence and looks at her husband. They smile at each other. I say I have to go take a phone call and head up to my room.

Earlier conversations, from women on the land, reflexively echo in my head.

Don't forget, you're still in the South.
It can be very white.
It can be very racist.
It can be spooky.
You don't have to go far in the South before you see our painful history. It's in the buildings and sometimes it's in the people.

It's the first time I wonder how the land would be if fifteen women of colour lived there. I'd guess that a women-of-colour lesbian land wouldn't be able to peacefully blend in here, nor in several other rural towns in the American South.

I lock my bedroom door and text Joni's mother, Ava, to ask if she can come to the B&B and take me back to the land. For the first time, I am thoroughly, utterly, spooked.

Ava and Emma*, along with their daughters Joni and Mia, and dog Kip, have lived here for over eighteen years – since Joni was a week old. Mia, now fifteen, was the first girl born on the land. The family house is just off the main trail that cuts through the woods, and is densely surrounded by towering pine, oak and pecan trees.

Theirs is a home designed for family, with a comforting smell of home-baked chocolate brownies. Monkey rings hang from the high ceiling, inviting you to swing across from the open-plan kitchen to the living area. Large windows open onto the wraparound porch, giving you a 360-degree view of the woods. Mia hugs me in a childlike, unguarded way that eases the discomfort of my earlier interaction with the Blondes.

Ava, Mia and I sit at the large dining room table near the front door, sipping Earl Grey tea, a plate of homemade espresso brownies in front of us.

'It's been a wonderful place to raise girls,' Ava says, apologising that her wife, Emma, is out of town and unable to meet me on this visit.

The girls' biological father, a surrogate, lives on the edge of the land, a fifteen-minute walk away. I'm surprised to learn that he was introduced to Ava and Emma through Lynn – and as I wonder how many lives Lynn has quietly changed, Ava continues telling me about raising her daughters on rural womyn's land.

'We've not had to worry about where they were, even as young children,' she says. The girls were invariably somewhere on the land, away from traffic. 'They were brought up with the luxury of safety.'

I wonder if that land is similar to the childcare embraced at the Michigan Womyn's Music Festival. School-age children there would be called 'wanderers' and given specific colour-coded armbands that indicated they were allowed to move freely in specific areas. If they wandered outside their nominated area – outside the colour code – a woman would notice and the child would be escorted back to a childcare tent in the designated area, where their mother or guardian could come to collect them. It's also similar to the country in *Herland*, where women care for each other's daughters. I ask if this is the reality here on the land, that a woman is available to care for your children?

This is a simplistic assumption on my part.

Ava tells me that this is not the case, that she and Emma never assumed the women on the land would be available for childcare. Not that neighbours weren't there for her, she adds. 'If I was really in a bind, like stuck in traffic, I felt thankful to know that there were neighbours I could call to see if someone could help me out.' But it's clear that parenting the girls is a responsibility that she and Emma took on themselves.

This is when reality punches through the bubble. I think I've been too romantic – perhaps even slightly patronising – to imagine a Herlandian world where motherhood is shared. Ava and Emma are the girls' primary caregivers, and their parents.

Their relationships are not tied to the women's community. They have a diverse group of friends, and they go on an annual holiday to the beach with their children's friends and parents – a wider circle that isn't connected to the land. When they're away, a woman on the land will feed Kip and take her out for walks.

I tell Ava that in my Zooms with her daughter Joni, she described a childhood of climbing trees and collecting eggs from a woman's chicken coop without asking if she could take some. It was a childhood full of safety and trust, Joni told me. It gave her the people skills to easily create a community of her own when she got to university.

Ava smiles and lets me continue. She instinctively knows there's a 'but' coming.

'But,' I go on, 'your daughter did tell me that she wanted to live in a more diverse community herself. Somewhere with different races and different genders.'

Ava nods.

'We're proud of that,' she says. 'Community should be diverse.'

Here in their conservative, rural corner of the American

South, no one has been openly hostile to them or their children, Ava tells me. Then she pauses.

'But that doesn't mean everyone is open-minded.'

During a state vote on gay marriage, she saw signs pinned to the lawns of several neighbouring fields that read 'marriage is between a man and a woman'. I ask her if this could've been a direct warning shot to the women on the land from lesbophobic people in town. But Ava doesn't think so. Even though the signs affected her more deeply than she would have expected, she tells me that she believes people can compartmentalise their beliefs. In small, conservative, community-oriented American towns, where people go to church and know all their neighbours, there may be prevailing political views, such as opposition to gay marriage. But those views often don't extend to their actual neighbours, who are seen as individuals and treated with empathy.

'They may see banning gay marriage as a purely conceptual and religious issue,' Ava says, 'and not connect a law like that to practical consequences in the life of their neighbours.'

Most of the kids, parents and teachers at the school Mia attends knows that she has two mothers, and it hasn't caused issues. In fact, it seems to have inspired some of the children.

'I know that our presence as the only openly gay parents in the community and school had some kind of effect for students who were coming to terms with their own sexuality. I remember one day I wore a T-shirt with a rainbow flag on it. I was walking through the cafeteria and some eighth-grade students I didn't even know stood up and told me how happy they were that I was wearing that openly.'

But not everyone is so accepting of other values they share.

In the summer of 2020, when around half a million

THE EVOLUTION OF WOMYN'S LANDS

people turned out in nearly 550 places across the United States to protest police brutality aimed at African American people following the death of George Floyd,[14] Joni made a hand-drawn Black Lives Matter poster. She planted it on the lawn of the land's private lane, which faces the main road. It was torn down and ripped apart by morning. Undeterred, she drew another BLM sign and put it in the same spot the following day. The sign was eventually ploughed over by a truck and damaged beyond repair. They didn't replace it after that.

Back at the bed and breakfast, Clare the farmhand sends me a text to say that Britt, the owner of the bed and breakfast, has returned early from his trip and is probably pottering around somewhere in the kitchen. Clare repeats that she's letting me know as she doesn't want me to be spooked if I see a stranger wandering around the farmhouse. This time I'm grateful. It's a fair warning after the Blondes, who've fortunately now taken off into the sunset, exploring new lands and crossing borders on their private plane.

Britt, a tall man with a thick silver ponytail, is pouring himself a coffee in the area where we have breakfast. He smiles widely when he sees me and asks if I'd like to join him. His wife, a talented weaver who has embellished the farmhouse with many of her bespoke pieces, is still away at an artists' fair, but he wanted to come back early and check in on the goats. He's technically retired and likes to spend his spare time tango dancing, a hobby he was inspired to take on after watching a news report that showed the Obamas dancing at a state dinner in Argentina. Although, he tells me, it is hard to fit in the dancing while overseeing hundreds of acres of farmland, which (like the womyn's land) is completely organic, with no use of chemical pesticides. Even though they have farmhands, Britt still likes to milk the goats in the evenings. You don't really retire from running a farm.

'Lynn had goats on her land too,' he says, smiling into his coffee.

She wanted to cultivate goat cheese and sell it at the farmers' market, Britt recalls. But after Yahoo died, before the rest of the women bought lots and moved in, all the duties on the land were overwhelming for a single woman. She asked Britt and his wife to take her goats. Now, more than thirty years later, they have a thriving goat farm.

Lynn's influence is clear. She has quietly changed the course of several people's lives, without taking credit. She inspired Britt to get goats. She introduced Joni and Mia's biological father to their mothers. She created a community where women can own their own homes at a time where polls show that the American dream of owning a house is slowly dying. US mortgage broker Redfin says that only 16 per cent of US home listings in 2023 were affordable on median income. It was 50 per cent in 2013.[15] Lynn sold all the lots on the land for around the same price she bought it for, $1,000 an acre, although its value has increased significantly. She isn't motivated by profit and she has helped over a dozen women afford to build their homes and live on their own land – in a world where women own less than a fifth of available land. Like Eliana Sousa and Dona Orosina in Rio, she has worked for the benefit of her community. It would have been special if she could have done it with Yahoo.

Just as I wonder how different her life, and so many people's lives, would have been if it weren't for Yahoo's mountaineering accident, Britt says, 'It was devastating for Lynn after Yahoo died.' He looks out the window to the three guinea hens, who are flopped on the porch, seemingly much more relaxed after the departure of the Blondes.

Britt tells me he and his wife became friends with Lynn and Yahoo soon after the two women bought the farmhouse. 'I remember the first time we went to their home for dinner. I remember seeing the two of them standing over the stove together, stirring a stew and laughing. I thought, "Look how happy they are, what a lovely couple. They'll build something beautiful here."'

I look at Britt and wonder exactly how I should phrase my next question, which is essentially whether people know that part of the town is lesbian land. But I don't feel the need to ask Britt the question after what he says next.

'We like good people who live honestly and are true to themselves. That's all you need from your neighbours.'

We go on

The lesbian womyn's land movement worked towards the ethos of symbiotic and mutual benefit. Their aim was to undo a male-led social system, where men made decisions and women did the caretaking and which was motivated by profit and dominance. It was an ambitious aim – to live by sharing land, sharing values, sharing responsibilities, rejecting profit, rejecting the notion of female submission to the rules.

Like Lynn, several women learned carpentry in order to physically enhance their environments. Using chainsaws and hammers was not a usual occupation for women in the 1970s and 1980s, even for women who had grown up in rural locations. In order to make rural communities a reality, women took on labour that was considered traditionally male.

Hundreds of women tried to set up womyn's lands, but few survive today. There are at least two reasons for this.

One is money. It's not always financially possible now to live full-time in a rural town – with fewer opportunities for diverse, salaried work. It was different in the 1980s.

'It was a different financial landscape,' says *Sinister Wisdom* editor Julie Enszer, referring to the time when womyn's lands emerged. 'You could work an average labour job for six months of the year and live on a womyn's land with what you'd saved.'

The formation of womyn's lands was especially enabled by the affordable cost of land in the 1970s and 1980s. Additionally, there was less financial burden on people when it came to education during the rise of womyn's lands. During the 1980–81 academic year, on average it cost students the equivalent of $17,410 to attend a private college and $7,900 to attend a public university, including tuition, fees, room and board.[16] By 2023–24, the average cost of tuition and fees had increased to a staggering $42,162 at private colleges, $23,630 for out-of-state students at public universities, and $10,662 for in-state students at public schools, according to data collected by *US News & World Report*.

As dozens and dozens of North American womyn's lands petered out, closing down after failing to recruit new members, Lynn and Yahoo's land has survived. It may not be what Lynn once imagined it would be. As one of the residents tells me, they are individual landowners living individual lives. They share certain resources (like the tractor, truck, lawnmower) as it's a practical use of resources. They are not intertwined with each other's lives on a daily basis, but unlike other womyn's lands, these have continued. Several other womyn's lands – especially those listed in Shewolf's directory – have no permanent residents any more, with some using their homes only as seasonal retreats.

Lynn says their land's longevity is thanks to the women on it reviewing their covenants every few months and learning to relax the expectations of what a community should be. While Lynn initially wanted pooled funds, she realised that financial independence is a vital pillar of feminism. It's important that the women own their own homes and exercise their own personal boundaries when it comes to visitors – including other women on the land. They will text ahead of time if they want to pop over to each other's houses. Each has close friends outside the land that they spend the majority of their time with.

Lynn too, spends several months in the year travelling across the country to see other friends. This land is not her sole community.

According to the World Economic Forum, women own less than 20 per cent of the world's land, despite over 400 million women working and living on farmlands.[17] Research shows that security and ownership of land could decrease the risk of domestic violence for some women, because economic independence means they are empowered to leave an abusive relationship.[18] Perhaps if more landowners, like Lynn, offered reasonable rates, that could be a reality.

The movement may not be over, however. Following the global coronavirus pandemic, several rural US states have reported a renaissance. After years of population decline, rural net migration rates in the first year of the pandemic (2020–21) were positive at 0.47 per cent, indicating that more people were moving into rural areas than out of them, according to US government data.[19]

The idea of living somewhere with fresh air, where you know that the people around you share your values, is an enticing one. Somewhere where someone has eggs and your daughters are safe. Maybe that is too simplistic, too wishful; it's a thought, though. Good neighbours can be found in several places, after all. Very few women live full-time on womyn's lands – not even Lynn, who had wanted an 'intensive' lesbian community the most.

I'll be buried here

Lynn and Doreen take me to the woods, past the communal pond and over a small makeshift bridge. I'm mostly looking down, navigating puddles that are filled with globes of frogspawn, keeping my grip on the carpet of brown leaves and moss that covers a trail that Lynn and Doreen know well. Piercing through the leaves are the red feathers of cardinals and dozens of hard, spiked balls of dried fruit that have fallen from the surrounding sweetgum trees.

I tell Lynn and Doreen that I grew up frightened of woods, petrified that if I ventured to one alone, something sinister would be waiting for me, ready to hunt me down. I say that a lot of my girlfriends were also taught to fear solitude in nature, especially in childhood.

'The media gives the woods bad publicity,' I say, 'especially for women.'

Lynn and Doreen agree. But it is not the case here. Joni and Mia grew up here, they remind me. And those girls spent their childhood roaming freely in safety amongst the thick canopy of trees.

We reach a plank of hand-shorn wood hanging between

two pine trees on thin metal rope. It reads 'YAHOO FOREST' – the fifty acres of land that is a forever memorial to Lynn's love. Carved next to the letters are four female gender symbols, the circle above the cross, representing a community of women.

We carry on for a while, then I look up to see that Lynn and Doreen have stopped ahead of me in a patch of land where a large oak tree has fallen. Its roots have pulled up the earth to reveal a depression that resembles a hole dug for a funeral casket.

Lynn points to the hole and says, 'I'll be buried here one day, in this very spot.' She has permission from the state to have green burials on the land. She'd like her body to be put straight into the ground without a coffin, and the earth over her planted with flowers and plants – maybe even acorns, from where a new oak tree might grow. There won't be a headstone or any kind of marking on her grave, similar to the eco-burial for Rain Queens in South Africa, and the relationship with Country as practised by First Nations women in Australia.

Lynn has planned for her death to share the same values as her life on the land. She wishes to have as little disruptive impact as possible on the environment around her. To only replenish it. This is an attitude that is underlined by several women-only communities. They share a sense of ecofeminism – understanding that there is a connection between women and the earth that they step on. Women should sustain and build on the environment with the aim of causing as little harm as possible to it.

Yahoo's ashes are scattered all through the woods, but Lynn keeps a small urn with her. She takes the urn with her in her RV when she leaves the land and drives across the country for a few months every year, during which she camps out in other womyn's lands, visiting decades' worth of friends – women who have been alongside Lynn and Yahoo in this unique life. The remainder of the ashes in that small urn will be poured into the final resting place Lynn has chosen for herself here, on the land that she and her love succeeded in building, deep in Yahoo Forest.

5
Oasis of Forgiveness

El-Samaha, Egypt, 1998

'We're here,' our translator says, pointing forward to a haze of sand and sun. Next to him, the driver slowly tackles the bumpy, uneven, untarred road that cuts through fields of feathery reeds – an invasive weed-like grass that can withstand salty soil. It's impossible to see anything past the five-metre-tall broadleaf reeds, but nevertheless I imagine the scene.

In my mind, dozens or maybe hundreds of women, surrounded by their noisy children, are collecting bread at the village's singular bakery. They are sitting outside their homes on their porches, washing vegetables in bowls, sipping sugary tea with large mint leaves floating on top. I imagine them smiling as we drive up, waiting to welcome us, eager to share how they run a remote North African village without men. Of all my visits to women-only spaces, the idea of El-Samaha village has excited me the most.

El-Samaha means 'forgiveness' in Arabic – a promise of transformation after unburdening yourself of resentment towards a person or circumstance that once wronged you. It means a new start, solace after heartbreak. El-Samaha is also the name of a tiny village that sits in Upper Egypt (which – confusingly – is in the south of the country), surrounded by the stretching Western Desert, over a thousand kilometres from Cairo. Search for El-Samaha village online and you'll find dozens of English-language articles promising a women-only oasis.

El-Samaha doesn't appear on maps, similar to Lynn's lesbian land, because the women would rather their homes were not a spectacle for visitors and to ensure their safety. I think back to Eliana Sousa, who lobbied cartographers and the Brazilian government to put Maré favelas on maps of Rio, to ensure that residents could no longer be overlooked and ignored by the authorities. Eliana wanted Maré women to be seen. A reminder that there isn't one shared ambition or desire for women's communities.

El-Samaha was built as a collaboration between the Egyptian Ministry of Agriculture and the World Food Program, in order to support single women and combat the country's stigma surrounding divorced and widowed women, who are often shunned by their local communities. The stated aim was to offer these vulnerable women a chance of autonomy – of owning their own home, making a living farming their own land, and earning their own money. The ministry invited mu'ila women – women without husbands; women who were the primary 'breadwinners' in the family – and their children to move into homes on around 1,800 feddans of land (a feddan is a unit of area used by Egypt, South Sudan, Sudan, Syria and Oman, which is roughly the same as an acre). The first women arrived in the village in 1997.

The Egyptian Ministry of Agriculture had granted women several short-term loans in order to purchase the land and houses, and they were also provided with fertiliser and farming tools. A representative of the ministry, Hamdi el-Kashef, told several news outlets that there were two rules: 1) no growing of sugarcane (as it drinks up too much water in the soil) and 2) if the women were to get married to men, they would no longer be eligible to live in the village – they would have to move out.

El-Samaha excited journalists, and positive press attention from English-speaking media followed. An article from 2017 on the World Economic Forum website spoke tantalisingly about this North African domain where women possessed all the power: a single-gender world like those written about in myth and science-fiction – a Herland. El-Samaha, one writer said, 'evokes the Amazons, the warriors of Greek myth who lived in a country where men were banned. Just like in the myth, El-Samaha village is home to warriors, but of a modern kind.'[1] Meanwhile *The Arab Weekly* described it as a haven from the patriarchal norms of the country: 'In male-dominated Egypt, El-Samaha is very different but it is a place that evokes all meanings about women's bravery, heroism and perseverance.'[2]

I couldn't wait to visit this desert-based society run by women, an anomaly in a country ranked 135 out of the 146 in the Global Gender Gap Index as of 2024. But I also knew a journalist couldn't simply turn up to a government-led project without an invitation. While Egypt's constitution ensures press independence and bans censorship, these rights are not always applied in practice. In 2023, Egypt was rated 166 out of 180 countries in the World Press Freedom Index and is one of the world's biggest jailers of journalists, according to Reporters Without Borders and the Committee to Protect Journalists. Human rights group Amnesty International has condemned the country for its 'relentless crackdown on media'. Technically, I was not visiting the village to report for a media outlet, but I was still a journalist who would be writing about it – and the authorities needed to know this. There could be serious consequences if I just turned up, and not just for me but for anyone who helped me. I've decided to keep all the Egyptians who helped me reach El-Samaha – the translators and drivers – anonymous for this reason.

It took years to gain access to the village, starting in 2022 when I posted a message in a private Facebook group that had been set up for some of the women in El-Samaha. A few weeks later I got a reply saying I would be welcome to visit but it would need to be arranged by the village supervisor – who was male, and was employed by the Ministry of Agriculture. No one picked up the phone at Egypt's Ministry for Agriculture, however. A Cairo-based journalist sent me a contact number for village supervisor Hamdi el-Kashef, who had been quoted several times in the media.

A male supervisor of an all-female village should have surprised me, but it didn't. In all my years of working in journalism, there were a lot of men put into government administrative positions to oversee women's projects. I assumed Hamdi was some kind of project manager.

I WhatsApped Hamdi and he replied the same day, sending a screenshot of a handwritten statement in Arabic. I later got it translated and it read:

> El-Samaha is a village for single divorced or widowed women. Each woman was given 600 feddans (a feddan is an acre) and a home to live with her children. The land has been planted with all kinds of summer and winter crops to support her and her children, to improve her economic situation and livelihoods. The village has multiple facilities including a school, a health centre, a market, and a bakery,

and an agriculture association, which is responsible for all their needs and for solving their problems. Women were located and have been living there for over 20 years with their children and relatives. The Egyptian government has been giving grants and aid to the families in El-Samaha village.

I thanked him and asked if I could visit El-Samaha. The double blue ticks indicated that he had read the message, and the three follow-up ones I sent, but he didn't reply.

Eventually, a male friend who lived in Upper Egypt offered to go to El-Samaha to ask if it would be okay for a Western journalist to visit and write about the village. I had considered asking a female journalist to go, but my friends in Cairo advised that it would be less risky for a man to travel to such a rural area.

My friend called me that evening to say that it had taken him over four hours to reach the village – via a train, a tuk-tuk and a bus – and a lot of sheltering under palm trees from the oily desert heat as he waited for the next transportation. Eventually he reached the edge of the sandy village, where he saw a building that looked like an office.

But it wasn't women that he found at El-Samaha.

Sitting on the steps was a man, dressed in a cotton thobe, who welcomed him with tea. The man told him that Hamdi el-Kashef had retired and that he was the new village supervisor and in charge of all the administration of the village, including arranging visits. The man assured my friend that I would be very welcome to visit El-Samaha whenever I pleased. The women would love to meet me too. Consider it arranged.

In the excitement of gaining access I ignored the slight twinge of anxiety in my chest that a man had granted us permission to enter a women-only village. I also ignored my close friend Alex, who had read *Herland* so he could talk about its themes with me. Alex asked if I should really be going to rural Egypt at all.

'Remember Peter Greste,' he said, referring to the Al Jazeera journalist who was found guilty and jailed for what the government claimed included spreading 'false news' and 'having a negative impact on overseas perceptions of Egypt'. But I ignored that, as well as the news of the detention of Egyptian feminists who had gathered outside UN Women in Cairo to protest in solidarity with women in Gaza and Sudan.

Instead I convinced myself that if I went to Egypt with Janey Starling, I would feel safe. Janey is a long-time colleague, a writer and an organiser with a focus on gender justice. She has run several women-only spaces, including peer support groups in multiple countries for women who have survived domestic abuse. When I initially heard of the women-only village in Egypt, I couldn't think of anyone better to come with me. Janey had been to Egypt several times and had friends and contacts in the country.

I felt that travelling with her, along with a translator and driver, would be totally fine. I convinced myself that the portrayals of an Amazon of empowered women, thriving in the Western Desert, were all true.

Upper Egypt is breathtakingly beautiful. We are staying in Aswan, metres away from where Agatha Christie based parts of *Death on the Nile*. Aswan moves at a dreamy pace, with feluccas sailing past walls of Nubian art, all soft orange and blue, blurry sun and sparkling water; the forty-degree heat appeased by the cool Nile.

The day we arrive it feels like the city is filled with women with frosted-blonde highlights and high cheekbones. It is the eve of the eighth Aswan International Women's Film Festival, the annual Egyptian film gala that celebrates cinematic works representing women's issues – amplifying the work of female filmmakers in the Middle East and North Africa. TV crews are interviewing glamourous women under palm trees, and posters around the city promote the films. One poster is inscribed with the Latin political slogan 'nihil de nobis, sine nobis'.

Nothing about us, without us.

It feels like divine timing – the promise of a female-empowered trip. That feeling stays for several hours, including when we leave the city and begin to drive towards El-Samaha village.

We laugh as our translator holds the melted chocolate bars we bought from the local supermarket, now liquid inside their plastic coverings, in front of the cold air blowing out of the car's air conditioning, hoping to solidify it for a snack. Aswan disappears behind us, the desert stretching out in front. My excitement continues past checkpoints where dozens of soldiers are holding large guns and staring into the back seat where Janey and I sit chatting. It remains when we cut through smaller towns lined with mango and palm trees, where young boys ride donkeys and old men with no front teeth sit outside their homes. We are quieter, more relaxed, a few hours into the journey, the towns evaporating behind us. Then it feels like we have reached another world, or a movie set – something out of *Star Wars* – as expanses of reddish-yellow earthy sand and rock engulf us.

I feel so lucky to be here. Just yesterday, our flight from Cairo was delayed for over seven hours due to a sandstorm in Aswan, and there was a chance that all planes to southern

Egypt would be cancelled. It reinforced the idea that this part of the world is incredibly hard to access. Luckily, the threat passed, and we were allowed to fly. Apart from the odd metre-tall dust devil, the desert around us is calm.

It is only when we pass the fields of reeds that border El-Samaha – and we see a cluster of terracotta-bricked houses coming into focus through puffs of desert sand, empty uneven alleys, and nothing but sandy fields for miles and miles and miles – that I feel a slight unease. My phone has no signal. What if our car breaks down, I wonder. Who would we call for help? How long would they take to reach us? Would we be okay out here, miles from anywhere? This is not a trip with a risk assessment.

And then, walking towards us, we see men.

El-Samaha village was designed with a clear and noble aim: to give women whose husbands had either died or abandoned them an opportunity to create financially solvent lives for themselves, in the safety of a single-gender space. There was certainly a need for a community that would cater to the needs of women without men, especially as single women were often rejected by their communities. Feminists have told me that divorced women in Arab communities are often confronted with derogatory labels such as 'kharrabet beyout' (meaning 'home-wrecker'), or even 'kharg beit' ('second-hand' – the sexist insinuation that they once belonged to another man).

'Egypt is a patriarchal and male-dominated society,' members of Ganoubia Hora, a feminist group from Upper Egypt, explained. Their name translates to Free Southern Women and they focus on the rights of women in that region of the country – especially Black Nubian women, and women from rural backgrounds. It helps single women who do not have the means to pay for lawyers. 'Many see the end of an unhappy marriage as a triumph but it is not always a win. A divorced woman can often be viewed with suspicion and judgement. She is almost always blamed for what went wrong, even if she leaves a marriage where she was abused.'

Additionally, these mu'ila – breadwinner women – bear a deep financial burden. Alimony is not guaranteed in Egyptian family law, and women are not generally earning enough money to support themselves and their families. Only 18 per cent of women in Egypt were part of the labour force, according to 2023 data from the World Bank.[3]

The need was clearly there for women to have a place in which they could live and earn, due to some surprising statistics: while divorce rates have declined across the US and Europe over the past few decades,[4] they have increased significantly in several Arab countries.[5]

In the twenty-first century, 40 per cent of Egypt's marriages have ended in divorce, according to the country's Cabinet Information and Decision Support Centre.[6] The Central Agency for Public Mobilization and Statistics estimates that a divorce in the country occurs every 117 seconds (about two minutes), which means an average of thirty-one divorces per hour, and 739 per day.[7]

Experts from Egypt cite three main reasons for this rise in divorce.

The first is a marked upsurge in independent feminist discourse, and grassroots organisations, following the 2011 Egyptian revolution – also known as the 25 January Revolution. Egypt has a long and rich feminist history including influential mid-twentieth-century feminists like Doria Shafik – who won Egyptian women's right to vote by secretly organising the storming of parliament with 1,500 women in the 1950s. Egyptian feminism has since seen the emergence of several women-led activist organisations that are vocally lobbying for gender equality.

The aftermath of the 2011 uprising, during the so-called Arab Spring, resulted in the amplification of several grassroots women's initiatives, many of which were spearheaded by young women with little former experience in political organising. One such group was Ganoubia Hora.

Then, along with an increase in women's education, financial independence, and the ability to assert their rights, Egypt's internet and phone infrastructure continued to improve. Women who knew their rights now had access and the ability to search for ways out of unhappy marriages. More than 70 per cent of Egypt currently has internet access, and more than 90 per cent of people have mobile phones.[8] As more and more women become connected, more women talk to each other, confide in each other, and realise that they do not need to stay where they are unhappy.

As well as this rise in some women's personal independence, the third reason cited by experts for the rise of divorce is the relaxation in Egypt's legal system that has granted women the ability to obtain a khula, or no-fault divorce. On 29 January 2000, then-president Hosni Mubarak signed a law granting Egyptian women the right to file for a divorce on the basis of incompatibility – without the burden of providing evidence of harm. Although the law was a significant step in giving women the power to leave an unwanted relationship, that's not to say this clause made obtaining a divorce easy for women. Feminists argue that women – especially rural women and women from lower income ranges – faced (and still face) several challenges in obtaining and paying for family lawyers, as well as a huge cultural pushback. According to author Nadia Sonneveld in her 2012 book *Khul' Divorce in Egypt*, cartoons and films in the first decade of the twenty-first century often portrayed women seeking divorce for irrational reasons, like being too lazy to cook dinner – women who were apparently heavily influenced by Western feminists.

The process of divorce is still an unequal endeavour between the sexes in the country. Unlike men, women can obtain a divorce only by a formal court action (tatliq). Men in Egypt are also permitted to divorce their wives through Islamic talaq, which translates as 'release'. They do this by saying 'you are divorced' three times. Men do not require their wife's consent to initiate the process. Over fifty Egyptian women's rights organisations published a statement in 2021 demanding that this method of divorce should be overhauled, and divorce should go through a formal legal process, but the proposal has been resisted by male religious leaders.

'The question of settling divorce should be in the hands of the wiser party, and that is men,' said chief judge Ayman Amin Shash of Cairo's National Center for Judicial Studies in 2004. 'Men are wise, which is why they do not have to go to court. Islamic law would consider the wise wife an exception, and you cannot generalise an exception.' Feminist organisers in Egypt have told me that the judge's view is not fringe, and is still repeated by many men in the country over twenty years later.

Even when women are able to get divorced, they face additional hurdles if they have children. There are more than 12 million single mothers in Egypt, according to the Egyptian Statistics Observatory, the majority of whom live with modest financial income. According to Human Rights Watch, 'divorced women with children receive monthly payments of

70 Egyptian pounds (US$11), while women without children receive 50 Egyptian pounds (US$8) per month'.⁹

Divorced women, left as the sole earners for their families and often socially shunned, needed help. A single-gender space where women could support themselves – and each other – seemed like a perfect solution to a growing problem.

At El-Samaha village, a middle-aged man with heavy eyelids and white stubble, wearing a graphite-coloured cotton thobe, introduces himself as Mr F*, the administrative head of the village. He doesn't live here, he tells our translator, but he's responsible for the running of the village, especially ensuring that tanks of water arrive every week. Mr F is short, with a continuous, unblinking stare. He stands next to another man, who is introduced simply as Mr F's colleague and whose name I never learn. They are outside the tallest building at the entrance of El-Samaha; it's three storeys with orange and red terracotta bricks. It is supposed to be the office of the Ministry of Agriculture.

I feel that this building was meant to be grand. It has a stately but slick contemporary design, with flat, clean lines and wide, looming openings to let in light. An extensive brick portico is a welcome shelter from the piercing sun, and this is where Mr F leads me, although we don't go in. The building is unfinished. The glass was never installed, and the light bulb at the entrance doesn't turn on. In fact, electricity has not been put in anywhere in the building, and the rooms were never decorated.

Mr F sits down on one of the wide rows of white steps outside the front door, under the roof of the portico, and pats a place next to him for me to join. He tells me that before I meet the women and see the village, he wants to have a chat.

'I don't like media reports that say women rule El-Samaha,' he says, looking at me and smiling. I break eye contact after several seconds. 'This is not a village where women are in charge. That's not the story.'

He says he'll show us around, and we begin our walk to the village, puffs of sand rising with every step. Janey, our translator and our driver walk slightly behind me and Mr F. If an artist were going to paint the village on a canvas, they would only need one colour palette – similar shades of orange, brown, caramel and stone.

El-Samaha has 303 one-storey houses, which look as though they were constructed hastily, with uneven bricks and flicks of cement. They sit side by side on unpaved, untarred roads. Each house in the village has the same layout and design: one floor, terracotta brick laid over exposed, bulging concrete, windows with shutters that open out without glass, and a tin roof. They each have a box-like living room, a bedroom, a hallway where most keep a second bed, a basic kitchen with a gas canister, an indoor bathroom with a pit latrine and bucket for bathing, and a small outdoor barn where a cow or two is tied up to a pole and groups of chickens wander freely. Each house has electricity, Mr F says proudly, but no plumbing.

We walk past a rusted gate, behind which sits an unused building with a sign saying 'Rural Women's Centre' in English. I wonder if it's in English to play to the English-speaking media, several of whom wrote giddy reviews about El-Samaha, the desert-based single-gender world full of 'warrior women'.

We turn right along the road past another vast, empty building. This one has a black and white gate, and a sign that says 'El-Samaha Preparatory School' in Arabic. Next to the sign, on the creamy wall, are two tiny black handprints, perhaps the work of a cheeky child. Mr F tells me that the school is in use, but I later find out – through Facebook messages with the women – that the school has not been open for a full week for several years, because it hasn't been possible for teachers with the appropriate skills to travel to such a remote village. They can't arrange transport in order to come to work.

Ahead of us, there's a small commotion. I look up to see no women, but rather groups of teenage boys. They are the sons of the mu'ila, Mr F says. The boys are standing with large plastic storage containers near a single-room, shed-like building with exposed brick. Through a glassless window I notice several large white tanks and a network of pipes that funnel back to three green taps outside. Water is delivered from the neighbouring city of Edfu to the white tanks a few times a week. It is then filtered through the pipes, and each house can collect purified water from the green taps when they need it. There is no maximum allocation of water, Mr F insists, and they have not run out so far.

The boys open the small taps and water trickles out, slowly and hypnotically filling their two-metre plastic containers. By now we're at the village's centre. We have seen no women so far.

The water building is next to another small building that I'm told is a bakery, but I cannot look inside. It is open twice a week, Mr F says, but not today.

'Does a woman run the bakery?' I ask.

'A woman's son runs it,' Mr F replies.

Opposite is the mosque, built in the 2000s, shortly after the establishment of the village; it is painted a subtle stoney lemon-yellow. The towering twenty-metre-tall pencil-thin minaret, surrounded by speakers from which the call to prayer is announced, is a stylistic reminder that Islam is the central value of the village. The men and women enter the mosque through different entrances and sit in different sections, a barrier dividing them. The women's section is smaller.

'Why would you need a male entrance at a mosque in a village built for women?' I ask.

'The sons will inherit the village,' Mr F replies.

I think about what he said earlier. The women are not in charge.

I thank Mr F for his time and say that I would like to go round the village to meet some of the women. He says that it's not necessary, as he has arranged for us to meet three women at the home of Aya*, one of the first women to move to El-Samaha. He walks ahead, and it's clear that we are meant to follow him. This will be a supervised visit, and Mr F will be there for all of it.

Aya is waiting for us just outside her front door, cocooned in a thick black abaya and hijab, but seemingly untroubled by the heat.

She's now in her mid-sixties, with an open and kind face. Aya's door is open and Mr F walks in. I follow him but take a moment near the door, along with Janey, our translator and our driver. Mr F tells Aya the foreigners are here, and she nods and beckons us inside. She pats the air down repeatedly, ushering us to sit on one of her four long sofas, with cushions on low wooden frames, which are backed up against each wall of the room. Mr F starts telling us Aya's story as she sits quietly next to me.

Aya moved to the village in 2001, a few years after it officially opened, when applications for the project began to be granted. She had heard about El-Samaha through her neighbours in Aswan. When her husband died, she needed a safe place to raise her daughter and two sons. The subsidised land at El-Samaha was on sale for a very reasonable price – under 40,000 Egyptian dollars (under US$900), which was less than 80 per cent of what it cost to buy in other parts of Egypt according to News Deeply, an online humanitarian news site based in New York. Aya's application was successful and she was given the house, five sheep and six feddans of land. She grew rice and hibiscus on her fields, which she sold to traders in the nearby cities. She supported all her children, and now they have all grown up and moved out of the village.

Aya does not live alone. Inside the front room, there are four other people. The one I see first is a woman who looks like she's in her early forties. She gently interrupts Mr F's monologue of Aya's story to ask if she can get us all mint tea. She looks a little like a lighter version of Aya – even her abaya and hijab are slightly paler.

Mr F introduces us.

'This is Jamila*,' he says, 'Aya's niece.'

Behind Jamila, two teenage girls linger by the doorway. They are Jamila's daughters, Mr F says. Then he introduces us to a man who remains sitting next to a full ashtray. Although the man looks around the same age as Aya, Mr F says the man is Jamila's husband.

The room is compact, and though the windows and front door are open, it is thick with the smell of tobacco. A ghost-like layer of smoke surrounds Jamila's husband.

The family haven't always lived with Aya, Mr F says, but they moved here in 2020 from Aswan, shortly after losing their income following the Covid pandemic.

'In the beginning, it was a village for women,' Aya says, now speaking for herself. 'It was difficult, but we were happy.'

There was no electricity in the beginning, she adds, and not all the homes were fully constructed. The women would stay in each other's houses while the building work was underway, and share meals of bean stew and eish baladi flatbread. They would accompany each other early in the mornings to their respective fields and work the soil with their poleaxes. On the days the supply teachers made it into the village, they would go via the school and drop their children there.

The teachers were more regular back then, Aya recalls, because the village had more attention and funding from the government. In the afternoons, when the viscous desert heat began to take hold, they would walk back to their homes and maybe take a short nap. In the evenings, the women would sit outside their houses and watch their children play.

At that time, the project's organisers would send regular deliveries, supplies, food, fertiliser and medical aid. They would also purchase crops tilled by the women, which were mostly hibiscus, wheat and rice, ensuring a regular income. But within a few years the officials visited less and less. The women had to walk a few kilometres to the main road, where they hitched a lift on the back of a van to head to the nearest town if they needed extra supplies or doctor's appointments. By 2010, the only regular visitors to the village were the water suppliers.

Then the gender dynamics changed. The women-led community became a traditional male-led one.

The sons and daughters grew up, married, and several moved their spouses into their mother's home. The men of the families — be they sons, or daughters' husbands — became the de facto heads of the village.

The women who had moved into the village were edged out of their own bedrooms as the men took over. Some of the women now sleep on single beds in the hallways of their homes.

I ask Aya what El-Samaha was like in the first few years. When it was a women-only village, when the sons were young and the women were in charge. As soon as our translator repeats the question, a rain of male voices falls around us; Mr F, Jamila's husband, and even our driver begin talking loudly and over each other, all at once.

'They say there is no women-led community in Egypt. Men look after women,' our translator says, but everyone is saying so much, so fast and so loudly, that it is impossible to translate it all.

Aya and I look at each other and she smiles. She is not given the chance to answer the question.

'She's not happy,' Aya's niece Jamila says, pointing to my friend Janey. Janey tells her that it's not true, she's fine and she's enjoying her tea, but Jamila's right. Even though Janey's demeanour is friendly, her face open in a smile, I can see that something's troubling her.

Before I get a chance to check in with Janey, two women are at Aya's front door. Mr F calls them in and asks them to sit down, as if it's his home, and they do. He introduces us first to the youngest: Anat* is thirty years old, and her husband has just ended their marriage, asking her to move out. She says she doesn't want to go into detail why, but Mr F interjects.

'Mother-in-law troubles,' he says, by way of explanation, adding that she moved to the village as her widowed grandmother already has a house here.

I ignore him and turn to the young woman, who is standing by the door, her head bowed slightly. I ask if she likes it here. She shakes her head.

OASIS OF FORGIVENESS

'If my husband wanted me back, I would go,' Anat says.

'Do you do anything with just the women in the village?' I follow up. 'Are there any women-only activities?'

'The women in this village get together alone if there's preparations for weddings,' Mr F cuts in, referring to the laylat al-henna, the night of a henna party. One of the most important Egyptian wedding traditions, this is when women gather for the bride to decorate her hands and feet with intricate, traditional henna designs.

'Or funerals,' says Jamila's husband, who has lit another cigarette.

'And sometimes prayers,' adds our driver – who has never visited El-Samaha before today.

I put my tea down on the well-trodden, mud-coloured rug on Aya's floor and stifle a sigh. It is impossible to do an interview with the women of El-Samaha with so many men present. As a reporter, I've been in plenty of scenarios where press officers are an unwanted and dominating presence during interviews, but they don't usually answer on behalf of the principal being interviewed. It would be one thing if it was just Mr F, who has a salaried job looking after the administration of the village, but Jamila's husband and even our driver have plenty to say too.

I turn to the second woman who came in with Anat, who has been looking at me with a slightly amused expression on her face, and go to shake her hand. Without waiting for Mr F, she introduces herself.

'Asimah*.'

I turn to our translator and say, 'Can we go somewhere else to talk with Asimah? It's noisy in here.'

I assumed he would ask Aya, whose home we are in, but he turns to Mr F, who replies that we can go to the back of the house. Aya and her family stay seated as Mr F gets up to lead us. Asimah and I follow him, along with the translator and Janey.

We head down a narrow corridor to a door that opens onto Aya's outdoor yard, where a gaggle of geese are pecking at torn-up pieces of toasted bread that Aya or Jamila must have prepared for them earlier. Then we round a corner and find ourselves in a small L-shaped room, where a single bed with a thin mattress has been placed against one of the walls. The cooking area is in the opposite corner and a small cluster of house flies are gathered round the saucepan where our sugary tea was brewing.

Asimah sits down on the bed and I join her, perching on the opposite corner. Janey takes a seat on the stool in the corner and our translator stands between me and Asimah, ready to translate. There are two closed doors that Mr F opens to show us. One is a smaller room with another bed, and the second is a tiny bathroom: a pit latrine next to a bucket of water.

Mr F says he will leave us to talk and walks out, seemingly back to the living room.

This is good, I think. Some privacy.

Asimah is thirty-eight years old and she applied to move into a house in El-Samaha in 2022, a few weeks after her marriage broke down. She had been living in an urban community in Aswan, near all her extended family. I ask Asimah what happened in her marriage. She raises her eyebrows and replies, 'It's a private matter.'

I've crossed a boundary.

Asimah smiles at my embarrassment and continues her story. When her husband told her to leave and take the children, she first turned to her brother for help. He told her that it wasn't possible for her, a divorced woman, to stay in their neighbourhood. A divorced woman brings bad luck to the community, he said. She would have to move in with their widowed mother in El-Samaha. The village was for women like her.

Asimah packed up a few suitcases and gathered her two young sons and daughter, and hitchhiked the six hours it took to reach her mother's home.

On her first night at El-Samaha, she sat outside her front door and thought to herself: I am a failure. I have failed at life. I have failed at my one job as a woman keeping a family together.

She looked around the village. It wasn't even for women, she thought, as she watched young men wandering the dusty roads and hanging around near the fields of reeds. How could she make a living here? The alkaline desert soil meant that if left unattended, crops would fail and the reeds would take over.

El-Samaha village was being taken over by an invasive species. Reeds or men, I wondered.

Asimah decided to forgo farming and offered to shear the sheep in the village, hitching lifts to the nearest town every week to sell the wool and bring back supplies for her family.

She has clearly managed to find a way to create a life in such a remote village.

'Do you think it would have been easier living here in the beginning,' I ask, 'before the men took over?'

Asimah looks like she's about to answer but catches herself and looks down. She is quiet for a few moments before finally saying, 'No, it's difficult for women to live alone. I would rather have men here.' Her eyes flick past my shoulder as she adds, 'I'm glad I have sons who will grow up and take care of me.'

I turn round. Mr F has returned and is standing in the doorway, listening. It's clear that Asimah won't speak freely any more. The interviews with the women are over, and it's time to leave El-Samaha.

El-Samaha was one of several villages opened by the Egyptian Ministry of Agriculture in the 1990s and early 2000s to offer subsidised housing for single and divorced women. They were all villages for women, but from what I can see this is the only one that was promoted to the English-speaking media as a women-only oasis. From my research, and speaking to several other women's activists, it appears that a number of women's villages were created for divorced women from more marginalised communities. They included Nubian women, who are an ethnic group indigenous to the Nile valley region of northern Sudan and southern Egypt.

A day after our visit to El-Samaha, Janey and I meet Shadia*, a Nubian woman who moved to one of these villages in the early 2000s, shortly after her husband left her. She now lives near Aswan.

'They said these villages were supposed to empower us, but it felt like they were hiding us away,' she tells me. 'People are suspicious of older single women.'

Shadia is originally from a village near Egypt's border with Sudan. Like several Nubian communities, hers was matrilineal – with a long tradition of women organising the economic and social agenda of the village. Men of working age left for the cities to work and were absent for extended periods, so by nature Nubian villages were women's villages. Traditionally the bayt, the extended family of at least four generations, was organised over large compounds.[10] But after flooding caused by construction of the Aswan Dam in 1964, more than 40,000 villages were relocated and the domestic unit became smaller. The relocation also disrupted women's unofficial status. They had run households on lands that didn't have deeds and were passed on through generations over thousands of years, but relocation meant they were now financially beholden to male members of the family as the government assigned land to men.

When Shadia's husband started an extramarital affair and left her and her son, Shadia's women-led family encouraged her to initiate a divorce. They asked her to stay with extended family, but she felt ashamed. A single woman who has been married is therefore sexually experienced, and is seen as a threat to other women, she tells me. 'Other women in my home village were suspicious of me. They would say that I couldn't be alone with their husbands.'

Then she heard that the government had started villages for divorced women to buy houses and land. It would be a place where she could be independent and safe, surrounded by women like her. She applied for a house and soon learned that her application had been accepted.

Shadia doesn't want to name the village but describes it as isolated and hard to access, with broken roads and terrible soil, much like El-Samaha. Men from neighbouring communities would skulk around the village, eyeing up the women, she recalls. She felt vulnerable.

Within a few years, Shadia sold her house and moved in with her sister's family near Aswan, where fewer people knew that she was a divorced woman. Today, we're sitting in her nephew's home, a multi-room layout built around a large open courtyard. Shadia's mother, her sister and her niece are all taking naps in different rooms. We're a short felucca ride from the city, where the brightly painted homes are built on a hill that slopes down to overlook the sparkling west bank of the Nile. Thousands of people live here and she is happy.

'In the divorced women's village, there were no police, no guards,' she says. 'And all women need the option of protection.'

Remote villages peppered in deserts aren't spaces built with women's safety in mind.

After leaving Shadia's home near Aswan, Janey and I walk around the market where a group of Nubian women are selling candles, spices and wooden keyrings. The walls of the street are filled with large murals, painted in crayon-bright and pop art colours. Several are postcards of daily life in the desert or by the Nile – men shepherding camels, women with water pails on their heads. Janey notes how so much of the imagery seems to show domestic duties, exoticising women's chores for Western tourists.

I think back to twenty-four hours ago, when we left El-Samaha in a hurry. When Mr F returned to the room where we were interviewing Asimah, it was clear that our unsupervised time was over. We were no longer welcome.

'Finished?' he asked, looking at me and then at Janey. As a village supervisor, he could say when the visit was done. We got in our car and headed back to Aswan, mostly in silence.

I had thought the trip to an Egyptian women-led village would help inform our own feminism. It did, but not for the reasons that I had anticipated.

El-Samaha, as a feminist project, has little chance of thriving. It is isolated with poor transport links. A feminist society needs structures to support women, who have lived most of their lives as supportive figures in male-led communities. Like the specialist support offered in places like Casa das Mulheres in Maré, which provides feminist lawyers and gender violence experts for the women in the Rio favelas. This isn't the case in El-Samaha.

The promise of women-only communities is seductive. Who doesn't love the image of a desert oasis ruled by women farmers? But El-Samaha wasn't conceived with the needs of these women in mind. On the drive back to Aswan I wondered who exactly it had been set up for. The fact that the articles I had read to research El-Samaha were all written in English strongly suggested that the audience was not the Arabic-only-speaking rural women the village claimed to cater for.

At the market, I ask Janey what she thought of our visit to El-Samaha village, as it was clear that there were parts of the visit she had found uncomfortable. She shares that she thinks women's development projects are often framed through a paternalistic lens, where funders make crucial decisions.

'Women-led spaces' is an enticing catchphrase. 'A development funding bingo card' of terms, as Janey calls it. Certain terms draw in donors who want an attractive headline. A village run by women in the desert? That's the kind of story that resonates globally. It's simple enough for donors to back, and compelling enough for journalists to spin into something hopeful. Yet women's spaces without specialist support leave vulnerable women dependent in a different way, and even more unprotected.

And few people would or could visit El-Samaha to verify the promise of a matriarchy in the Western Desert for themselves.

*

About a week after I return to London from Egypt, a Facebook message from Upper Egypt pings into my inbox. It is from one of the women in El-Samaha. She says she heard about our visit and while she doesn't want to reveal any details about herself, she wants me to know something.

She says that a small group of women in El-Samaha meet several times a week in secret, and they use their time together to discuss what is needed for the village. Some of the organisation is mundane, like making an inventory of all the new tools needed for farming and pooling funds to buy in bulk. They then take their proposal to Mr F. They make other subtle suggestions to him too.

'We plant ideas that he can say are his own.'

Other times the women meet and discuss the welfare of other women who live in the community. Does anyone seem a little more withdrawn? Maybe she needs a visitor, someone to drop by and chat to her.

'El-Samaha is an isolated place, and sometimes you feel this is where they hide the women they are ashamed of,' she writes, 'but we try to help each other.'

The issue is that the men do not ever let the women publicly lead, even in this village for women. The running of a women-led society is dependent on what the patriarchal system allows. She says that as rural women with little opportunities to earn a living, they don't have the means to leave and survive in other places – even if they wanted to.

That is the last message she sends me, and the several replies I send her go unanswered.

'In Egyptian societies, there is a lot of shame around women who don't have husbands,' feminists from Ganoubia Hora told me, 'so the motivation to help single women is a noble one, but a robust follow-through plan has to be set up with the women's welfare in mind. That wasn't the case with El-Samaha.'

The women from El-Samaha all come from patriarchal communities where they showed deference to fathers, husbands and sons. After divorce and widowhood, they were placed in a village in the desert, with a male supervisor, while remaining in the same mindset. Many wanted to return to husbands who had left them, like thirty-year-old Anat, the shy woman who Mr F spoke over when we met her in El-Samaha.

'Women exercise self-stigma,' the organisers from Ganoubia Hora said. 'Women are trained to accept that men rule over them.'

This mentality mirrors an Arabic saying that often goes viral on Instagram: 'The irony of pain is that you often want to be comforted only by those who hurt you.'

A thriving women-led community could have emerged if a few issues had been given better consideration. Perhaps women who have experienced disempowered lives need to be around women who are examples of empowerment. Maybe El-Samaha could be a happier place if a woman were appointed as the village supervisor. A woman supervisor who would centre the needs of women and maintain connections with feminist organisations who could regularly visit the village and offer outreach. Such organisations could prepare women for divorced life, offering support and a space for women to talk. They could host the meetings in the Rural Women's Centre, the empty and unused building we walked past. As it stands, no feminist organisation has access to El-Samaha to meet the needs of the women who live there, be it their mental and physical health or their financial situation.

'Very rural villages in the desert are difficult for feminist organisations to gain permission and access to visit,' a feminist lawyer from Cairo, Nesma Al-Khatib, explained to me. 'They operate by their own rules. I am not confident that feminist organisations would be safe if we did or said something that upset the male supervisors.'

Nesma runs an organisation called Sanad (meaning 'support'), which helps vulnerable women – many of whom are the victims of domestic violence and abuse within marriages. Her aim is to set up a series of divorced women's communities within cities where women can still be part of a wider society and around people they know, but also have specialist support as they navigate single life. She's of the belief that women-only spaces can only be empowering if they are within wider communities – not places of confinement, where 'unacceptable' women are hidden away from everyone else.

And elsewhere in Egypt, more and more women-centred spaces are emerging, designed and led by the very people they serve. Ganoubia Hora runs a 'feminist school' – a series of online and in-person workshops in Upper Egypt to inform women about their rights, including women who are in unhappy and abusive marriages. The organisation also runs separate workshops where they educate men on becoming better allies to vulnerable women they may know, including how to examine their own behaviour and not dominate conversations. They hope it will help people to rethink gender roles within the country. I wonder how Mr F, and our driver, would cope in these workshops.

Less official collectives include the private Facebook community Egyptian Single Mothers, run by its Cairo-based founder Nermeen Abousalem. She started the group in April 2016, and more than 2,000 women joined within that month, seeking support and fellowship.

Now, the group has over 100,000 members, and there are more than 5,000 women on the waiting list. Nermeen told me that she doesn't accept donations, and the group is not a formal charity. 'I am trying to create a healthy safe space for women to exchange knowledge, experience and advice. We are trying to change attitudes towards single women through talking. When women talk, things change.'

Egyptian Single Mothers has a vibrant community of volunteers who look to help women who are struggling with several aspects of single life – including widowhood and divorce. 'Anyone who can contribute with a service, product, a piece of information or even a word is welcomed in.' Several single women whose husbands have abandoned them and their children with no financial support post about their concerns, and they are then helped by lawyers (many of them also women).

Nermeen explained that one of the group's objectives is to build up women's knowledge, skills and confidence, and empower single mothers to find economic independence. The group also calls for family law reviews in order to protect women and children from domestic violence. They aim to have an impact on media, policy and public opinion, in a culturally sensitive manner.

'We aspire to get as much support from everyone in the community. So we invite everyone to join: doctors, lawyers, teachers, life coaches, psychologists, even organisations – schools, nurseries, hospitals, sports and activity centres – to support single mothers in every possible way.'

It is a truly influential women-led space, started by an Egyptian for Egyptian women.

*

The day we returned from El-Samaha, and drove back through Aswan, we passed the Tulip Hotel where the International Women's Film Festival was about to begin. A group of women organisers wearing headphones and chic trouser suits were fluffing up vases of flowers and removing flecks from the red carpet, organising the final touches. Women were directing the show. We once again passed the poster with the Latin political slogan 'nihil de nobis, sine nobis'.

Nothing about us, without us.

In my more than decade-long experience as a journalist, I have seen many initiatives created for vulnerable communities and women's spaces set up by organising committees. Some have slick, clever, marketing strategies, but it's clear when they lack committee members who are actually from or who currently live in those spaces. Villages for divorced and widowed women, designed by divorced and widowed women with women's leadership, would be an entirely different Herland.

The desert is a perfect place for hibiscus, and El-Samaha once had a reputation for growing some of the best hibiscus in Upper Egypt. But nowadays the hibiscus often struggles to survive. It's hard to organise the delivery of fertiliser, and their farm tools are old, so the reeds and dandelions have taken over.

In another world I imagine a divorced and widowed women-only village would have packaged and marketed the hibiscus tea, creating a thriving business which would have generated regular income for the women. As it stands, the men have already taken over.

My experience at El-Samaha left me thinking back to a previous trip, to a women's village in rural Kenya – a place where women built their own space and made bold changes when hierarchy and male influence started to creep in.

6

Villages for Single Women

Kenya, 1990

A few months after our Egypt trip, Janey texted me to say that she had been talking about El-Samaha village with a South American feminist friend who had then recommended a Nicaraguan novel called *El País de las Mujeres* by Gioconda Belli. I couldn't find an English-language copy (and I can't read Spanish) so I had to rely heavily on Google Translate. It was worth it. The story, published in 2010, is set in the fictitious South American country Faguas, an androcentric culture in which male violence reigns – until, that is, an act of nature rejigs society. An unexpected eruption of a volcano results in a significant reduction of testosterone production in men. They become meek and docile, and a group of women form a political party called PIE, which soon takes over the running of the country. PIE stands for the Party of the Erotic Left; 'erotic' refers to Eros, to life, and women are linked with life since they are responsible for giving it. The party flag shows a female foot with red painted nails. It's a symbol that plays to sexist politics, unapologetically reclaiming a feminine identity.

The five women leaders, from different parts of the social strata, share the aim of restructuring the male-centred social system by tackling the most urgent issues affecting

Faguas – the most urgent of the urgent being male violence against women.

The PIE leaders introduce a series of bold measures including mandatory education courses on domestic violence prevention. They increase surveillance and street lighting. Every rapist has a 'v' (for *violador* or 'rapist') tattooed on his forehead. Every Thursday, male abusers are exhibited in cages in public. Each cage has a sign revealing the crime committed by the man against a woman. The controversial goal is to present gender violence as a bestial act, an act of animals in a zoo; an act that a civilised society will not tolerate.

The PIE party leaders insist that they want a felicísimo – a feminised culture where both women and men are happy, and free of violence. So they devise a culture by local women for local women and put it in motion themselves.

Umoja Village, Kenya, 2018

It was an American tourist who first told me about 'the land of no men'. I was captivated by the epithet, learning much later that the tourist was quoting the headline of a *Vice* article. I'd met her in the garden of the Nairobi guest house where we were both staying, and although I was tired, she had my attention. The trip to the land of no men – what a dazzling concept.

The American tourist had been on safari at Samburu National Reserve in northern Kenya when her tour guide asked her if she would like to see a village where men were not allowed. Of course she said yes – who wouldn't say yes? And so she was driven there, right to the banks of the Ewaso Ng'iro river, where dozens of women wrapped in vermilion cloth and beads and anklets met her by their huts. It was wonderful, one of the single most memorable experiences of her life . . . Wait, was she describing too much? Would I want to go discover it for myself?

'I want to see it myself,' I replied.

It was 2018, and I was on a visit to Kenya where my days were jam-packed, but the American tourist convinced me to change my schedule.

A few days later, on the six-hour drive from Nairobi to Umoja village, I thought how accomplished a saleswoman the American tourist had been. It was only later that I realised she herself had been the customer for a particular type of commercialised feminism. So had I. An eager customer whose belief system was being directly marketed to.

Like El-Samaha, the desert village for divorced women, Western media loved Umoja, an off-the-beaten-track women-only village that was enticing, exotic and empowering. It's a story that's easy to market to a news editor. The top line: women have built their own world to escape domestic violence. Over the past decade they've been visited by the UK's *Guardian*, Germany's Deutsche Welle, CNN and NBC in the US, and the Australian Broadcasting Corporation. Umoja was a rare positive news story centring the voices of women from the global south.

In order to reach the village, you first have to travel north from Nairobi, for more than 180 miles, to Samburu County. The most chaotic part of the six-hour drive is the hour it takes to leave the capital on the eight-lane Thika Superhighway, which is filled with overtaking and undercutting boda bodas and minibuses, or stationary matatus and cars taking a rest on the sides, with a police checkpoint every ten kilometres or so.

Things got calmer as we reached the market town of Nanyuki. The roadside kiosks selling potato chips and pay-as-you-go phone cards were more frequent, but there were fewer vehicles on the road. We weren't stopped at the checkpoint near the small settlement of Archers Post, where the landscape begins fading into desert.

Archers Post is parched scrubland, where vast sand-like flats are broken up by the occasional acacia tree or deciduous shrub. It's fed by the Ewaso Ng'iro river, which is seasonal in its flow. People mainly pass through Archers Post on their way to Samburu National Reserve, but both the British and Kenyan military have training camps nearby. Other than that, there's little else. In the distance are the Ndoto Mountains. *Ndoto* is Swahili for 'dream' – a hope for a better tomorrow.

When my driver, Malcolm, reached the market centre, we stopped to buy soft drinks from a stall painted lime green with a flying tin roof portico to protect from the suffocating dry heat. The young man at the stall could speak English, and he told us that it was not possible just to turn up at Umoja women's village. We would have to go to a guest house where staff would liaise with the women from Umoja on when it would be convenient for us to go there. It should only take a day or so, the young man said.

It made sense. I wouldn't want a stranger to pop over uninvited to my house either.

The Samburu women

The Samburu are an indigenous ethnic group from the expansive arid shrublands of northern Kenya. They are a warrior race of cattle-owning pastoralists – one of the

Maa-speaking peoples, of whom the Maasai are the best known. Their dialect is spoken in a more rapid manner than that of the Maasai but includes many words that are common to both.

Samburu County is also one of the most challenging places in Kenya to be a woman, according to women's groups. The UN Environment Programme reports that Samburu women are amongst the many millions of women around the world who produce up to 80 per cent of food in developing countries, yet own less than 20 per cent of land worldwide.[1] That figure is even less in Kenya, with only 1 per cent of Kenyan women owning land – and even fewer in tribal communities, according to the Africa Data Hub.[2]

Gender status within Samburu communities is strictly enforced, favouring men, and this grows more pronounced with age. Older men decide who marries whom and who owes whom, and this is essentially how individual families and the wider community are run. Men are allowed to take multiple wives, with the younger ones having little say in the running of the household. Yet even being an elder wife offers little power, and they are excluded from decision-making and community councils. Men largely spend their days together, tending to cattle. Women herd animals too, but are responsible for cooking and childcare within their traditional huts, the manyattas.

Similar to gatherings in El-Samaha village, the sole specific women-only spaces in traditional Samburu culture are the rituals before a girl or woman marries.

A special manyatta is built for the girl and she is taken there by the women in the village. On day one they shave her head and put a paste of red ochre on her face and neck. The colour is associated with celebration and life, a victory over tribulations. The women stay together in the hut and on day two the bride-to-be is circumcised.

A female elder cuts the bride's genitalia in the manyatta as a cow is slaughtered outside. The old practice is said to make a girl ritually pure for her husband, preparing her for the sexual demands expected of her in marriage. Samburu Women Trust calls it a 'barbaric' and 'heinous' practice, and although female genital mutilation (FGM) has been legally banned in Kenya since 2001, grassroots organisers say it is still prevalent in Samburu culture. According to the 2022 Kenya Demographic and Health Survey, approximately 76 per cent of Samburu women aged 15–49 have undergone FGM, compared to a national average of 15 per cent.[3]

'Girls are ruled by their fathers,' a Samburu woman who fights for indigenous women's rights told me, 'and then expected to marry young and submit to their husbands, and later their sons.' It's a theme that women in China have written about in their women-only language of Nüshu as the 'Three Obediences': following the wishes of fathers in childhood, husbands during marriage, and male children in later life.

For Samburu women, FGM is not the only threat. There is also the everyday violence – the physical battering and psychological torture. 'In the presence of men, Samburu women have some of the fewest rights you can imagine,' the campaigner added. 'It is only away from the structures that men rule that rural women find their voice.'

One such place was Umoja village, which opened in 1990 after Kenya's government donated a patch of land to sixteen Samburu women who were survivors of male violence.

The initiative was led by Rebecca Lolosoli, a Samburu

woman born in the 1960s. She did not want to be interviewed for this book, but Rebecca has told her story over the years to sources including *Daily Nation*,[4] UN Women, the *Guardian*, Vital Voices and the *Washington Post*.

Although her childhood was spent in a polygamous and male-heavy community, she was one of the few girls who thrived in school. Rebecca was one of the less than 30 per cent of Samburu residents who could read and write,[5] a number far lower than Kenya's national average of 82 per cent.[6] She attended a girls' primary school and then later joined the Catholic nursing training centre, but dropped out as she could no longer afford her tuition fees.

Rebecca married as a teenager, at eighteen. Her husband provided her family with a dowry of seventeen cows. As a wife, Rebecca began to notice something: women around her were being abused, either at their homes by their partners or by British and Kenyan soldiers who were training in the barracks nearby. When women would go to collect firewood, men in green uniforms, camouflaged against the shrubs, would ambush the women and sexually assault them.

Rebecca began to quietly ask the women in her community about whether they had been attacked, and she found their answers shocking. Soldiers at one Samburu village had allegedly raped more than a dozen women, who were subsequently shamed by their community. Rebecca visited these women and offered to help them report the offences. But her activism angered many in the community, who felt she was disrupting accepted gender norms. At one point, she was so brutally physically attacked by a group of men, who insisted that she must stop bringing attention to their community, that she needed to be hospitalised for several days. This was when she decided to leave her village, leave her husband, and offer women a place of safety.

In the 1990s, gender-based violence was already an ongoing crisis in Kenya, with over 40 per cent of women experiencing intimate partner violence.[7] Yet there were few shelters then – or even now – which offered rural women an escape.[8] Even in larger cities, gender violence recovery resources were scarce. There were around fifty formal women's shelters in Kenya as of 2024, according to a report issued by Kenya's Generation Equality Secretariat. Only two were funded by Kenya's government.[9] Such shelters are mostly located closer to Nairobi, with hardly any resources for abused women in rural regions like Samburu County. No wonder a women's village emerged.

It was at the hospital, recovering from the physical abuse that had been meted out against her for simply asking about domestic violence, that Rebecca realised she needed to create a safe space for Samburu women. She told the BBC's Swahili service that she wanted it to be a place for sisterhood. She called it Umoja, the Swahili word for togetherness.

A sign in English

It was a day later when the reception staff at the Archers Post guest house told me they had been liaising with Umoja village and the women were now ready for me to visit.

Entry would be 1,000 KES per person, so less than $20 for me and Malcolm, and the village was around two kilometres away. On the five-minute drive, we passed dozens of young men walking along the sandy road on their way to the market stalls. October was the wet season in Samburu County, but the day was forgiving, a dry and mild heat. We passed a painted white stone with blue capital letters.

WELCOME TO UMOJA UOSA WOMEN CULTURAL VILLAGE & MUSEUM

A small arrow pointed left. We were 100 metres away.

In 2018, I didn't question why the sign was written in English, instead of the native Samburu. But I did think about it years later, when I saw the English sign at El-Samaha village in Arabic-speaking Egypt. Umoja, like El-Samaha, was packaging itself for a foreign audience.

Behind a fence of thorny shrubs, around ten traditional Samburu huts made of wood twigs and cow dung (the manyattas) were arranged several metres apart. We were allowed to see inside one of the huts, which had a bare mat on the floor where the women and children slept. There was a stove, which would later be taken outside to prepare meals, usually maize and pulses. The women generally prepared their meals to eat together in an outside communal area, which looked almost like a bus stand with a roof, with mats on the floor. Aside from that, there were over ten acres of sandy shrubland. The land was shared with a local school as well as a campsite for tourists, which had fully furnished guest cabins with running water and flushable toilets – and was fully booked.

There were around six women sitting on the woven mats, tending to toddlers and babies. Before I could ask how a women-only village was producing babies, the sonorous singing started.

Another twenty or so women were walking towards us, a mist of dust around their feet as they thumped the ground rhythmically. This was a welcome dance. They clapped in time and it was lovely, although I hadn't expected it. Being there felt less like seeing how people lived and more like watching a staged performance.

The women were each wrapped in red cloth and a white sash, along with multicoloured beaded jewellery: earrings, bracelets, anklets. Their necks were encircled by dozens of beaded collars held together by elephant hair which bounced as they danced. The women had short, cropped hair, and wore intricate beadwork caps that looped around the eyes and nose. The bead pattern for each woman was unique, with the colours representing various Samburu pastoral necessities: green for the grass, white for purity, red for sacred cow's blood, yellow for peace, blue for water. The younger women wore red necklaces, and those of the older women were multicoloured.

Our greeter told us the beads were signs of each woman's connection to men. Her first loops would be given to her by her father. Later, her boyfriend might give her a collar as an indication of his love, but this had to be returned when the girl became betrothed to the man of her father and uncle's choice. We were told that around fifty women and their children lived in the village – more than 200 people in total. There were fewer than twenty manyattas in front of me, and I wondered if multiple families shared each hut.

I asked the women what a typical day looked like in the village, and one of them replied on behalf of the group. They woke before 6 a.m. and headed to Ewaso Ng'iro to collect water. Then they would cook maize. Afterwards, they would bead jewellery, which they made and sold to sustain themselves, and wait for visitors. The jewellery was available to purchase online from around the world. Their main income came from Western tourists.

VILLAGES FOR SINGLE WOMEN

The women in Umoja allowed male tourists. They also employed male labourers – there was a man selling the jewellery and another man herding a group of goats to a boma. But they were keen to reiterate that Umoja was a village for women. The presence of small children made it clear that the women certainly had encounters with men, but they insisted – to this holidaying foreign journalist at least – that men never spent the night.

'When you are attacked by men all your life, you do not know which man is an attacker,' another woman said, 'so it is better that no man stays here.'

They told me that a women-only space was an essential signal, to let women know that this was a place their male abuser could not harm them.

The busiest time for Umoja village was between July and October – tourist season. Vans of sunburnt, sweaty muzungus (white people) would visit on their way to or from the safari at Samburu National Reserve. They would expect a tour of the village, a visit inside a manyatta, some songs and jewellery.

As well as the entrance fee, we were encouraged to pay 500 KES ($5) to each dancer. The necklaces cost around 2,000 KES ($20). One of the women shared that all the earnings were given to the village's matriarch, who then divided the total amongst each household, in proportion to how many people lived in the manyatta.

After around three hours, my time with the women was up, made clear when they started singing a parting song. We took our cue and headed out, deciding to leave Archers Post and make the journey back to Nairobi. As we drove away, we saw about a dozen women leave the thorny gates of Umoja to walk towards Archers Post. I assumed they were walking to the market, but my driver had other suspicions.

'Maybe they don't all even live in Umoja,' he said. 'They may be local women who come to dance for tourists.'

Years later, I would learn that he was somewhat right. Not all the women I met in Umoja permanently lived there. A few women in Archers Post said they had been recruited to pad out the choir of singing women when tourists were visiting. They were happy that Umoja gave them an opportunity to bead necklaces and bracelets, sing, and feel a sense of purpose. But in 2018, driving south back to Nairobi on Kenya's A1 highway, I felt mixed emotions.

The Umoja women, led by Rebecca Lolosoli, had clearly done something incredibly powerful and radical in setting up a village for women to escape abuse. Yet the village I had visited didn't feel like a village. In total, I'd spent less than a hundred dollars for the entire experience, but that's what it felt like – an experience. It didn't feel like visiting a community. It was like a living, breathing exhibition, although one with a vital social cause at its centre: the urgent issue of violence against women. Our visit had felt like we were following a curated programme – a staged performance for outsiders.

Years later, while researching for this book, I asked to visit Umoja again – through my Kenyan friend, journalist Michael Kaloki. Michael was told that it would be a fee of over $200 just for entry, and more to talk to any women. I would also need the permission of Rebecca's son, Sammy, who was running the campsite. Just as with El-Samaha in Egypt, you now needed the permission of a man to arrange a visit to a village where women were said to rule. I declined the offer. Although Umoja was undoubtedly a safe haven, it was also a show for tourists – a bit of a Disneyland of feminism, where a hierarchy had crept in, overseen by a man. Sammy didn't respond to requests to speak with him.

'Umoja is not like it was when it was first set up. It's now run like a tight ship,' a resident of Archers Post who asked not to be named said. 'It's a commercial enterprise now.'

And there was growing dissent.

Unlike in El-Samaha, where many of the women had adapted to a patriarchal order and believed men were in charge, several women in Umoja were not willing to accept being told what to do. They wanted to live in a women-led land, but they didn't want a matriarch, or a matriarch's son, as their ultimate decision-maker – the gatekeeper of all funds. Not all women in Umoja wanted to live with this kind of leadership.

Although I didn't know it in October 2018, some women had taken matters into their own hands. About a kilometre down the road, a new village for women had emerged – one with a more egalitarian outlook. It was called Unity.

Life at Unity village

The women say that when they decided to leave Umoja, they wandered the nearby area looking for available land with access to the river. They found two clear acres closer to Samburu National Reserve and decided this would be where they would build their community.

In Samburu culture, women are responsible for building the manyattas, with older women – women with the prefix 'Mama' in front of their first names – instructing younger women and girls on how to construct a stable home.

The Unity women started by first clearing and levelling out the land, chopping down bushes and patting down the sandy earth. Then they gathered large timber poles from nearby areas and arranged them in an oval framework, anchoring the thicker sticks deep into the ground. They built the walls as a lattice of smaller branches, which were then plastered with a soup of water, mud and newspapers, and secured with corrugated iron and cloth. The next step was the roof, a boat-like version of the main frame, and finished with grass that had been collected in the bush.

In the old days – the Umoja days – the Samburu would use cow dung and urine to form a type of water-resistant cement, but the Unity women have adapted and phased that stage out. Each manyatta is around 3 metres by 5 metres, with a height of 1.5 metres. There are usually two sleeping areas and a living area – enough to house a woman and her children. There are no windows, but there are some small holes where light peeks in. The air inside is often thick with the smoke generated from burning wood and a stove cooking ugali, the typical daily meal of a pulpy maize-flour porridge.

Every woman's hut is unique on the inside, decorated to her own taste. 'The houses we build are similar to each other. What differs is who is inside,' says Mama Leah, who was one of the first women to move to Unity. 'Every woman has their own decorative style. We build with the same materials, but inside it's different.'

Although you have to stoop to enter through the door, someone over six foot tall can comfortably stand up inside a manyatta. The living areas are where the plastic bottles used to gather water are stored, and the sleeping areas are cordoned off by wooden poles tied together. The women and their children sleep on mats on the floor made from cowhide. The manyattas, even in Samburu and Maasai communities that include men, are the domain of women. Men visit, but rarely spend the night, often choosing to sleep outdoors.

At Unity, the women built each of the manyattas together. It took them a full week to build one manyatta. The first four were for the older women, including Mama Leah. Then, over the next few weeks, another seven manyattas were erected. Over three months, the women built a new village – their own women-only community. Each woman has her own story of survival that she is happy to share with you in the communal shed, where they meet to talk with visitors.

Their days follow a similar pattern. The women wake up early, before 4 a.m., and pray for an hour, wishing for security. Then they tend to their goats before getting the children ready for school. Unity village has water tanks, but the water in them can often taste chalky, so the women go to the river to fetch water. Nothing beats fresh river water. They also cut firewood, and take the excess wood to sell at the market in Archers Post. In the evening, they bring their goats inside the shared boma. They watch their children play and eat together.

'If one mama does not have money to buy food for her family,' Mama Leah says, 'the other mamas share their food.'

They talk together in the open shed. The older women go to sleep early, around 8 p.m. Then, the next day, they wake up and do it all again. More than twenty women and fifty children have lived here – and followed this simple routine – since about 2011.

Unity receives international visitors and they also make money from beading. Money is divided up equally amongst all the women who live in the village.

Elizabeth speaks English and is happy to translate for the other Unity women. Now in her twenties, Elizabeth had her education sponsored when a group of American women met her at Umoja. She had made it there after a childhood of mistreatment. She was physically assaulted by an aunt she lived with, who punished her for excelling at school. Her aunt destroyed her school books and arranged for her to be married to a much older man when Elizabeth had just turned thirteen. However, Elizabeth's sister, also a survivor of abuse, wanted to protect her sibling. She had a home at Umoja village, and she helped Elizabeth to move there with her. A classic example of women helping women to break the cycle of abuse.

Forty-year-old Alice also came to Umoja seeking a safe haven. She had been regularly and ferociously beaten by her husband, her skin ripped with the sticks and rocks he would use in his abuse. Often she would lose consciousness. Once, he found her taking a rest under a tree from herding cattle and beat her to the point of collapse, using a wooden Maasai walking stick called an eng'udi. He would often deprive her and her child of food. In desperation, Alice would brew a potent illegal spirit called chang'aa, and sell it to local men in order to earn some money for her family. It was while doing this that a woman from Umoja passed by and approached her. She told Alice about a village where, instead of selling chang'aa, she could make necklaces and sing for tourists – a place men could not harm her. It was at Umoja that Alice met Elizabeth, who was then barely a teenager, and also Mama Leah.

Mama Leah isn't sure of her age, but she thinks she's around fifty-five. Her face is deeply lined, with skin folding over her eyelids. She could be a decade older, or more.

'The Samburus don't measure time in days,' she says.

Mama Leah's story is the story of many rural and impoverished women around the world. She grew up in a cycle of abuse. Her father had three wives and she watched him abuse them all, putting a knife to their throats as he screamed and punched them. Then, when she was still a child, before she developed breasts, Mama Leah was forced to marry an older man, becoming someone's third wife like her mother had before her. Her husband was abusing her from the start of their marriage.

'It is usual within the Samburu culture,' she says, 'because men see a woman as being less.'

There was no one Mama Leah could speak to about the violence. You could tell the male village elders that your husband was beating you, but they rarely intervened. Cultural norms meant that women rarely approached the local police – and even if they did, the male officer would tell them to return to their husbands.

'When women are together, we talk,' she adds. 'Sharing our experiences helps identify patterns.'

The pattern was domestic violence. Each woman at Umoja and Unity is a survivor of abuse, and their women-only village is their shelter.

A safe space

In Unity, as in Umoja, the women are free from male violence against women, a phenomenon so prevalent that UN Women call it a 'shadow pandemic'.

Traditionally, a Samburu woman is seen as the property of her father and then her husband. In this way her body, subjected to female genital mutilation, is rendered almost incapable of experiencing abuse. An owner cannot abuse their own property.

'Domestic violence is a creature of gender inequality, but it intersects with all forms of discrimination, including poverty, location-isolation, cultural expectation,' former executive coordinator of UN Women, Purna Sen, told me. 'This shapes who is being abused, and who is excused as the abuser.'

But some men I speak to in the Archers Post area deny outright that abuse occurs.

'There is no domestic abuse in Samburu culture,' Lemax, a forty-five-year-old father of four, who is sitting on a dusty road outside a hotel near the market, insists defiantly. 'None.'

Lemax is suspicious of the value of having a women-only space, and feels that it is an issue that the male elders in Samburu communities could help end. 'You tell a couple of elders, or a council of elders, and then they settle the problems.'

Then he adds knowingly, 'The school in Umoja has a German name.' He's referring to Umoja Muehlbauer Academy, which educates around eighty rural girls. The school makes all parents take a pledge that if their children are to be pupils there, they will not be made to undergo female genital mutilation or early marriage. For Lemax, though, the European name is simply another indication of the erosion of his culture. So is the existence of Umoja and Unity – they are unnatural villages, polluted by Western ideology.

'How can you live just a lady and a lady together, without men?' he asks. 'Maybe in Europe you can, but not here. Here you need a man and a woman together.'

Lemax is also convinced that Umoja, and to some extent Unity, is made to attract Western tourists and their money. 'Economic reasons,' he says.

His cynicism makes me feel defensive of the women. The commercialisation of a women-only space doesn't take away from the achievement of setting one up. The women who first moved to Umoja and El-Samaha were pioneers who showed that it is possible to create a world where women feel safe from abuse, saying it is safer to live without abusers. Yet over time, any ecosystem can be taken over by predators – those who are naturally at the top of the hierarchy. Every domestic violence specialist I have talked to insists that because of male-led social environments, women's spaces are vitally needed so women survivors of male violence can recover from domestic abuse. Even if not all men are abusers, most of the predators at the apex of abusive structures are male.

Rebecca Lolosoli created a space where Samburu women could escape violence through sheer will – a remarkable, brilliant achievement. And what is wrong with generating income from Western tourists for such a place? Having her son oversee the management could be how the community has chosen to evolve – which all communities do, eventually.

Perhaps Unity village is also part of the evolution of an idea. Unity has taken the foundations of Umoja and adapted them, clarifying the concept of equality and emphasising the idea that every woman should feel a sense of ownership. At Umoja, Rebecca and her son Sammy have the final say. At Unity there is no leader. Every woman has a stake in the community finances.

Both Umoja and Unity are sanctuaries for women escaping gender-based violence, forced marriages and female genital mutilation. They have faced several challenges and much criticism, including backlash from local men. They are also heavily reliant on tourism, on the sale of their jewellery and crafts, which makes them the recipients of criticism from people who say they are a commercial venture. Yet their existence is a symbolic reminder that women do not have to endure abuse.

Elizabeth says that she wants women to know that if they ever find themselves in the area, they should come and visit both villages – and see that women can build more than one successful neighbourhood of peace. Both communities provide specialist services for vulnerable women: they are culturally sensitive spaces in which to share experiences and foster confidence. Unlike a women's refuge, they are open to visitors, but they are also places in which women seek refuge. They have been created by women for women's safety. Spaces like these will be essential as long as violence against women exists.

7

Girlboss Island – and a Club for Africa's Elite

Fjärdskär, Finland, 2017; Lagos, Nigeria, 2021

Fjärdskär island was once called 'an exclusive women's oasis for superwomen' – echoing the gushing descriptions written in press releases about the villages of El-Samaha and Umoja. But unlike El-Samaha and Umoja, which were set up for the most vulnerable of women, who were often without independent resources, Fjärdskär served women at the top of the executive strata. It was a women-only island open to the most financially successful, accomplished women leaders.

Fjärdskär is tiny – only 8.47 acres. So tiny it's more accurate to call it an islet, although no one does. It's one of over a thousand that make up the labyrinthine archipelago of Raseborg, rising from the inky green waters of the Baltic Sea just off the coast of Finland. For a while, Fjärdskär was known as SuperShe Island.

In another timeline, another universe, SuperShe could have been a real-world mini Themyscira, the home of Wonder Woman – an isolationist nation of mythic Amazon women who possess advanced technological knowledge. The fictional Themyscira is ruled by Aphrodite's Law, which promises immortality on one condition: no man must enter their sacred domain. Men, and their way of doing things, contaminate the values of Themyscira.

In our real world, between 2017 and 2023, only women were allowed to set foot on SuperShe Island. To reach its pine-tree-bordered harbour, you would be taken on a power boat from the coast of Finland. Your captain would also be a woman.

Like Themyscira, SuperShe attracted leaders who excelled in male-dominated spaces. SuperShe visitors held cultural power. They were tech bosses and oil company magnates. They were assertive, competitive, ambitious women. They were tired women. On SuperShe, they could be with women like themselves.

Then, everything changed.

A private club for the elites

Before we delve into exclusive private members' clubs for women that exist in the real world, it would be helpful to see how they are depicted in literature. Fiction can sometimes offer deeper insights – creative licence allowing for more truth than snippets of reportage permit. Other than Themyscira, fictional realms where powerful women have shaped law and policy include gender-role-reversed worlds like the one in *Egalia's Daughters*, a 1977 novel by Norwegian author Gerd Brantenberg. In the fictional country of Egalia, women enjoy dominance in every way, including language. Women are called 'wim' and men 'menwim', making the man the prefix. Menwim exist to support the wim.

The novel features a luxurious private members' club where the most powerful and privileged wim spend their evenings, making important decisions away from the docile menwim in their lives. The wim-only den is called the Narcisseum Club for Gentlewim, and it is here that the wim arrange jobs for each other's children and influence what subjects make it onto the syllabus at schools. The powerful wim lament the diversity hire of minorities, including timid menwim, at their workplaces. They discuss politics, and lobby for laws that suit the ruling class, including tax breaks and more maternity pay on top of a full salary and bonus.

Of course, in the real world, we know that single-gender clubs have long existed for men in several cultures. The Dogon people of Mali, for example, erect a togu'na which only the community's male elders are allowed to enter.[1] Here the male leaders discuss pressing local matters and pass laws that affect the whole community. Discussions are often heated, so the togu'na design accommodates this. The building has a low roof, inviting the men inside to remain seated. This avoids any physical fights when disputes inevitably escalate. In some cultures, if a local woman enters this space, she can fall under a curse. The curse doesn't apply to people outside the community, however.[2]

Another club, over 3,000 kilometres away from the Dogons, has been the focus of recent controversy. The Garrick Club, deep in London's theatre district, is a short walk away from Covent Garden tube station. It's a grand nineteenth-century Italianate palazzo-style private members' club, with decorative mouldings and a sweeping staircase with an ornate cast-iron balustrade. For almost two centuries, the Garrick – with its bust-lined corridors, oil paintings, intimate bars, libraries and dining areas – was reserved only for England's most privileged men. 'Overwhelmingly white and predominantly elderly,' as the *Guardian* described its members.[3]

For years, the club resisted motions to admit women as members. But that changed in 2024, when its 1,300 members – including the head of MI6, several MPs, senior judges and actors, and King Charles III – voted to allow women to join permanently. Actresses Dame Judi Dench and Dame Siân Phillips were fast-tracked as the first women members. When their names were announced, there was said to be spontaneous clapping from the men.[4]

The Garrick isn't the only such elite and exclusive members' club. The Australian Club in Sydney, established in 1838 and considered the oldest gentlemen's club in the Southern Hemisphere, continues to allow only male members after a 2021 proposal to admit women as members failed to secure the necessary votes.[5]

Who knows what is settled in these rooms of male influence. What kinds of decisions are made when a politician and judge enjoy a private conversation over a casual cognac? Defenders of these men's clubs insist that they should be applauded for maintaining a cultural consistency as the world changes at breakneck speed. 'The endurance of the traditions of the private members' club is something to celebrate, not condemn,' argued the politically conservative UK magazine the *Spectator* in 2024.[6] Women may not be allowed to become members of men-only clubs, but they are allowed as guests of the men who are. So what's the issue?

'It's not trivial because it does actually damage women in their careers if they can't associate with more powerful people in their industries; it's often the informal meetings that lead to job offers and promotions,' Mary Ann Sieghart, author of *The Authority Gap: Why Women Are Still Taken Less Seriously Than Men* told the *Guardian*.[7]

As some men's clubs maintained their exclusionary

policies, women began to question why they were begging for inclusion in these spaces. Why face rejection from clubs that aren't interested in you as a member, when you can build your own? Women, as we've learned, are excellent at carving out their own spaces when they are excluded. And when I started looking for them, it didn't take long to find exclusive spaces for influential women – women who chair board meetings, enact policy and law, and spearhead culture.

SuperShe Island

SuperShe attracted a certain type of woman. A woman who could afford to pay 4,000 euros to camp for a week. It took an hour and a half to drive there from Finland's capital, Helsinki – or less than a thirty-minute helicopter flight if you were being especially fancy, which many were. Then, a short motorboat ride later, you would be transported to a private jetty on the bay of an island with pine trees, yurts, a sauna and your thoughts.

At any one time, ten women could stay on the island. Each day varied, but this was a time for relaxation and connection. No one wore make-up. There was no alcohol. Guests ate low-carb, dairy-free, farm-to-table food. They swam in the cold Baltic Sea and decompressed in a sizzling luxury Finnish sauna. They talked under the stars. They took power yoga classes and went kayaking. They exchanged numbers and agreed to work together in the future.

Founder Kristina Roth was born in Germany, to a family where men led and women supported. She describes her mother as a strong woman, yet she became subservient around men. It was a quality that Kristina observed carefully, and one she didn't want repeated.

Kristina studied computer science at university. There were five women in her class of around 400 men. It was, she says, a boys' club – women accounted for less than one-third (32.8 per cent) of the total number of people employed in the EU's high-technology sectors in 2022.⁸

She and the few women in her class became fast friends, though each was motivated by her own individual ambitions. They supported each other, grouping up as a study community and sharing lecture notes. 'We were like a SWAT team,' Kristina told me.

In 2002, she moved to the US with two suitcases to pursue the old-school American dream: upwardly mobile economic prosperity, available to any man and the occasional woman. The idea that – with enough gumption and ambition – anyone, from any background, can achieve material success.

Kristina eventually settled in the sprawling tech hub of Seattle, within its ecosystem of start-ups, setting up her own consulting business, Matisia Consultants. It was a success, landing her a spot on the Women Presidents' Organization (WPO)'s annual list of the fifty fastest-growing women-owned/led companies. By 2015, the company's annual revenue was more than $40 million.⁹ But this success came at a price. Kristina was exhausted from the hours spent working and networking to build her company.

To unwind, she would sometimes book herself into wellness retreats, yet she couldn't always relax. And she found the issue was men. If men were present at the retreats, the women changed their behaviour. There was a performance, a type of peacocking, even amongst the most accomplished leaders.

'The women would start getting their lipsticks out, and I'm not saying I wasn't one of them,' she joked when we spoke.

'If there's a sexy guy around, the retreat immediately gets this, like, you know, has like a hunting component in it. So I thought, "If there's a retreat, I really would like to do it just for women."'

Kristina told me that she hadn't ever been a separatist craving permanent women-only spaces. 'For me, men were not all predators and women were not all amazing. I think there is a healthy balance.' Yet there was clearly a market need for a women's space and a community. A place where leaders in high-pressure jobs could meet women like themselves in a low-key environment where they weren't obliged to wear power suits and deliver presentations.

Kristina sought out the company of women like herself, launching an online platform called SuperShe. It mainly spotlighted women like her in leadership positions, and evolved into a networking community with thousands of members from more than a hundred countries. Then in 2017, she decided to expand this digital community into a real-world piece of land. She had often holidayed with friends in private spots like Sir Richard Branson's Necker Island, and found herself thinking, 'If Branson can have an island, I can have an island myself too.'

And so SuperShe Island was born. It was a place where women could breathe in crisp air and watch the star-studded sky and talk about resetting their boardroom. Women who wanted to get together and talk.

'I think that there is a tremendous power in female communities if you know how to harness it,' Kristina said to me. 'It's up to you to get the best out of it [and] focus on the positives – there's always going to be a downside with everything.'

I told Kristina that I would love to visit SuperShe Island.

She replied that I'd be most welcome. I could have access to the entire island and meet her all-women staff: the boat captain, the chef, the yoga instructor, the masseuse.

Unfortunately, it never happened.

Rise of Girlboss Feminism

To understand more about the motivation behind SuperShe, we have to rewind slightly, to the beginning of the 2010s, when a certain type of feminism emerged onto the global stage.

This was a decade where well-known women were proudly promoting women's rights. In 2012, Nigerian author Chimamanda Ngozi Adichie delivered a powerful and viral TED Talk in London titled 'We Should All Be Feminists'. Then in 2014, British actress Emma Watson stood at the UN headquarters in New York and said that, although the word was unpopular, she was a feminist.

But this was also a decade of glamorised feminism and targeted messaging that centred the needs of individual women rather than collective empowerment. This digital age feminism was photogenic, and armed with hashtags and stylish Instagram filters. It invited women to assert themselves in a system built by men, which largely catered to the comfort of men.

Although it was not a touchstone cultural moment by any means, when I think of this time, I personally recall the 2011 trailer for *The Iron Lady* – Hollywood's interpretation of British prime minister Margaret Thatcher's life – having a particular impact on my personal perception of women in the workplace. The clip ended with the actress Meryl Streep as Thatcher standing up in a room of male heads of state and asking in a commanding semi-growl, 'Gentlemen, shall we join the ladies?' The message was clear: now the important people had reached agreement on important matters, in a male-only domain, they were free to join their home-making female spouses for trivial chitchat. I remember watching this and actively thinking that success meant sitting in a room of powerful men.

It's widely reported that in real life Thatcher thought this too. If she had wished for other women leaders in those decision-making rooms with her, she didn't say it out loud. Besides former Indian prime minister Indira Gandhi, Margaret Thatcher actively omitted any admiration for other women leaders in her autobiography. And as noted by Jenni Murray, the former BBC *Woman's Hour* presenter, Thatcher didn't welcome questions about why she didn't use her immense power to reconfigure a male-dominated political world and invite more women to the table. Thatcher brushed over her good fortune that – unlike other women around the world – she had a supportive husband and domestic help.

'Thatcher's answer, when pressed on her tendency to pull the ladder of equal opportunity up behind her, was invariably that none of the women was good or experienced enough to rise through the ranks,' writes Murray. 'If positive action to include women was suggested it was dismissed.'

'A woman must rise through merit,' Thatcher would insist. 'There must be no discrimination.'[10]

The same year Margaret Thatcher died – 2013 – *Lean In: Women, Work, and the Will to Lead* was released. The book is a guide on how to assert yourself in the workplace, written by former Facebook board member Sheryl Sandberg. It is a manifesto that argues that women can move to the head of the board table if only they better advocate for themselves while sitting at the fringes. *Lean In* soared onto bestseller lists around the world. It should come as no surprise that millions of women, looking for a manual for success, bought copies.

This 'you can make it by yourself, girls' directive was further compounded the following year when businesswoman Sophia Amoruso popularised the term 'girlboss'. It was soon folded into popular vernacular. The girlboss was a self-made woman, a feminine empire-maker in heels, who somehow had enough time to raise children and get a blow-dry.

Girlboss feminism – or 'neoliberal feminism', as coined by gender studies Professor Catherine Rottenberg[11] – was a hopeful road map to a social and corporate ascent. Yet unlike other waves of feminism that prioritised community gain, it focused heavily on individual achievement. It suggested that individual action was enough to dismantle systemic gender discrimination, a concept that seems at odds with the collective and community-based feminism espoused by women like Eliana Sousa in Maré and Elizabeth at Unity village in Kenya.

The 'lean in' philosophy arguably fostered a certain type of mindset – one that Canadian YouTuber and cultural critic Broey Deschanel described as 'Me and My Girls' feminism.[12] It places an overarching focus on issues that only affect the girlboss and her immediate circle. This form of feminism acknowledges workplace sexism, but assumes that all women experience misogyny the same way. It prioritises challenges facing cisgender, heterosexual, able-bodied, white and privileged women, and assumes that equal rights for these women will uplift *all* women.

An example is legacy millionaire Ivanka Trump's 2017 book *Women Who Work*, another guide to making it in the workplace. Here she acknowledges some challenges facing the few women who have made it into leadership positions, while offering smudgy solutions on gender parity. Women, more than men, are denied opportunities to negotiate a raise, she concedes. Yet Trump's advice is for women to prove their worth to their employer. She acknowledges that work-life balance is a challenge and argues it should be fought for, but only fleetingly mentions the help she receives that other women may not have access to – including nannies, personal assistants and house staff.

This mentality was in stark contrast to collective social mass movements happening elsewhere in the decade. Movements like Me Too and Time's Up, and also Ni Una Menos (Not One Woman Less) – the mass protests that took place in Argentina, Peru, Uruguay and Chile in 2016, following the murder of a teenage girl in Argentina the previous year. It was described as a 'collective scream against machista violence'.[13]

Girlboss feminism also brushed over the systemic challenges and barriers women face in pursuing career success. Barriers like societal expectations placing a disproportionate burden on women to shelve careers and cater to the individual caretaking needs of parents, spouses and children. According to the Trade Union Congress, 1.46 million women are kept out of the labour market in the UK because of their caring responsibilities, and women are seven times more likely to leave the workplace for caring responsibilities than men.[14]

And if a woman does rise to a leadership role, there are often very few like her in the room. According to the McKinsey *Women in the Workplace 2023* report, women represent roughly one in four C-suite leaders, and women of colour just one in sixteen.[15] The C-suite refers to top executive roles beginning with 'chief', such as chief executive officer (CEO), chief financial officer (CFO), chief operating officer (COO) and chief marketing officer (CMO).

Over the Christmas holidays in 2024, my family found out a surprising fact about women in leadership positions after going down a rabbit hole. My cousin Rohan (an accountant and Excel sheet whiz) and I were looking through the latest data for S&P 500 companies – the top US companies according to market capitalisation (meaning the value of US stock market shares). We found there were more CEOs named John, David and James (forty-seven in total) than there were women CEOs (forty-one).

If you're a woman, leadership positions are rare – and arguably more challenging.

A 2022 survey of 40,000 employees by McKinsey and LeanIn.org found that women in the top jobs were leaving their companies at the highest rates in five years. Around 43 per cent of women leaders reported burnout, compared to 31 per cent of men at the same level.[16] Women were feeling overwhelmed, under-supported and under-recognised, trying to crack systems set up by men. Systems where they were often the only women leaders at a table of men, without a community of other women around them.

A leader who vocalised this was New Zealand prime minister Jacinda Ardern, during her shocking resignation in January 2023. 'I know what this job takes and I know that I no longer have enough in the tank to do it justice,' she said, her voice giving way slightly. She was two minutes into a speech at a press conference that many had thought would concern little more than her political party's yearly housekeeping.

GIRLBOSS ISLAND — AND A CLUB FOR AFRICA'S ELITE

The story predictably trended around the world. Google Trends reported a rise in the search for the word 'burnout'. Article after article wondered if Ardern's gender had played a part in the decision. *Telegraph* columnist Judith Woods summed up the mood best with her headline: 'Jacinda Ardern has shown how hard it is being a woman in a world built for men by men'.[17]

It's little surprise that in a world not built for women leadership, an island like SuperShe emerged. There was clearly a market for women who wanted a retreat from the daily fight for survival and domination in a hostile ecosystem, and the wellness sector has been booming in recent years. The global wellness tourism sector was valued at $814.6 billion in 2022, and is expected to expand at a compound annual growth rate (CAGR) of 12.42 per cent from 2023 to 2030, according to Grand View Research.

Which is why, when I called Kristina in January 2024 to say I'd love to come visit SuperShe, I was so surprised at her reply.

'I've sold the island,' she replied cheerfully. 'The world no longer has a women-only island.'

Like several start-up projects that are branded and built for profit, SuperShe was vulnerable to shifting market needs. Covid had curbed sales, and fewer women were booking high-end retreats.

'People don't understand that running an island is expensive,' Kristina told me.

While it was undoubtedly a project with somewhat of an ideological mission, SuperShe was still a business. And when businesses don't make money, they fold. Ever the entrepreneur, Kristina had moved on to other projects, including a non-alcoholic drinks brand aimed at women.

Women-only members' clubs

SuperShe Island is not the only fallen artefact of the girlboss era. Another is The Wing, the US co-working space for women that opened its first branch in New York in 2016, at a time when most of the world thought Hillary Clinton was about to become president. It then rapidly expanded to eleven other cities, with the aim of advancing women and allowing them to form more meaningful connections through shared workspaces. It charged around $2,000 a year for membership, so it certainly wasn't something every woman could afford – but then it wasn't really for every woman. It was for girlbosses trying to make it in fast-paced (male-led) industries.

By 2020, there were rumours that it too had fostered a toxic workplace culture. Frenchie Ferenczi, The Wing's director of community, admitted in an op-ed that she had been too focused on business growth, rather than on the very real concerns of The Wing's members, especially women of colour.[18] The start-up's mission had been lost in the push for growth, and The Wing ceased operations in 2022. *Business Insider* reported on its demise with the headline 'Gone Girl(boss)'.[19]

While high-end women's clubs like The Wing and the UK's Grace Belgravia have closed, others have emerged in their place, including Zabeel Ladies Club in Dubai (launched in 2013). More private members' clubs have opened in London in the past four years than in the three decades following the 1985 opening of the iconic Groucho Club, according to property agency Knight Frank.[20] Private clubs are therefore the fastest-growing subsector in the real estate industry.

The global private members' club market is poised to be

worth an eye-watering $25.8 billion by 2027, according to research and market analysis firm Mordor Intelligence. Market analysts predict that following the Covid-19 pandemic and hybrid flexible working, which combines office and home, private members' spaces will only grow.[21] These should include women-led spaces.

The reasons people are willing to pay for private communities based on identity vary. Perhaps it's a desire for community connection in a world of digital and disjointed fellowship. Or perhaps, in an age of Instagrammable highlights, it's a way to join an exclusive and sectioned-off village. Maybe it's a way to weed out people with different values. Or, if you're a woman entrepreneur, it might be easier to have your ambitions supercharged by other women going through the same experience.

And this is not just a global north or a Western phenomenon either.

Africa's first private members' club exclusively for women quietly opened at the tail end of 2021, billing itself as a haven for the top 5 per cent of the continent's C-suite women leaders. It's called Gaia Africa, named after the Greek goddess – the feminine personification of all life on earth. Gaia emerged from Chaos, the mythic void before creation, and represents a self-conscious and benevolent balance, a hope for a stabilised future following the emptiness of the abyss. The symbolism is obvious. A feminised, woman-led world could be a soothing balm to the chaos of before times.

You're guaranteed a sea view when you reach Victoria Island, one of the more affluent areas of Nigeria's largest city, Lagos. You can drive there over three bridges from the mainland, leaving behind the densely populated city – some areas covered in makeshift tin-roofed structures – and entering a different world. Everything here looks, well, expensive. Victoria Island, along with its neighbours Lagos Island and Banana Island, is home to Forbes-listed millionaires, designer boutiques and corporate headquarters, while Lagos Island remains the historic core of the city, with its colonial-era buildings and traditional markets along the Gulf of Guinea. Victoria Island is also home to financial institutions, multinational corporations and several foreign embassies, including those belonging to the US, Germany, the UK and Russia. In 2022 Nigeria was Africa's largest economy, with a GDP of $477 billion. Its billionaires almost certainly have sealed business deals in buildings on Victoria Island. And this is where Gaia's clubhouse sits – a symbol of a future that includes more women in business.

Gaia House is a 900-square-metre, three-storey, pastel-coloured, modern minimalist building, with large windows and clean, geometric lines. When you enter, you see original artwork by some of the continent's most exciting creators. The centrepiece is a striking work called *Gaia Woman* by contemporary artist Ayobola Kekere-Ekun, which uses a technique called quilling – involving rolling, shaping, and gluing thin strips of paper together. *Gaia Woman* is a modern take on those regal portraits you see in castles: it's a side-profile portrait of a confident yet cartoon-like woman with circular eyes of black, green and brown. Some of her hair is braided and tied in a bun, with other strands flowing naturally. Around her are waves encasing circular shapes – symbolising egalitarianism, popular in women's spaces.

The ground floor features Gaia's reception and a five-star restaurant, which is open to the public, including men. The rest of the building is for the sole use of Gaia's female members. The goal is luxury and connection. There's a multi-purpose room called the Hub for screening films, seminars, private dinners, brand activations and so on, and the meeting rooms feature high-speed internet with outages prevented by a back-up generator. There's a wellness area for steams, scrubs, facials and massages, as well as an exclusive members-only lounge and bar called the Haven, with a high ceiling, sputnik-bulbed chandeliers, mood lighting, expansive wingback chairs, and vases of seasonal flowers. The walls are adorned with elegant artwork, and there was a terrace separated behind frosted glass. Once outside on the terrace you can see Victoria Island's well-paved streets lined with high-end restaurants and men in suits. Beyond is the Lagos Lagoon, and beyond that is the Atlantic Ocean.

The club has more than 130 women members, including tech leaders, high commissioners, lawyers, actresses and authors. Anyone is welcome to apply for membership but they will be screened by Gaia's existing members before they are accepted. Membership fees range, but can be over 3 million Nigerian naira, which translates to around US$2,000 as of mid-2025. By contrast, the national minimum wage, recently raised to 70,000 naira a month, is just a fraction of that cost.[22] While there's no one standardised method to measure the average salary in Nigeria, and top-tier professionals in executive management can earn a significant amount, only the country's most financially prosperous can afford the Gaia membership.

Gaia Africa is the brainchild of Olatowun Candide-Johnson, a lawyer who worked for decades as a general counsel for a large multinational oil and gas firm in Lagos. The first time we speak is while she's on a business trip in Dubai. I ask her if she's had time to experience any of the UAE's many women-only facilities – the beaches or the carriages in the

Dubai Metro system, or the pink taxis that are women-driven cars exclusively for women passengers. She says she hasn't, although she can see why women might feel more relaxed using any of those facilities, and it is one of the reasons why she created Gaia Africa – to be a 'safe' space for women like herself, leaders in their chosen fields of endeavour.

'Women-only spaces are essential because women have been deliberately excluded from so many spaces where decisions have been made about us and for us,' Olatowun says. 'Excluding women in the first place has been the impetus for us to create our own rooms and build our own tables.'

The aim of Gaia is to change the culture of women giving all to the workplace and then rushing home to give it all there too. It invites women to take time for themselves – to stop for a drink, relax, and talk to their peers as well as grow their businesses.

Olatowun smiles, sipping her coffee. 'A man would call this networking, and part of the working day.'

She acknowledges that Gaia Africa is an exclusive space. As well as the cost, there is a highly selective membership process, requiring invitations from existing members, potentially limiting diversity within the club. And a place like Gaia is not accessible to a large number of Nigeria's less privileged women – those with less disposable income for luxuries like private members' clubs. According to women's rights groups like the Girls Opportunity Alliance, women are less likely to be given the opportunity for further education all over the world. Over three-quarters of the less well-off women in Nigeria have never been to school. Consequently, they have less of a chance to reach corporate leadership positions.

Olatowun, however, believes that spaces like Gaia can change the dynamic for all working women in the country.

'An empowered woman empowers other women,' she tells me. 'Changing leadership dynamics to include more women, rather than one woman, the girlboss, will lead to a society where there is equal opportunity and treatment for all women.'

The club supports and contributes to various charities, including one working to eliminate sexual violence against women. Gaia also offers mentorship and support programmes for younger women in business, such as entrepreneurs, industrialists and those leading commercial enterprises. One initiative is the Gazelles Breakfast Series, a curated networking and knowledge-sharing platform where emerging female leaders can engage with more experienced professionals across sectors. The series aims to provide younger women with guidance on scaling businesses, navigating leadership challenges, and building influence in traditionally male-dominated industries.

A lot of the meetings that happen at Gaia could happen online, of course, but having the anchor, the north star, of a physical women-only 'clubhouse' is essential, Olawatun explains. 'The more we connect physically, the quicker we build relationships and trust. Trust is a critical element in everything that we do and hope to achieve. This notwithstanding, when you belong to a powerful network of women leaders, there is nothing that you cannot achieve.

'Women and men go through different challenges in the workplace. Having a physical space where women can go and vent, brainstorm about those challenges or just relax and let their hair down is vital. Until workplace equality measurably improves, Gaia is needed. Having said that, it goes beyond the workplace. Women simply enjoy each other's company, but it's time to turn that into an opportunity.'

Members are encouraged to first consider collaborating

with another Gaia member on any of their own businesses and personal endeavours. The reasoning is that, because men are dominant in most fields, women need to be intentional about including other women in those spaces and giving them the opportunity first.

I wonder out loud if they are creating a parallel to the classic 'old boys' club' – the informal system in which wealthy men around the world help each other consolidate their social and financial advantages by keeping opportunities limited to their own contacts list. Is this a mirroring of male structures instead of creating a new one?

'Perhaps it is in some ways, but I like to think that we are creating an alternative to the old boys' network,' Olatowun replies. 'One with a different set of values. Our dealings are guided by the Gaia Honour Code. We are also more inclusive than the men.'

The Gaia Honour code, she explains, includes three tenets:

- mutual trust
- integrity
- authenticity

Women seek other women in times of turmoil. A UCLA study suggests that women's bodies respond to stress by releasing the hormone oxytocin, which encourages us to seek other women for comfort and support.[23] The study, which involved collecting data over fifty years, concluded that, for a woman, not having women friends could be as harmful to her health as being overweight or smoking.

Women-only private members' clubs aim to foster a new type of decision-making community – one where women have access to a trusted network with whom to do business.

'A women-only private members' club is about the

empowerment that comes from a woman-to-woman connection which first builds relationships and then trust,' Olatowun says, 'After this, the magic happens.'

Places that offer empowerment allow for the exchange of knowledge, experience and resources.[24] Environment is particularly important for women who have experienced gender-based forms of marginalisation – including workplace harassment and discrimination – according to psychological, sociological and organisational research published in journals such as *Psychology of Women Quarterly* and the *Journal of Vocational Behavior*. Women who then went on to receive support from other women stated that they felt a higher level of self-esteem and a higher perception of autonomy in both their personal life and their workplace.[25]

In 2021 I interviewed Samoa's first woman prime minister, Fiamē Naomi Mata'afa – an especially meaningful moment as there are fewer women in politics in the Pacific Islands than in any other part of the world.[26] Fiamē, as she asked me to call her, introduced me to her 'margarita circle' – a group of around a dozen women who were her closest friends and confidantes.

They meet several times a month and share a drink, cook, talk, take private salsa classes and remind their friend, the prime minister, that she has a support system. They travel the country with her, and helped organise her roadshow when she ran for the leadership of her party. 'It was hilarious to watch the reactions as these good-looking and glamorous women, my friends, turned up with me to village council meetings with male chiefs and religious leaders,' Fiamē told me. 'The men definitely sat up straighter when they arrived.'[27]

'We're not an organisation and we're not a registered charity, we're a support system,' Fiamē's friend Alise Stunnenberg added. 'Every powerful woman needs a support system of powerful women.'

This is also the ethos of Gaia, says Olawatun Candide-Johnson. She is proud to have founded Africa's first space for professional women. She hopes there will be more.

One Thursday a month, Gaia holds 'Gentlemen's Thursday', an event to which they have a male guest speaker and members invite their male colleagues, partners and allies – including those eager to support women. It is a convivial evening where business connections are made, and important conversations are had over drinks and light bites.

It makes me think about the 2011 Thatcher film trailer. Gentlemen's Thursday is the opposite to that. At Gaia, you'd be more likely to hear, 'Ladies, shall we join the gentlemen?'

8

The Troll Feminism of Megalia

South Korea, 2015

It was the spring of 2015 when an online homeland for South Korean women emerged from the bubbling lava of decades of anger. Digitally savvy feminists who had been born in the 1990s and were exhausted with the drip-drip of daily sexism agreed to code a discussion board that centred their perspective. It would be called Megalia and it would be anonymous, leaderless – and angry. It was to be a social territory where women could lead conversations that mattered to them, when their real world was openly hostile.

Megalia wasn't a physical country with borders and rivers and cities, but it had some markings of a land with an identity. It had a controversial logo (a hand with pinching fingers, the universal sign for a tiny penis), which remains a meme. It had its own words and phrases – for example, 'Hamheung Jaji', used to describe a man who abandons his family.

Although Megalia's roots went back decades, the direct trigger was in 2015, after an outbreak of a coronavirus plunged South Korea into a state of emergency. Many people felt that the Korean government was not forthcoming with the details they had about MERS (Middle East Respiratory Syndrome, so named as it had been first identified in

2012 in Saudi Arabia) and people naturally turned online for information. South Korea already had a reputation for being one of the world's most 'wired' nations. Over 80 per cent of the country had access to the internet in 2012 (by 2024 that would have increased to more than 97 per cent), and South Korea had one of the fastest connection speeds in the world. A popular destination to seek out information on the coronavirus was the MERS Gallery, a bulletin board on one of the country's most popular social media sites, DC Inside.

The outbreak in South Korea was traced back to a sixty-eight-year-old man who often travelled to the Middle East on business.[1] He had exposed over 740 people to the virus, and transmitted it to at least 28 individuals,[2] and yet he was not the target of the most anger in the MERS Gallery. Instead, the vitriol was saved for two young women.[3] They had travelled to Hong Kong on holiday, been exposed to the virus, and on landing back in Seoul had evaded quarantine. They were soon found by authorities, who put them into isolation for fourteen days and fined them.

The women inspired an outpouring of anger on the male-led online forums of South Korea. They were called 'kimch'inyŏ' (kimchi woman) and 'tocnchangnyŏ' (bean paste girl) – pejorative slang about basic women who are motivated by consumerism and obtaining material goods.

Such was the force of the rhetoric against the two women that female users of the MERS Gallery decided it was time to create a new online space for themselves. The domain name Megalian.com was registered.

Megalia was careful to label itself an explicit feminist website created by women, for women. After all, a women-led online world was desperately needed to allow South Korean women to share women-centred information. Topics included where to obtain the morning-after pill, how to get support for gender-based violence, the rights of sex workers, and perhaps the most recurring and anger-inspiring topic of discussion – the rise of digital sexual abuse against women.

The identities of Megalian.com's founders have never been revealed, but according to one of the site's first users, who goes by the pseudonym Tae-ok Ahn, it was created by two women. One was the primary programmer and manager for the site, and the second acted as its main funder. Once Megalian.com was active, several hundred women immediately migrated to the site.

'In short, Megalia was an outburst of fury of women in my generation,' Tae-ok Ahn tells me. 'It was a grassroots movement.'

It also had real-world consequences.

A *Los Angeles Times* article in 2021 described one such instance: an argument that broke out between young men and women at a pub in Seoul in 2018.[4] The women shouted '6.9' – a Megalia meme based on a 2003 study that claimed South Korean men had an average penis size of 6.9 centimetres – which was lower than the global average of 8.8 centimetres. The study had been posted in Megalia in response to male-led forums like DC Inside stating that South Korean women had small breasts. '6.9' had become a rallying cry – a way to shut down misogyny.

The men in the bar then retorted by calling the women 'megal bitch'.

As it turned out, the discussions on Megalia had invited not just the curious and then furious attention of South Korean men, but also the country's media – and, before long, its politicians and eventually the police.

Daughters of Egalia

The name Megalia is an amalgamation of two ideas that mattered to its foremothers. The first part refers to its birthplace, the online social media messaging board, the MERS Gallery. The second – Egalia – was inspired by *Egalia's Daughters*, the Norwegian satirical novel we have spoken about earlier in which gender roles – and vocabulary – are reversed. In the book, the wim (women in the real world) dominate the menwim (men), who act as supporters to the wim. Menwim take birth control, wear penis-supporting underwear that is similar to a corset, curl their beards and wear dresses. They feel nervous when attention is on them in rooms (a theme my cousin Tushanka pointed out when she told me about 'Sultana's Dream', which describes a world where women are in charge and they find the timidity of subordinate men amusing). The menwim look after children after the wim give birth.

In Egalia, wim also possess all the crude qualities that come from socialised dominance, including inflicting violent and sexual abuse on men. When Petronius, a teenage boy in Egalia who dreams of the life of freedom that his sister enjoys, is gang-raped by three women, his mother asks what he did to lead them on. She urges Petronius to keep the assault to himself, warning that revealing it may harm his reputation. As one might expect, the abuse against menwim in Egalia mirrors the abuse against women in the real world.

Data from the World Bank shows that, in forty-four economies, 49 per cent of women who have experienced any physical or sexual violence never sought help to stop the violence, and never told anyone.[5] Women often do not seek help due to the fear of reputational damage resulting from socio-cultural norms, and because they worry that they will be denied.

This is precisely what happened to a Megalia user, whose online pseudonym is Dooboocat, when she finally mustered the courage to speak about her assault.

It took Dooboocat over ten years to tell her parents about the man who had raped her when she was twenty-one, in 2011. It was during Covid-19, and Dooboocat and her family were living together. She thought sharing it would be a moment to heal, Dooboocat tells me over a video call from her apartment, with Seoul's noisy traffic honking outside.

She pauses to take a sip of water.

'Their reaction was exactly what I feared it would be. They asked, "What did you do to encourage him?"'

It had been this way since her childhood in the outskirts of Seoul. When she was seventeen, a female teacher told her that the best way to avoid unwanted sexual advances from men was to 'destroy the mood'.

'My teacher said, "Put food in your teeth! Fart in front of him!"' Dooboocat tells me quietly. 'She said, "Don't make it awkward by saying no. Just put him off you."'

Dooboocat and her female school friends didn't speak about this with each other. No one wanted that awkward conversation. The responsibility to not be attacked was on them. 'Girls are expected to quietly accept the bad behaviour of boys. I wanted to speak with women who understand what I have been through, but I didn't know how to verbalise myself out loud.'

A world where she could talk freely, though, did exist. There was a virtual forum where women in South Korea could discuss their experiences without being judged. She didn't even have to reveal who she was; she could make up a name like Dooboocat (a portmanteau of two of her favourite things: tofu and kittens). Online, she could share her most painful experience and be validated by women who had gone through the same.

Yet, as it turned out, the digital world was no safer for women than the real one.

As in the rest of the world, traditional Korean society in the 1800s expected women to be limited to the home. Yet this was to change significantly throughout the twentieth century.

Girls' schools — which had the specific goal of offering a high school education — opened in the early part of the century. Women began to enter the workforce, predominantly as teachers. According to the Asia Society, this period also saw the participation of women as activists in the independence movement against the Japanese occupation. Then, in 1945, Korea was divided into South and North following its liberation from Japanese colonial rule.

When the Republic of Korea (South Korea) was established in 1948, women were guaranteed the legal rights already enjoyed by men, including the right to vote, drive, and own and inherit properties and assets — on paper at least. In reality, there was still a barrier to true equality.

Under Korea's hoju system, in place since 1898, the man was the legal head of the family.[6] When a husband died, he was usually succeeded by his first son, not by his widow. When a daughter got married, she was transferred from her father's hojeok (family registry) to her husband's. Children were automatically added to the father's hojeok, and even when a couple divorced and the mother retained custody of the children, they kept their father's surname and remained in his hojeok unless he gave them permission to transfer. The system would only be formally replaced in 2008.

Following the Korean War of 1950, the agriculture-based economy of the republic experienced a period of rapid economic growth when the country was opened up to international markets. As a result, more women entered the labour force.

With an increasing number of women in professional jobs, in 1987 the government passed the Equal Employment Act to prevent discriminatory practices against female workers in regard to hiring and promotion opportunities. A vital move for women. On paper, at least.

By the 1990s, things seemed to be advancing even more. And under the new democratic government that came to office in 1998, feminist objectives saw a number of victories. A Ministry of Gender Equality and Family was established to promote a more gender-equal society.

South Korean men, who had to perform mandatory military service after the age of eighteen for a minimum of eighteen months, had been given certain privileges when applying for jobs when they returned to civilian life. One was additional points in the government's civil service exam, which gave them a head start over women who were applying for the same jobs. However, after pressure from women's rights groups, this advantage was scrapped.

By the early 2000s, the terms 'alpha girl' (a female student attaining high grades in school) and 'gold miss' (a single woman earning high wages and enjoying a professional career) had become popular expressions in South Korea. But with this growth of opportunities for women, resentment was brewing.

The rise and fall of South Korea's women-only spaces

For much of Korea's history, women-only spaces outside activism were generally informal and organised by women from a community with close physical proximity to each other.

One example of this is the kye – an informal money-lending system in which a group of people, often all women, pool cash in a communal pot. Its origins are said to date back to Korean farming villages in the sixteenth century, where it was a means of raising capital for those who would not otherwise have access to loans.[7] After a certain period – say a month – one woman gets the entire pot and is able to use it however she wishes. The group then starts over, each donating the same amount again. At some point, every woman will have got the lump sum, and all members remain in the kye until each woman has collected the pot.

'This system of community amongst women involves a sense of trust and fellowship,' gender studies academic at Stanford University Haein Shim, who has been researching South Korea's feminism, told me. 'I've been doing this with my girlfriends since we were in our twenties.'

But as more women entered the public sphere, through work and education, a number of formalised female-only spaces came into existence. These ranged from study cafés and gosiwon (dormitory-style flats) to guest houses and gyms. In 2022, a women-only camping site in Cheonan, South Chungcheong Province, was opened for women who wanted 'to enjoy a quiet and peaceful experience in the absence of men', according to its organisers.[8]

While these spaces were largely accepted, others became

the subject of heated debate. Women-only transportation in South Korea was one such controversial subject. In the 1990s, several women's rights groups lobbied for women-only carriages in the subway system, arguing that rush hour was a source of particular discomfort.[9] Groping and sexual harassment was an ongoing issue, with the *Korea Times* reporting that sexual harassment on the subway in Seoul increased by 26 per cent between 2008 and 2009.[10] And another particular fear was emerging at this time – molka, the secret and illegal photographing of women with spy-cams. These tiny cameras would be hidden in public restrooms, hotels and changing rooms. The images they recorded were then uploaded to websites, where men would pay to access them.

More than 30,000 cases of filming with the use of hidden cameras were reported to police in South Korea between 2013 and 2018, according to the BBC.[11] Secret filming in subways, where cameras or smartphones were used to take pictures under women's skirts, was especially popular. The only way to tackle this, some feminists insisted, was to have spaces where women didn't have to fear this type of violation – and single-sex spaces on public transport was one idea.

South Korea wasn't the first country to try this; several countries across the world had attempted women-only public transportation with varying degrees of success. In 2008, Mexico City launched a series of bright pink 'solo mujeres' (women-only) buses. They were popular, but only operated at certain times with limited service. In India, women-only buses did not achieve sufficient ridership, according to Sonal Shah, an urban planner in New Delhi who specialises in equitable and sustainable transportation. The Indian women she spoke with told her that they often wished to travel with male companions, and these buses didn't allow them to do that. Shah argues that women-only transport solutions, when not considered through the lens of what women actually want, may inadvertently fail to address safety concerns.[12]

Japan did see more success with its efforts. In 2005, female-only subway cars were introduced after it was revealed that up to two-thirds of women between twenty and thirty years old had been victims of some form of harassment on trains.[13] There was hardly any pushback from Japanese men, and the women-only carriages are still available in major cities in Japan. In Indonesia, however, women-only carriages lasted just a few months, and then were discarded due to impracticality. Mixed trains became overcrowded during rush hour, while the women-only cars were largely empty. A similar scheme never took off in Brazil, where it was met with open hostility from some men who refused to observe the single-sex train carriages and boarded them anyway.[14]

In Busan in South Korea, there were complaints of 'reverse sexism' by men when the city adopted carriages for women and children on metro trains during rush hour. But the women-only carriages, unsubtly painted pink, remain in Busan – unlike similar efforts in the capital, Seoul.

Seoul Metro implemented two rush-hour women-only carriages (out of eight) in the 1990s, but discontinued the programme after male passengers were clearly disregarding the rules and boarding the cars. They tried again in 2008 and 2011 – but again, the project was abandoned following criticism from men's rights groups.

These men's rights activists dedicated a lot of time to finding and critiquing women-only spaces on online message boards until they reached the attention of the mainstream. Women-only parking spots in Seoul – which were positioned nearer buildings so women didn't have to walk as far – were first introduced in 2009 following a series of attacks against women in basement car parks. Jean Mackenzie, the then Seoul correspondent for BBC News, reported extensively on this, finding that Seoul city council proposed that 'car parks with more than 30 spaces were required to allocate 10% to women – just under 2,000 of the 16,640 public parking spaces', in order to tackle this violence.[15]

Although the programme was largely accepted in its first few years, it became a renewed topic of discussion on men's online message boards in the mid-2010s. A common charge was repeated: 'Reverse sexism'. By 2023, Seoul's mayor said these spaces were no longer required and the spots should be reserved for families, despite government figures showing that two-thirds of violent crimes committed in Seoul's car parks were sexual crimes against women, including rape.[16]

The car parks weren't the only women-only spaces in South Korea that were modified to include men following online criticism. After a petition filed by a men's rights group in 2012, the National Human Rights Commission of Korea said that a women-only provincial library in Jecheon, North Chungcheong Province, was inherently sexist and went against a gender-equal society. The library had existed since 1994 – and was women-only because its private donor had stated they wanted to fund a place where women of all socio-economic backgrounds could read in peace. But following the criticism, the library opened its doors to men in 2012.[17]

Ironically, and perhaps unintentionally, these men's rights groups developed the skill of finding and amplifying women-only spaces – even small, quirky and obscure ones, including a 'women-only smoking zone' at a rest stop along the Mokpo–Gwangyang Expressway in South Jeolla Province. In reality it was just two chairs and a table arranged outside, under a pink sign, but it was still singled out and angrily condemned on the website Ilbe Storehouse. Photos of solitary men sadly smoking next to bins were uploaded as a comparison.

The campaign against women's spaces on Ilbe was, in many ways, a primary motivation for the birth of Megalia. But perhaps the most important impetus for Megalia, as with many origin stories for women-only communities, was rooted in economics.

An economic catastrophe

In 1997, South Korea, along with most of East Asia – which had enjoyed steady economic growth over several decades – was ravaged by the Asian financial crisis. The crisis caught a lot of economists and policymakers by surprise, and South Korea found itself on the brink of default. Its vulnerabilities had been masked by years of rapid domestic credit growth, inadequate supervisory oversight, and doubtful loans.[18]

The job market was decimated, and the economy was forced to adapt. South Korean corporations overhauled the traditional working structure, introducing flexible (but insecure) contracts. The domestic market, which had once favoured in-country labour, was forced to open up internationally.

The generation that came of age following the 1997 crash was nicknamed 'the N-po generation', meaning they'd had to give up numerous things – jobs, financial security, the ability to buy a home, and the hope of a better lifestyle than their parents'.

Everyone was affected, but women bore the disproportionate brunt. Women, particularly those in temporary or irregular positions, were often the first to be laid off as companies restructured. Additionally, societal expectations led many women to withdraw from the labour force altogether to support their families during the economic downturn.[19] In the years that followed the crash, South Korean women university graduates faced significant challenges, including lower employment rates and a substantial pay gap compared to their male counterparts.[20] There was a duality in expectations: while some women were pressured to leave the workforce to fulfil traditional domestic roles, others, particularly from lower-income households, were expected to enter or remain in the labour market to help sustain their families. Women who had previously been primary caregivers and homemakers had to seek other jobs in order to support their household. The Korea Labor Institute reported that, in 1997 alone, approximately 500,000 women joined the labour force as part-time and temporary workers – many of whom were compelled to work after their husbands were laid off.[21] This signalled a significant cultural shift. The Korean male was no longer the dominant breadwinner, but the Korean female was still expected to be the traditional homemaker on top of being a co-breadwinner. Many women were still expected to carry out all the household chores when they were at home, a situation their daughters observed.

'These young women became the Megalia generation,' Dr Youngmi Kim, an academic who specialises in online populism, told me, 'and these women witnessed asymmetry against their mothers from their childhood.'

At the same time, it was also a volatile time to be a man. Male-solidarity coalitions began emerging that were openly enraged by women-only spaces. One men's rights activist, named Sung Jae-gi, launched a group called Man of Korea in 2008. The group campaigned against laws that it believed discriminated against men, and demanded the abolition of the Ministry of Gender Equality and Family. Sung openly criticised female-only train carriages as an example of discrimination. He said that only men were forced to do military service, as well as financially provide for the family. Men were the true victims of gender inequality, Sung insisted. In 2013, he tweeted that he would be jumping off a bridge over the Han River in Seoul, to raise funds and get more publicity for his group and its causes. On 26 July, he did. Three days later, Sung's body was found by police in the river, over a kilometre from the bridge.

Men's rights activists were furious at his death.

Unsettling times lead to stress, and stress often demands a scapegoat, and there was a perfect venue in which to channel their anger.

By the 1990s, South Korea's government had decided tech would be a priority. It pledged to invest around a trillion won in its Science and Technology Promotion Fund by 1996 and become one of the global leaders in the information and communication technology sphere.[22] According to Statista, by 2024 around 94 per cent of the country had access to high-speed internet and the mobile communication penetration rate was above 1, meaning there was more than one mobile phone number registered per citizen (which is more than the US).[23] This had all been achieved in under twenty years. Why is all this important? Because it meant that the Megalia generation – the same generation that experienced the brutal shock of the Asian financial crisis – were growing up with access to the internet. Online, they had the means to express their thoughts anonymously.

DC Inside, South Korea's largest and most popular online forum, emerged in 1999. Its different 'galleries' hosted conversations on current affairs and entertainment, allowing users to share images, videos and words. Prior to 2007, it was completely anonymous – and even after that, a user did not need to reveal any personal details in order to post. There were no consequences for misogyny.

A study commissioned by the Korean Institute for Gender Equality Promotion and Education found rampant misogyny on the forum.[24] It cited posts like one that expressed an 'urge to kill' plus-size women when seeing them in public. Although several people criticised the sentiment, some responded by commenting 'I can't agree more' and 'these women deserve to die'.

Although discussions on DC Inside were not regulated, several threads – both controversial and benign – were deleted by admins after a certain period of time. Some users considered this a design flaw, stating that discussions should be archived. The splinter group Ilbe Storehouse was set up in 2010 to enable users to do this. To begin with, Ilbe's main feature was bookmarking the 'best' posts from DC Inside – especially the most controversial ones. But the site was soon populated by men's rights activists and absorbed into the 'manosphere' – a web of online men's communities advocating against the empowerment of women.

Apart from misogyny, Ilbe also became dominated by venomous discussions around foreign immigrant workers, LGBT people, and the political and social left. According to Seoul-based journalist Kelly Kasulis Cho, Ilbe was mostly frequented by young men who felt powerless at a time when youth unemployment was alarming.[25] In 2007, ten years after the Asian financial crisis, the global economy had suffered a huge blow when the US economy took a similar battering. The largest recession since the Great Depression, and a global financial crisis followed. Unemployment rates reached 11.2 per cent amongst 15–24-year-olds in April 2012.

This cluster of young men who were chronically online

and angry soon caught the attention of the mainstream South Korean media, especially as the wider manosphere was inspiring global intrigue. Sites like English-language board 4chan and Japan's Futaba Channel were attracting a largely male user base: 4chan claims on its advertising pages that around 70 per cent of its users are men.[26] And young men on these forums were displaying the kind of sexist views that many hoped had died out.

Ilbe was a universe dominated by trolls with a victim complex. The topics were crude and graphic, dripping with in-jokes and memes. Slang like 'kimchi woman' and 'bean paste girl' soon became part of the vernacular. Boys at South Korean schools would use these terms in everyday conversation. 'They would say "I'm not a user of Ilbe but . . ." and then say something that mirrored Ilbe's value systems,' Tae-ok Ahn, the early Megalia user, tells me. 'They were reproducing the thoughts of Ilbe.'

Other posts veered from anger at the death of men's rights activist Sung Jae-gi to praising a man who had been jailed for killing a woman he had suspected of cheating on him. The term 'samilhan' was often used, short-hand for 'women must be beaten every three days'.[27] According to the *Korea Herald*, another discussion topic – 'the perfect wife' – listed desirable traits in a woman, including obliging her husband whenever he wants to have sex, 'being ready for physical punishment if her husband's shirt is not ironed every morning' and 'only listening when her husband speaks, without interfering or questioning'.[28]

'Ilbe became a dumping ground, a concentration camp of human trash,' says Tae-ok Ahn.

And then there were the sex crimes. The photos of women – and girls – taken without their consent or knowledge.

The foremothers of Megalia

Hyena lies on her stomach on the bottom bunk of a bed, in a room that is overflowing with books and notepads. She shares her Seoul apartment with a friend, a fellow feminist. Hyena's glossy bobbed hair is tucked behind her ears and I notice that she doesn't touch it during our conversations. I, on the other hand, fiddle with my hair a lot. Coiling it as a distraction, or to help anchor my thoughts.

Hyena occasionally closes her eyes, waiting patiently for our translator to relay her thoughts to me.

Her activist name, Hyena – after the tireless and dangerous scavenger – seems at odds with her serene composure. Hyena is now in her thirties and has been active on the internet since she was a child. Her laptop was a 'magic box', she tells me – one her parents wanted her and her brother to use to expand their education. At the age of ten, she opened a file her brother had saved on their laptop that was titled 'rag' – and when she opened it, she saw a graphic sex video. At school, boys would ask girls if they were rags; she quickly learned that the word referred to women who were objectified by men. Women whose bodies were used to soak up male sexual desire – often without their consent. The internet, the magic box, contained dark places.

By the time she became a teenager, Hyena was looking for a place to connect, for a place of her own, but on chatrooms she experienced sexual harassment from older men.

'They wrote, "Do you want to meet in exchange for pocket money?"' she says.

DC Inside and Ilbe 'poured over with misogyny'. Hyena remembers seeing posts praising the dead men's-rights activist

Sung Jae-gi. She trembled with fear at what was written about women. She wanted to exist somewhere else.

After our conversation, Hyena emails me diary entries from when she was desperately searching for a place online where she wouldn't feel under attack. In her diary she referenced Virginia Woolf, writing that she was looking for an online 'room of my own'.

'The internet is not a place where everyone is equal and free,' she wrote, musing about the gender imbalance. 'A hundred years ago women also wanted a space to be a "content producer", a space where they could think only about themselves and convey and spread those thoughts. In other words, a room of their own, and a way to manage and create that room.'

Then, in 2015, a room emerged. It was called Megalia.

When you accessed the site megalian.com, you entered a white page with a green banner on top (the pinching hand representing a small penis). There were multiple sections on different topics – all gender-related news – everything from period poverty to sharing experiences with ex-boyfriends. There were several new discussions posted every day. Users didn't reveal their names but said they were South Korean women from around the world – from Seoul to Toronto.

Hyena, by now nineteen, had found her home. She was one of its foremothers. One of its first organisers.

Unlike several other social websites in South Korea, Megalia centred women. Aside from daily, sometimes hourly, discussions of shared experiences, Megalians hosted successful fundraisers for domestic violence charities.

Hyena found herself taking part in real-world activism organised on Megalia.

One such project involved Post-it notes. Megalians started

scribbling messages about a female-led future – what a women-led world would look like – on Post-it notes, and stuck them inside the toilet stalls of public bathrooms. According to women studies academic Euisol Jeong, more than 700 Megalia Post-it notes were found in locations around South Korea.[29]

Hyena threw herself into Megalia's discussions and projects. This was the sisterhood she had craved.

'Was there any way of knowing for sure that Megalia was a women-only site? No,' she admits, 'there was no real way of knowing for sure, but as women shared personal stories of harassment and abuse, there was an understanding. Even in digital anonymity, a woman recognises a woman.'

Posting under her pseudonym, Hyena soon found that she became a high-profile and popular user.

The mirroring of misogyny

As children, we are often taught to display kindness when faced with rudeness. To turn the other cheek, so a perpetrator may learn from our virtue. Yet this is not a tactic that is always practical. Megalians especially were not willing to be a wilting flower in the face of online abuse from men.

Megalia mirrored the language of misogyny within its boards. Body shaming against men was especially popular: 'I heard the average penis size of Korean men is 6.9? It's smaller than my dog!'

This is a strategy called 'mirroring', and Megalians deployed it with relish. They developed their own slang, which was a reflection of derogatory expressions used by men on other sites. 'Kimch'i-nam' (kimchi man), was a term for shallow men who obsessed over a woman's appearance. A 'kkongch'inam' was the male equivalent of a bean paste girl. It translates as 'mackerel man', and meant someone who coasted off money he didn't earn. '6.9', of course, referred to the small penis study.

Hyena was part of all this. But she would go on to play an even more vital role in Megalia's culture and history.

'Herstory,' she corrects me, closing her eyes again.

Hyena destroys Soranet

There was an even uglier place than Ilbe on South Korea's internet: Soranet. It had existed in the online underbelly since the early 2000s; Korean media stated that at one point it had more than a million users.

Soranet hosted thousands of videos and images of illegal sexual abuse, including women who had been secretly filmed at public locations and even in their own homes. Hyena first heard about the site when she was thirteen, and when she logged in at the age of nineteen, nothing could prepare her for what she found.

There were images of underage girls, sleeping with their tops raised and nipples exposed, posted by men who said they were related to the girls. There were images of unconscious women where the photographer had placed knives and cigarettes near the woman's exposed vagina. There was spy-cam footage from tiny cameras hidden in changing rooms, bathrooms and even schools.

Hyena felt her pulse quicken and a sick feeling rise in her stomach. She watched in real time as the view count on some of the images rose to over 10,000. Comments mocking the unconscious girls accumulated underneath.

Hyena didn't trust the police. She had previously sent them screenshots of older men approaching underage girls online and had been ignored. She had no idea how she should approach what she was seeing on Soranet.

She posted a tentative message on Megalia.

'I want to organise and document women's abuses on sites like Soranet. Maybe go out and hand out leaflets. Would you like to join me?'

She received several messages. Megalians wanted to help. She set up a private group chat.

By October 2015, Hyena was part of a sub-group of women on Megalia who were determined to shut down Soranet. The group, who didn't know each other's real identities, spoke daily on group chats, sharing disturbing images they were finding on the site.

It was gruelling work, looking at image after image of what was clearly abuse. Hyena soon learned that Soranet used a code word for the most graphic images: golbaengi.

'Golbaengi referred to women who were incapacitated after being drugged,' Hyena tells me. 'If you searched this term, you found image after image of rape.'

Some women on Hyena's monitoring team quit the group, too traumatised by what they saw. Others had to seek the help of a psychiatrist. But still, Megalians were working. They shared images on Twitter and Facebook and raised funds for a billboard advertisement alerting people to spy-cam crime in a subway station. They lobbied and supported a politician, Chin Sŏnmi, who pressured the National Police Agency to investigate Soranet.

Nothing happened for months, and the site remained active and fully functional. But Megalians continued collecting evidence and monitoring the site and posting screenshots on Twitter. Their actions caught the attention of the media and in particular SBS (Seoul Broadcasting System), one of the leading South Korean television and radio broadcasters, who produced a documentary on Soranet and the danger it posed to women. Pressure was mounting, and even the National Police Agency commissioner Kang Shin-myung acknowledged that Soranet was an issue.

'We are considering closing down Soranet,' he said tentatively in November 2015 in the National Assembly, but it would take several months before anything happened.

Men on Ilbe, DC Inside and even Twitter reacted with expected venom. Tae-ok Ahn shared messages she collected from the time.

Soranet represents freedom of having sex and enjoying porn.
Megalia is more harmful than Soranet.

But despite the male fury, the women were angrier. They ensured that the conversation refused to die down. Following an investigation conducted with Dutch cyberpolice, in April 2016 South Korea's police shut down the core server of Soranet, deeming it the largest pornographic site in the country. Several people were arrested for hosting the site, but it was Soranet's founders that people were after.

A few years later, a co-founder was sentenced to four years in jail for aiding and abetting the distribution of obscene materials, and ordered to attend sexual violence prevention education.[30] The co-founder was a woman. She said that she'd had no idea what Soranet was, or the abuse it hosted. Her husband had been in charge of running the site, she insisted. The South Korean authorities agreed that he had been as – if not more – responsible for Soranet, but there was no way to locate him. He had fled South Korea, and left his wife to face the consequences. No man has yet shouldered the full punishment for Soranet's crimes against women.

For Megalia, Soranet's shutdown showed what was possible when women worked together. The work continues. Hyena went on to form DSO – a civic organisation dedicated to the elimination of online sex crimes. I'm told that other former Megalians now also work for KCSVRC – the Korea Cyber Sexual Violence Response Center. The organisation was established in 2017, and advises the Ministry of Gender Equality and Family on how to tackle cyber-abuse against women.

'People talk about the shutdown of Soranet like it was heroic,' Hyena tells me. 'I don't think of it as heroic. We did what we had to do, because no one else was going to do it for us.'

Hyena was just nineteen years old, and already a soldier. She may not have been on a physical battlefield, but taking down Soranet had been a fight, and the images she saw left lasting scars and resulted in immense personal trauma. Hyena and the other women of Megalia went to war to defend women facing a type of gender violence that was specific to their generation.

The shutdown of Soranet was not an unequivocal win though. It has not ended the illegal filming of women. In June 2021, Human Rights Watch named South Korea as the country with the most spy-cam digital sex crimes.

Megalia goes too far

In October 2015, at the same time as the campaign to take down Soranet was underway, a post was shared by an anonymous writer on Megalian.com that shocked and repulsed even the most ardent feminists.[31]

The post was initially written on 17 October on a private board, and then made public eleven days later, on 28 October.[32] In it, the woman wrote that she wanted to sexually molest a 'jonnini', which is Korean slang for a very young boy. She went into detail about how she would like to 'devour' the child, in a post I have read and choose not to repeat any more of other than it concluded: 'I'm going crazy holding back.' The message soon spread through various online communities, with people expressing their disgust.

The media began referring to the poster as 'Ms A' – the 'scarlet letter' anonymous woman. A few days after her post went viral, Ms A wrote another post. She said she understood that her previous post had caused distress but it had been an example of Megalia's tactic of 'mirroring'. This strategy was aimed to inspire an emotional reaction, or even overreaction, from male users who didn't care about abuse against women.

Young girls were being targeted across South Korea's male-dominated social media sites, Ms A said. Ilbe referred to young girls as 'lolini', a portmanteau of 'Lolita' – a reference to the 1955 novel by Vladimir Nabokov that depicts the sexual desire of the narrator for a twelve-year-old girl – and 'eorini' (child). When she wrote of jonnini it was a mirror of lolini, Ms A explained. She was a survivor of childhood sexual abuse herself, and had been trying to make a point.

The explanation didn't assuage anger against Megalia. Feminists insisted that child sex abuse, against any gender, couldn't be wielded to make a philosophical argument. Mirroring had its limits.

A search was organised by online sleuths to identify Ms A. It didn't take long to find her. She was a freelance kindergarten teacher. South Korean government officials, who were still taking their time looking into Soranet's abuses, were swift to act against a Megalian offender. Ms A, who was from Daegu, was arrested by the police.

Megalians who had been watching the events unfold online felt a wave of complex emotions about the arrest of Ms A.

Tae-ok Ahn tells me that on one hand she felt Ms A's post had taken mirroring too far. She herself attended teacher training college, majoring in pedagogy. So had Ms A. She knew the ethics involved in being a teacher. 'The post crossed a line,' she says.

Yet at the same time, she couldn't help feeling sympathy. Ms A said she was a survivor of childhood sexual abuse and Tae-ok Ahn felt that South Korea didn't have suitable and accessible systems to offer support for victims of abuse.

Either way, it didn't matter. In the eyes of thousands of people, including many feminists, Ms A – and by proxy, Megalians – were no different to the trolls on men's forums.

Megalia shut down

Criticism didn't just come from the outside. Megalians began internally arguing over strategy, mirroring, the use of words, and the inclusion of trans women and gender minorities in their world.

Megalia had changed the landscape of feminism in South Korea. As well as shutting down Soranet, the organisers on the site had done so much for women who needed it. They had raised money to finance lawsuits brought by women against men they alleged had ill-treated them, by selling a T-shirt with the slogan 'Girls Do Not Need a Prince'. They had organised a protest of thousands of women outside Gangnam station in 2016, to protest the murder of a woman in a public toilet by a man.

Megalians had rewritten the rules of how a generation of Korean women could form a community. They had demonstrated several strategies for how women could have their voices heard. One was boryeok – the Megalian practice of adding so many feminist comments in the comments section of a digital news story, while also upvoting each other's comments, that any negative comments about women were drowned out.

But then it became too much. Tae-ok Ahn, who had been there since the beginning, watched as chaos ensued.

'The bulletin boards went out of control. Megalia had been run by the manager's good faith and effort. She hadn't charged anyone. It had not brought her any financial benefits. Now there were angry mobs. How could it continue?'

Early organisers and volunteers like Hyena and Tae-ok Ahn stopped contributing. The infighting caused several Megalians to abandon the site.

Just over a year after it had started, the country of Megalia was nearly deserted – it was becoming a ghost world.

A global survivor-led movement

Following the exposure of numerous sexual abuse allegations against Hollywood film producer Harvey Weinstein in October 2017, thousands of women across several professions and countries shared their own experiences of harassment and assault with the hashtag #MeToo.

The kindling for South Korea's Me Too was ignited by a

woman named Seo Ji-hyun, a prosecutor at the Tongyeong branch of the Changwon District Prosecutors' Office. In January 2018, she uploaded a post titled 'My Hope' to E-Pros, an internal chat system for Korean lawyers. In it, she stated that her boss, former senior prosecutor Ahn Tae-geun, had drunkenly groped her at a funeral in 2010. She had promptly reported it, but the Ministry of Justice did nothing. She claimed that Ahn Tae-geun had then handicapped her career by not granting her the promotions that she was qualified for. In the weeks following Seo Ji-hyun's televised interview, there was a 23.5 per cent increase in reports of sexual abuse and domestic violence, as recorded by the Korea Women's Hotline.[33] Women came forward.

Then, in March 2018, South Korea was rocked by another high-profile political scandal when Ahn Hee-jung – a provincial governor, and a leading presidential hopeful was accused of sexually assaulting his secretary on five occasions over the course of a year. The survivor, Kim Ji-eun, revealed that Ahn had assaulted her even after he mentioned the growing Me Too movement to her.

This was an avalanche. Social media sites KakaoTalk, Daum Cafe, Womad, and even DC Inside were filled with women talking about how to make their voices heard.

Widespread demonstrations followed. The streets were filled with young women showing solidarity with victims of sexual abuse. South Korea was experiencing a shift, it seemed.

Women-only online

Dozens of women-led communities sprang up online following the collapse of Megalia. Several users had migrated to the new site Womad, which was explicit in stating that they were a forum for 'natal' women – gender minorities and trans women were not welcome. Others joined group chats on KakaoTalk, discussing how best to continue the many wins they had achieved with Megalia.

'Megalians were a generation of women who forged an online bond, but these women rarely ever took these friendships offline,' says JiMin Nam, an interdisciplinary researcher in social anthropology, Asian and gender studies at the University of Oslo in Norway. JiMin grew up in Seoul, and has observed several of the region's women-led online communities.

'When these women who got to know each other on Megalia did meet offline, they were doing so to directly protest anti-women policies,' she tells me.

The KakaoTalk group chats populated by ex-Megalians were alive with a proposal called 'escape the corset', a movement to take a stand against rigid beauty ideals – unlacing the metaphorical corset. Analysis from News1 showed that purchases of cosmetics, hair products and other beauty-related apparel by South Korean women in their twenties dramatically declined between 2015 and 2018. Make-up sales went down by 53.5 billion Korean won (over US$38 million).[34] This was not a coincidence.

Then there was the political activism. One anonymous online feminist community, mostly daughters of Megalia, was B-wave. These were young women who had used Megalia and were looking for a new home with a clear purpose. A user who wanted to remain anonymous told me that B-wave was focused on overturning South Korea's anti-abortion policies. Taking the momentum of Me Too and the spy-cam protests, hundreds of women who had organised on B-wave met in the streets of Seoul to demand a change in the law. They protested over a dozen times, wearing face masks and throwing sunflower seeds into the air. The sunflower seeds, the user who attended the protest told me, represented the tiny size of a seven-week-old foetus.

'They were saying that South Korean society was valuing sunflower seeds more than the wishes of women,' JiMin adds.

Additionally, the B-wavers carried signs insisting that they were not 'baby vending machines', borrowing from the stark and graphic descriptions used in Megalia. And the B-wave feminists made a further pledge: 'We will have no sex with males until the legalisation of abortion!'

In all likelihood this led to the birth of the 4B ideological stance, which is the rejection of four traditional values that represent traditional female roles – all beginning with the letter 'B'. The first, bihon, is the refusal of heterosexual marriage. Bichulsan is the refusal of childbirth, biyeonae is saying no to dating, and bisekseu is the rejection of heterosexual sexual relationships.

In 2019, South Korea's Constitutional Court overturned the country's decades-long abortion ban, and abortion became fully decriminalised in 2021. This was a win, but several women continued with the 4B pledge.

One is Siwon. She talks to me from the library of her women-only university in Seoul, stopping to wave at her friends who pass. This isn't a silent library; the women talk confidently and laugh with gusto.

'This library is what happens when women are without men,' she tells me. 'South Korea is not a country for women,' she adds, shaking her head. 'Don't let Instagram pictures of an advanced nation fool you.'

And while the country is a technological giant, home to

Samsung and LG electronics, women are still behind. According to the World Bank, they are paid on average a third less than men, giving South Korea the worst gender pay gap of any rich country in the world. Male decision-makers still dominate boardrooms, and in 2022 BBC News reported that women hold just 5.8 per cent of the executive positions in South Korea's publicly listed companies.[35]

'And we are still expected to take on most of the housework and childcare,' adds Siwon, 'so you can see why we don't want to get married or even have sex with men. We need to irritate men, shock them, and use radical tactics like 4B to disengage with them. We do this in women-only spaces.'

The women-only promise of 4B captured imaginations. Research published in 2021 by Yonsei University reported that 43 per cent of female respondents to a survey titled 'Seoul Sex Life' said they hadn't had sex in over a year.[36] 'Statistics that actually prove the 4B movement,' a popular South Korean feminist called Cat tweeted, after sharing the study.

Videos about the 4B movement took TikTok by storm in 2024, although several South Korea-based journalists have said that it is still a niche phenomenon that interests mainly Western feminists.

It is lazy to assume that South Korea's birth rate, one of the lowest in the world, could be linked to an internet trend started by some millennial women, they argue. South Korean women are more likely not to have children due to the country's pay gap and the high cost of education.

Yet 4B has undoubtedly had an influence. In the hours after Donald Trump was elected as president of the United States for his second term, 4B began to trend in the US. Young North American women started posting about the South Korean feminist movement. They said that they too feared the loss of abortion rights and were dismayed at the election of a man who at least twenty-six women have accused of sexual harassment.

Women-only online spaces from South Korea had given them the vocabulary to protest a culture that seemingly did not respect them.

The backlash

If the 2010s were a time that digital feminism galvanised South Korea, the 2020s should have been the period in which it thrived. Instead it has become the decade where the backlash took hold and decades of wins were undone.

Firstly, feminism remains the 'unpopular word' Emma Watson said it was at the UN in 2014. In May 2022, the Korean marketing and research firm Hankook Research did a study of over 3,000 men in their twenties and thirties. The study found that more than 77 per cent of men in their twenties and more than 73 per cent of men in their thirties were 'repulsed by feminists or feminism'.[37]

Dozens of women said that they had lost jobs for supporting issues that women-only online groups championed. One was a female illustrator who was fired from gaming company Project Moon after her social media accounts revealed she had liked old Megalia and B-wave tweets, including support for legalising abortion and protests addressing spy-cam crimes.[38] The tweets were sent to Project Moon by men's rights groups.

The 2020s also ushered in a new president who openly rejected women's issues. The former president Moon Jae-in, who was in office between 2017 and 2022, called himself a feminist – even though women MPs only accounted for 19 per cent of the National Assembly.[39] However, the new president as of 2022, Yoon Suk-yeol, played to the rhetoric of men's rights groups. Structural sexism, he insisted, was 'a thing of the past'.

As he started his term, President Yoon quickly got rid of gender quotas for government jobs. He appointed just three women to his nineteen-member cabinet. He made it clear that he wished to abolish the government's Ministry of Gender Equality and Family, which supports women and victims of sexual assault and is often advised by former members of Megalia. Yet his tenure was short, lasting only three years. In December 2024, MPs voted to impeach President Yoon after he declared martial law in the country in an act of defiance against the opposition-controlled parliament – only to cancel it hours later. In January 2025, he became the country's first sitting president to be arrested and questioned over an attempted power grab.

Feminists tell me that although they hope South Korea's new leader will be more supportive of women's rights, they expect rules that prioritise men. Instead, they look for support in each other.

Four young women could pass each other in the streets of Seoul and not know that they were all once natives of a land where women changed the rules, setting a dynamic in motion that altered the course of how young women in South Korea thought of themselves.

Megalians were careful to maintain their anonymity in a country where it is still taboo to call yourself a feminist. In 2023, a man in his twenties assaulted a convenience store worker in the city of Jinju after suspecting she was a feminist due to her short hair. In 2024 he was sentenced to three years in jail.

Tae-ok Ahn, Hyena, Siwon and Dooboocat are daughters of parents who survived two financial crises. They have seen South Korea's gender dynamics shapeshift and alter their own households. Their mothers worked. Their fathers were not the sole breadwinners. Yet they were expected to follow centuries of cultural expectations in a world that was rapidly changing. With the internet, they were voyagers who formed lawless and edgy settlements. Megalia was not perfect, but it was the fire and volcano that formed dozens of other islands of women. They may have fragmented into smaller spaces, KakaoTalk group chats and Instagram groups, but Megalia gave them a unique experience.

This South Korean women-only space inspired a women-centred approach for a generation that had grown up in the early years of the internet. Megalia gave them an online experience where they had the opportunity to push back against the harassment they faced as young women. Megalia was a movement where the female gaze dominated.

'Megalia confronted deeply rooted misogyny and gender discrimination in my country,' says gender studies academic Haeim Shim. 'It was a bold approach to challenging power dynamics.' She adds that, to an outsider, the forum used shocking tactics. Megalians used graphic metaphors about castration as a solution to male violence, and not everyone liked this method. However, these words were meant to serve a purpose. 'This language was meant to mirror the misogynistic rhetoric often used against women.'

The daughters of Megalia may have made some mistakes, but as Haein tells me, it served as more than just a discussion space; it was a springboard for online activism, empowering many young women to take real action. Megalians weren't prepared to accept online harassment in a society that did little to protect them. And so they worked together – in an anonymous women-only space – to embody a bold and liberating type of feminism.

Four women in Seoul might not recognise each other if they passed in the city's streets today, but they are pioneers who designed an audacious, controversial space for women – one that continues to influence women around the world today.

9

The Babayagas and New Ground: Co-living in Elderhood

Paris, France, 2012; London, UK, 2016

Three years after I visited the Maré favelas to meet the teenage historians, I received a DM on Instagram from Tereza Ona, who was part of Casa das Mulheres. Tereza wanted to tell me about a project called 'Tea with the Grandmothers' – a form of intergenerational female connection where young women from Maré would spend time with older women from the neighbourhood, to share stories and get each other's advice. The initiative was so popular that Tea with the Grandmothers had begun to visit schools around Rio, with older women speaking to young women from all social classes about the importance of looking out for each other. Tereza said she wanted me to know that sisterhood between women happens at all ages, and women find community in each other at all stages. This is on my mind when I arrive in France to meet a group of women who are reimagining elderhood. They call themselves the Babayagas.

The Babayagas live together in a six-storey apartment block designed for single – and independent – women over the age of sixty, six kilometres from the centre of Paris. This is not a retirement home where carers time every meal and movement.

Nor is it a community that is hidden away from the life and pulse of the city. The Babayagas live in Montreuil, in the eastern suburbs of France's capital. They are a stone's throw away from Rue de l'Église, a road alive with a footfall that reflects Montreuil's international population. A fruit stall sells custard apples, sharon fruit and Medjool dates. The rotating kebab spits of shawarma restaurants let out hisses and sizzles. A Malian man behind the counter of a fried chicken shop asks where in India I am from, and begins counting to ten in my native Malayalam when I tell him. There are over a hundred different ethnicities living in Montreuil, and it feels like they're all here on Rue de l'Église. Then there is Maison des Babayagas, a building for independent women of retirement age, at the heart of this much larger, dynamic and diverse urban community.

This elder women-only community was the vision of Thérèse Clerc, a feminist and activist who insisted that she didn't want her independence to disappear with age. She made it clear to her family that she didn't want to spend her final years in a care home, bound by timetables set by others, and nor did she want to rely on her children for support.

Thérèse insisted that there needed to be a radical rethinking of where and how older women – especially single women – live when they reach retirement age. Her idea was an apartment block with shared facilities. She called it an 'anti-retirement home', where women would remain independent members of society and care for each other. She died four years after she made her dream – twenty years in the making – a reality.

When Maison des Babayagas opened in 2012, it immediately excited the press. It was described by reporters from all over the world, from Jordan to South Korea, as a feminist utopia for a rapidly growing demographic – older women.

By 2050, the global population of women over the age of sixty will have nearly doubled from the current 605 million to 1.14 billion.[1] Women all over the world tend to outlive men by an average of five years.[2] Over the last hundred years, women have lived longer than men in almost every country. According to the UN Population Fund, in countries like Russia, Belarus and Ukraine the gap is large – it averaged more than ten years in 2021. In other countries, such as Nigeria, it is less than two years. This increase in the older-female share of the global population leads to significant challenges. The data shows that older women will be financially more vulnerable and be alone longer than their male counterparts.

In every country, older women have faced economic struggles due to societal expectations of free labour; women of certain generations have served as primary caregivers to both children and parents, leading to a huge gap in savings. According to the ILO *Global Wage Report 2018/19*, women earn on average about 20 per cent less than men.[3] And a global gender pay gap will lead to a pension pay gap. The Geneva Association estimates the worldwide pension gap to be US$41 trillion.[4]

A study in 2019 found that while families in countries in the global south – including Tanzania, Kyrgyzstan, Indonesia and Brazil – mostly still lived in multigenerational homes, older women in Western countries were likely to end up alone. This, according to the study's authors, was due to atomised and culturally more individualised societies in the global north.[5] In a 2023 advisory, the then US surgeon general Dr Vivek Murthy stated that there was an 'epidemic of loneliness' facing older women in the global north.[6]

However, women like the Paris Babayagas, who have been

majorly short-changed by society, are coming up with their own solutions for how to tackle older age with independence and companionship.

The rise of co-housing

Maison des Babayagas is an example of co-housing – a residential complex intended to foster community through shared values. Although residents in such spaces have their own private units, there are communal facilities that may include gardens and laundry rooms. The values of Maison des Babayagas are on a retractable banner as you enter the common room that opens onto their shared garden:

- Autogestion (self-management)
- Citoyenneté (citizens – referring to how the Babayagas are part of the community of Montreuil)
- Féminisme (feminism)
- Écologie (sustainability)
- Laïcité (secularism)
- Solidarité (unity)

The first community to be defined as 'co-housing' was established in Denmark in 1972. Saettedammen, just north of Copenhagen, included multi-generational families and male and female residents; the community is still thriving today, and more than 50,000 people now live in co-housing in Denmark.[7] The concept soon attracted feminists. In Sweden, the philosophy of the 'kollektivhus' (collective house) was strongly supported by the feminist movement of the 1970s, which argued that a democratic and communal style of living would encourage a division of labour between the genders.

Since its inception in Northern Europe, co-housing has spread globally. American architects Kathryn McCamant and Charles Durrett introduced the concept to America in 1991 with the development of Muir Commons in Davis, California, the first co-housing community in the US. According to the Washington Commons there are currently over 170 established co-housing communities in the US nationally, with nearly that many in the formation stages.[8] And around the world there are more than 2,000 communities, according to the UK-based community-building organisation A Fairer Society.[9]

No two co-housing communities are exactly alike, and there is no minimum resident limit or unit of land. Some are consciously designed for families, others focus on sustainable living, and some are set up to welcome LGBT residents specifically.

An emerging demographic has been women-only co-housing communities, examples of which include a block of flats purely for single mothers in Uruguay and an ecovillage in rural Colombia built for and by women who have suffered displacement as a result of the country's fifty-year civil war. But the most popular are homes for women residents over the age of fifty-five who want to stay in urban areas, close to cultural activities. Women like the Babayagas, who wish to remain in a major city – even if living together in a women-only space isn't always an easy lifestyle.

It's a crisp day in February when I arrive at Maison des Babayagas, and we're drinking coffee in the common room that overlooks the large garden. But I'm distracted.

It's hard not to keep looking at the gaping hole in the corner of the ceiling. It cracked open following a roof leak in 2016, the year Thérèse Clerc died. The Babayagas have tried to fix it. But when they call the local government office, they are told it is the responsibility of a co-housing maintenance office. That office doesn't reply. The hole only gets bigger.

I'm here with my friend Laure Cometti, a journalist who lives in Paris. She has come along to help with any rapidly spoken French I may not understand. However, the Babayagas, used to international visitors – especially holidaying feminists who ask to drop by – speak slowly and deliberately, making themselves understood. A young woman who writes for an Italian women's rights website drops in while we're chatting, quietly joining our table and pulling out her camera. She spots the hole in the corner and gets up to photograph it.

Flora Fernandez, the president of Maison des Babayagas, looks from the Italian journalist to me and Laure, and unpins a small black and pink badge on her sweater.

'Don't idealise us,' she says as she hands the badge over to me, smiling as I put it on my coat. 'Things have gone wrong, but we are a success.'

The badge is only slightly larger than a button on my duffel coat, but it demands to be seen. White block letters spell out 'Montreuil Girl Gang', with three pink fists raised in a power salute underneath. The badge is not a logo for an association. There is no organised girl gang in Montreuil that meets regularly; it's a vision, not a club.

Flora is in her eighties, and as soon as she tells me this, she gets up to bend down and effortlessly touch her toes, her thick dark hair – cut in a bob – falling to cover her face. She's agile and she's rightly proud of it.

Flora put in an application for one of the studio flats shortly after watching a TV report on a proposed women-only residential block in the east of Paris. The report featured

Thérèse Clerc, introducing her as the building's founder; she was a smoker with a chic messy grey bun, who spoke with ferocious bullets of passion.

Thérèse's vision was of a group of single women living together in a building close to the heart of urban life in Montreuil. But they would be more than just people who happened to share a building – they would be a community. Each woman would have an individual studio apartment with her own kitchen and bathroom – which would be disability-friendly with handrails and a step-free shower. Although they would meet every week to discuss issues that needed to be dealt with at Maison des Babayagas (from maintenance and building works, to requests to host events, to the health of fellow Babayagas), if they didn't want company, they could retreat to their own home and shut the door. If they did want company, they could head down to the common room and they would find friends there with whom they could go to the cinema, or a fruit stall, or see a doctor. They could grow strawberries in the two gardens, and enjoy a coffee together. Without the need for formal arrangements, the majority of the women would see each other almost every day. They would notice if they hadn't seen someone for a while and could check in on her. They would care for each other.

'The aim is to change the way elderly women look at themselves, elderly women look at society, and society looks at us,' Thérèse told the reporter.

Flora, an immigrant to France from Chile, was mesmerised by what she was hearing. She was on her own after two relationships that had devastated her. She had ended her first marriage when it became clear that her husband was more focused on his work than on her – a decision he didn't fight, adding to Flora's devastation. Then she fell in love again in her forties, with the hope that this time it would be different. For a while it was, but problems started when they were unable to conceive a child together, and they too ended their relationship. Flora then decided that she no longer wanted a serious romantic relationship with a man. When she saw Thérèse on TV, talking about a community for single women, it felt as though she was speaking directly to Flora. She has been living at Maison des Babayagas since 2012, the year it opened.

Flora points to where a photocopy of a six-page handwritten letter from Thérèse is taped to the wall. In it, the community's founder recounts its origin story and her hope for the Babayagas.

The idea for Maison des Babayagas came to Thérèse Clerc in the 1990s, after five years of caring for her elderly mother. Thérèse was in her sixties by then, divorced and still working. Her own children were distracted by 'turbulent' marriages and caring for their own children. She felt devastated for her mother, once an independent and headstrong woman, now completely dependent on her daughter.

In the days following her mother's death, Thérèse pushed herself forward leadenly, as if on autopilot. She emptied drawers and packed up clothes, divided up heirlooms, and slowly, sorrowfully, disposed of a lifetime of trinkets and souvenirs – all those her mother hadn't got round to clearing out. The kind that would be of no use to anyone else.

'It was an extremely difficult time,' Thérèse's letter recalls. She felt alone in her avalanche of grief and responsibility.

Going through objects her mother had cherished in this world and deciding whether they had any further use, Thérèse made a vow: 'I swore to myself that I wouldn't let my children go through all this.'

So, grabbing some paper, Thérèse scribbled out her plan, her manifesto: a shared block of studio flats, with communal areas, for women over the age of sixty. The idea behind it was simple: older age would be less burdensome on an individual if she had a community of several women.

'She said women of a certain generation had been made to cater to male comfort all their lives,' Thérèse's friend, the journalist and biographer Danielle Michel-Chic, told me over Zoom. 'She wanted to spend the last few years with women.' And when Thérèse discussed her idea with friends Monique Bragard and Suzanne Gouëffic, they said they would help her dream become a reality.

Thérèse, Suzanne and Monique knew just what to name their group: the Babayagas. The women in the woods that men have deemed past a desirable age but who still have value and purpose in their community. The Baba Yaga is a folklore character who has existed in Eastern European oral storytelling for hundreds of years, and first popped up in print in 1755. Her name roughly translates as 'grandmother witch'.

In stories written by men, the Baba Yaga is an undesirable elderly woman with iron teeth and drooping breasts and a nose that touches the ceiling when she lies down to sleep. In some stories she is a crone who kidnaps and eats children, planting their bones as a picket fence around her home. In others she provides guidance to a younger woman character, giving her the tools with which to escape an unhappy life. She's unattractive to men, but she has sisters – also named the Baba Yagas. Their cat will scratch you if you attempt to enter their home uninvited, their dog will bite you, the birch tree will gouge out your eyes and the fence will lock you in or out. The Baba Yagas work with their community, and their community is fiercely protective of them.

'The Baba Yaga was an old woman who didn't care how the world saw her and didn't care about the rules created by men,' Thérèse Clerc's granddaughter Petronille told me. 'The Baba Yaga created her world, and existed for her own pleasure. Of course that character inspired my feminist grandmother and her feminist friends!'

Thérèse registered their association with the administration of Seine-Saint-Denis, the department of France in which Montreuil is located. Seine-Saint-Denis is the most deprived area of mainland France, according to the country's office of national statistics, INSEE.

Thérèse did not want the Babayagas to be a private building that only wealthy women could afford; she wanted the flats to be affordable for any single older woman who needed community and wanted to be active in Montreuil life. In order to do this, the community needed to be be partly funded by the local government.

The local government had questions. Firstly, why did older women even need a place?

The three Babayagas had data. A lot of data.

Older women, like most women in Western countries, are likely to live alone. According to INSEE, by the age of sixty-five, 71 per cent of men in France have lived with a partner, compared to only 45 per cent of women.

If heterosexual couples of older age groups break up, men are statistically more likely to re-couple sooner than their former partner. According to *Population and Societies*, a journal published by the French Institute for Demographic Studies, men are much more likely to re-partner following death or divorce than women. Approximately 37 per cent of men aged 50–59 reported 'probably or certainly' intending to form a new romantic union following a divorce, bereavement or separation, versus 24 per cent of women in this age group. In the age 70–79 group, the proportion is 10 per cent for men compared to just 1 per cent for women. When men established new relationships, they generally re-partnered with younger women, the same report showed.[10]

The older women who are alone are vulnerable. An example of this occurred during the 2003 heatwave, which marked the hottest summer in Europe since 1540. Roughly 87 per cent of the 15,000 victims were over seventy, and were mostly women. Scientists have different hypotheses for why the mortality rate amongst women was 15 per cent higher than for men, including reduced sweat production amongst elderly women, a higher core temperature, and more physical activity within the household.

As the Babayagas presented this data to France's local government, the officials were forced to agree that older women were indeed in need of community-based housing.

Yet, they still had questions. What about Montreuil? If the council was helping to fund the house, the space would have to be of use to the whole neighbourhood. How would the Babayagas benefit Montreuil?

The women would do ten hours of local community service monthly, Thérèse suggested, such as hosting lunches for their neighbours, allowing visitors to take in the gardens, teaching classes, and running informal play groups for local children.

'That doesn't mean you can dump your kids on us when school is out,' Thérèse would regularly remind her neighbours, keen to underline that she was not prepared to take on the free labour expected of women her age. 'We're not free babysitters.'

Fair enough, the council conceded. The Babayagas would undoubtedly be a benefit to the community of Montreuil.

However, if funding was partly going to come from the local government, it wasn't possible to open an entirely single-gender building. That was discriminatory and exclusionary, the French government argued, and they wanted no part in that.

Again, Thérèse offered a solution. The Babayagas would make four flats on the ground floor available to young parents who were in need of social support, or immigrants, or those fleeing violence.

A great idea. Who could argue with that?

By now France's media had heard enough of the proposed project to have questions of their own. Were the women vowing to go sexless? Were they saying they would not take on lovers?

Of course not, Thérèse would reply, amused. Older women were obviously going to have sexual partners, and no one would police who spent the night at this women-only block in Montreuil. The lovers just weren't permitted to permanently move into Maison des Babayagas.

Once again, Thérèse's answers were satisfactory. It was going to happen – the house was going to be a reality.

But there was now trouble amongst the three founding Babayagas. Suzanne and Monique were increasingly uncomfortable with Thérèse's vision, especially the inclusion of immigrant women and those on social welfare, as several women privy to the arguments between the three have told me. The project was clearly more than a block of flats for older women; it was now a kind of social, maybe even political, statement, and that's not what Suzanne and Monique had envisioned.

'Also, Thérèse was a strong personality and she was the one always invited by the media when they started being interested in the project,' her friend Danielle Michel-Chich said. 'Monique and Suzanne felt they were being left aside.'

The two withdrew from the project. Yet Thérèse was not one to give up. Life had taught her that building her own world would be necessary for survival.

Far from conforming to traditional roles, Thérèse Clerc certainly wasn't a typical grandmother, either. 'She would talk to me about the political power of the clitoris,' her granddaughter Petronille, her chestnut brown hair piled up in a messy-chic bun like her grandmother's, told me over Zoom, laughing. 'She thought that it was wonderful that a body part existed purely for female pleasure.'

Thérèse wasn't always that way, however. She had been born in 1927 to a middle-class family in Bagnolet, an eastern suburb of Paris. In those days it was expected that women would marry – and so she did, at twenty, still a virgin.

Over the next two decades she had four children and settled into life as a stay-at-home mother and housewife – going to church, masking her bisexuality and following the rules. This was around the same time that the French intellectual Simone de Beauvoir wrote her ground-breaking book *The Second Sex*, arguing that women were discriminated against and dominated by men, and judged only in relation to men. Thérèse didn't engage with the book at the time of its publication in 1949, being the typical disenfranchised housewife case study Simone was writing of, but later she would echo its sentiments, speaking of how her generation of women were under the financial and social control of the men in their lives. Women around the world, Thérèse said, were forced to pimp themselves out to their own husbands.

'I remember the money my husband gave me every month,'

Thérèse revealed in the 2014 documentary *Rebel Menopause*. 'It was extremely tight. Some months, when the children needed things, I ran out by the 20th, so I had to be extra nice to him for extra money. That's why I believe, in those days, marriage, all over the world, was like a whorehouse.'

When she turned forty, Thérèse fell ill with a lung infection and had to be admitted to hospital for over a month. It was a turning point.

'She found community there,' Danielle Michel-Chic told me. 'She spent her days talking with the doctors and nurses, the other patients. She realised then that she couldn't return to a life of just caring for family. She wanted more.'

A few months later, in May 1968, Paris was swept up in a sea of violent protests led by students, who were later joined by workers and eventually over 9 million people. The protesters, later known as Les Soixante-Huitards – or '68ers' – were calling for social and cultural change, and decrying economic inequality, unfair working conditions and government corruption.

Thérèse was there.

She would walk to the demonstrations at college campuses and marvel at the women in the streets, twenty years younger than her, screaming for access to abortion and demanding the dismantling of sexist laws that allowed men full legal decision-making powers concerning their children. Thérèse was transfixed.

'My grandmother had come from a conservative world where women sat quietly, clutching their handbags as shields,' her granddaughter Petronille told me, 'and here protesting, there were young, wild, free women refusing to accept the norm. They inspired the woman in her that was ready to come out.'

'Thérèse would say she was born twice,' explained Danielle Michel-Chic. 'December 1927 and May 1968.'

Thérèse moved to an apartment in Montreuil and threw herself into the community and activism, with women's rights centred as a particular passion. Women found Thérèse through a whisper network of other women. Her friends and family told me that by the early 1970s Thérèse learned to perform clandestine abortions through a doctor who would attend her dinner parties, which she carried out on her honey-wood kitchen table. The table now belongs to Petronille's mother, Agnes, who keeps it in her living room so that everyone who asks (which is everyone) can see it. Petronille texted me some photos of it, and I noticed that it was smaller and more delicate than I'd imagined: two planks of stained wood, with delicate cabriole legs. I replied that I hoped Petronille would inherit it one day; she responded that she did too.

Thérèse's Montreuil apartment was open to her neighbours. By the 1980s and 1990s, she was hosting regular discussion evenings, at which the eclectic local community would turn up with bread and cheese, ready to talk about what they needed most. One idea was a drop-in day centre for women to talk, drink coffee, play the piano and relax. Maison des Femmes opened in 2000, on Rue de l'Église, the road with the shawarma restaurants and chicken shop, when Maison des Babayagas was still just an idea being argued over. Today the sign outside says 'Maison des Femmes Thérèse Clerc'.

In most projects, if two of the three founders withdraw, it's usually a sign that the venture is in huge trouble. But by the time Suzanne and Monique left the Babayagas, it almost didn't matter. Thérèse had enough momentum on her side, and a growing number of supporters.

'Maison des Babayagas would not have come into existence

if it wasn't for the sheer tenacity of Thérèse,' recalled her granddaughter Petronille. 'Her mission was the health of the community, the collective. The individual was a dirty word to her.'

By late 2012, with over 4 million euros raised from over half a dozen donors, as well as commitment from the cohabitation board of East Paris and the local government, plus a flurry of positive press, Maison des Babayagas opened its doors. Twenty-one single women over the age of sixty moved into twenty-one studio apartments.

The Babayagas were pioneers, but they were not alone. Women in England, just a short train ride across the English Channel, were making a similar journey around the same time.

New Ground, London, 2024

It takes around forty minutes to get from my home in London to New Ground, and I feel an involuntary flush of 'home envy' as Jude invites me into her flat. Londoners experience this a lot, but mostly when we leave the city to visit friends who own homes that don't rattle when the overground goes past.

New Ground is London's first intentional community created just for women over the age of fifty, and Jude's flat is certainly not rattling. New Ground sits in Chipping Barnet, a charming market town with independent cafés and a mixture of Victorian and Georgian architecture interspersed with clean new-builds. It's just over twenty minutes on the Northern line to central London, I will find myself repeating in the pub when I meet up with my friends that evening. The jackpot.

Once you enter New Ground from the main entrance, the shared meeting area is to your right, just past a noticeboard that spells out the weekly activities: yoga, a showing of an Irish documentary on co-housing communities called *Reimagining Elderhood*. The common room is large, with a kitchen, dining area and a wall-mounted flatscreen TV for movie nights. Glass doors offer a stunning view of the south-facing landscaped communal garden. Each flat has been built to enjoy a view of the expansive garden. It's just so rare to have this kind of space in London, I find myself saying over and over again.

'We know we're lucky,' Jude says when she sees my eyes widen at the further connecting meadow, where planting beds of different heights (depending on how low you want to bend) have been sown with vegetables and fruit. A small summerhouse, with a kitchen and bathroom, is available if you need a break while gardening. Water tanks are sunk into the lawn to harvest rainfall for irrigating the garden. The whole complex is due to have solar panels installed soon.

In January 2024, World Habitat, a housing NGO, awarded New Ground the Bronze award for creating a groundbreaking model of community living that provides a supportive environment for older adults.

'It's so well thought through,' I say.

'We worked very closely with the architect to make sure they understood what we wanted from this community,' Jude's neighbour Hedi replies.

Jude's flat is a similar size and layout to mine, with a roomy kitchen that opens onto a living room with large windows, two double bedrooms, wooden floors, and lots of light. But her interior design choices – such as understated tiles in rows above a single line of bold pattern – take hers to another league. Jude's home could be featured in *Architectural Digest*. She smiles as I admire a carob-coloured wooden-framed square mirror hanging between prints.

Jude still works in art education. In fact, several residents of New Ground remain active in the London workforce. Her three neighbours join us in the flat for coffee: Hedi, Charlotte and Ann, whose ages vary from mid-fifties to mid-nineties. They all write, edit and advise for various projects in and around the capital.

I tell them that while doing research for this book, several women told me that I must talk with the ladies at New Ground, and Hedi gently corrects me.

'We say "women", not ladies. Calling women "ladies" or "girls" can feel undermining.'

I'm embarrassed. I realise that these aren't nouns I use often, so I'm not sure why I did just now. Do I have an internal bias when it comes to older women that I haven't fully explored?

Calling women anything other than 'women' can seem especially patronising when you're meeting them to discuss their pioneering work and what it means for women everywhere. I'm reminded that in a world with substantial inequality between genders and generations, language matters.

New Ground opened in 2016, emerging from an idea that took almost twenty years to make a reality.

One of the early planners of New Ground is Maria Brenton, an academic and a UK Cohousing Network senior co-housing ambassador. She tells me that she has been researching models of community for single older women for decades.

A memorable one she visited in the 1990s was an all-women's trailer park in Arizona. It was full of groups of women 'snowbirds', mostly lesbian, who would jump into their eighty-foot-long RVs and migrate to warmer regions during the winter months. They wouldn't let men into the trailer park; they insisted that their community had to be free from the directives of men.

These particular snowbirds were women who had served in the US armed forces. Maria says she initially found some of the women to be 'a bit domineering'. But soon she discovered that they had set up highly organised and compassionate forms of community care for those that needed it the most. The best example was a woman who was in the latter stages of cancer. She had a rota of neighbours dotted around the trailer park who looked after her in shifts.

'There was solidarity within the trailer park,' Maria recalls. 'They were caring for each other in illness, preparing to look after each other in old age.'

But a trailer park is a transient model of living – one that is hard to replicate around the world. Visits to Denmark and the Netherlands, however, introduced Maria to co-housing. It was these that served as the main inspiration for New Ground.

After her research visits to co-housing communities, Maria received funding to set up workshops in 1998 to brainstorm how to adapt the Netherlands model specifically for older women. Two of those in attendance were Shirley Meredeen and Madeleine Levius, members of Growing Old Disgracefully – a national network aiming to inspire women to challenge conventional views of ageing. After Maria's workshop, they all went to the pub together and decided to establish Older Women's Co-Housing, a group that would meet regularly to share meals, socialise, and begin the search for a place to live together. They set out their values for OWCH: equality, companionship, mutual support and self-reliance.

Hedi says 200 women attended the OWCH meetings, expressing their interest in moving into what would become New Ground. Maria thinks the number is closer to 400. It took the group eighteen years to finally find their site, eventually securing funding from Hanover, a non-profit housing association. They also worked together on designing their homes alongside architects from Pollard Thomas Edwards. They wanted shared amenities, including a laundry room and greenhouse – facilities that would place community interaction at New Ground's heart. Eventually twenty-six women moved into the two- and three-bedroom flats in the multistorey building.

I ask Maria the most obvious question. Living together and looking after each other in older age makes sense, but why without men?

'The very strongest voice I have in my recollection is [New Ground founder] Madeleine Levius. She expressed her views very vociferously,' Maria replies. 'She said, "We've been told what to do by men all our lives. And I, for one, am not going to tolerate it in old age."'

Madeleine died in 2005, more than a decade before New Ground opened. Shirley Meredeen, another founder, enjoyed six years at New Ground before her death.

Like the Babayagas, the group has received floods of attention, including visits from women looking to set up similar communities. Maria remembers a group of young women from South Korea, who called themselves the 'Never to be Married' group, coming along to ask how they could replicate New Ground back home. Maria has also been approached by women from all over the UK, from Hastings to Manchester, who have asked her to advise on setting up their own women-only co-housing. But she's not confident that we'll see a huge rise of older-women-only co-housing around the

UK, because as it stands, local governments do not help make the process easy.

'In Holland you can get help from local authorities, provincial authorities, and from the government to finance someone who will guide you through the whole process of getting a group mortgage, borrowing the money, hiring the architects,' she says. 'The Dutch government will fund a process consultant, to help you as a group get through all those tricky areas that you've not got any familiarity with. But that doesn't happen in other parts of the world. It doesn't happen here.'

And not all the attention they've received has been positive. Some have criticised the project's lack of diversity, because no women of colour were photographed in the press materials for New Ground. Having met the inhabitants, I find this claim reductive. The New Ground community is diverse. They are from varied socio-economic backgrounds, and some came to the UK as refugees.

'Diversity takes lots of forms,' Hedi adds, noting that eight flats are rented out as subsidised homes, and have housed women from Iran and Ukraine.

And data from the UK's Office of National Statistics from 2011 and the Pew Research Center from 2022 has shown that Asian and Black women are more likely than those who are white to live in a multigenerational family household. Older women of colour, therefore, often continue to live with members of their family and might not need these co-housing spaces.

Everyone has a role, if they want

By 2030, two-thirds of the world's population is expected to live in cities, with many urban areas in the global north having

25 per cent or more of their populations aged sixty and over.[11] Community is hard to cultivate in cities, and academics have suggested that residents in urban areas often experience lower levels of connectedness and interactions with their neighbours.[12]

Charlotte tells me that this is not the case for New Ground. 'Living in New Ground allows us access to diverse cultural experiences, and we're lucky that we get to enjoy that within a community.'

Each woman who wants a role has one waiting for her at New Ground. There is a communications team, a membership team, and a finance team with a reserve fund for women who will live at New Ground in the future. They don't see each other every day, but the teams have regular meetings – and the residents have regular visitors. A sociological definition of community is a group of people with a high degree of interaction and a shared purpose. New Ground fits that definition. And their shared purpose is independence.

I ask the women what community means to them – and each agrees that it is a moveable, living, breathing concept, which is open to change if it doesn't work. For example, when they initially moved in, they wanted all decisions to be made using a consensus model where the whole committee agreed – but some decisions were taking far too long to action. Now they've moved to a majority vote. This made me think of the women of Unity village in Kenya, who, when living at Umoja no longer suited them, decided to leave. Their community was also a concept that could be changed.

Jude interrupts my thoughts. 'We run ourselves like a business,' she says. 'Obviously not with the transactional coldness of a commercial project, but we organise ourselves.

We look after each other. We let our families know if each of us needs extra care.'

'When people come here they often say, "I think my mum should move somewhere like here", but they should be thinking about it for themselves,' Ann adds. 'You should be thinking about where and how you want to live for the later stages of your life by your thirties.'

This catches me off guard. My friends and I often fantasise about a future a stone's throw from each other as neighbours, but we've made no concrete plans.

Growing old with girlfriends

My friend Claire, whom I've known since we were eleven years old, lives in a beautiful cul-de-sac in South Yorkshire. Almost every time our group of girlfriends catches up, we reiterate a fantasy. Over the next few decades, we will edge out Claire's neighbours, one by one, and take over the homes. This way, we will grow old together. We've seen each other through school and university, marriage and divorce, the loss of family members and the births of babies, grappling with sexuality and gender identity, career lows and highs. We'll see each other through the rest too. I know ours is not a particularly original conversation. I bet almost every group of women friends have at some point discussed moving in together, or close to each other, when they are near retirement.

There's a viral YouTube video we shared in our group chat in 2019. It showed a group of seven girlfriends from Guangzhou in China with a similar plan, and garnered millions of views. The friends were staying in a beautiful mansion they said they had bought together. They were in their thirties, but they insisted they would move in together when they reached their sixties. It clearly captured the imaginations of a younger, digitally engaged audience. The comments section was alive with women saying they would love to do the same thing with their best friends, insisting it would stave off loneliness in older age and rethink the traditional gender-binary family dynamic.

I'm not certain that the video is genuine. It may just be clever marketing, because the mansion is available as a holiday rental – and despite an initial tour on Zoom, the women do not respond to requests for interviews.

But I know that co-housing communities like New Ground and the Maison des Babayagas are not the only models of older-women-only communities. In 2019 a woman named Pat Dunn in Ontario, Canada, set up a group called Senior Women Living Together, to help women look for housemates for shared living in a traditional home. The group has over 2,000 members and there are active discussions on harmonious living – including whether lovers are allowed to spend the night. Pat's own three-woman household has a strict no-overnight-guests rule.

Other communities offer alternatives. The Sharing with Friends organisation in Australia, for example, places women over the age of fifty-five into groups of five. Each woman has her own one-bedroom unit on shared land, and the group also has access to a separate building for shared meals, doing laundry and watching movies. Still, older women choosing to live in communities without men is still very much a Western phenomenon.

There are ashrams in Vrindavan, a pilgrimage city in India, that look after more than 20,000 widows. However, the women are housed in these ashrams by governments and charities, due to being socially outcast. Some denominations in Asia regard widows as spiritually unlucky, and they are marginalised by their communities and families. Isolated and shunned, these women disappear inside the ashrams. However, not all widows have negative experiences; for some, ashrams provide a sense of belonging, spiritual purpose, and autonomy.

'Today I am happy to have all these women around me, I am not alone any more,' a sixty-year-old woman told BBC Travel. 'We have learnt to live together, to help each other. We became friends, true friends, as we all know what we've all been through. We look ahead, we try to never look back. We never talk about the past.'[13]

Back in the Babayaga common room in Paris, Flora pours me a syrupy black coffee that has been brewing on a camp stove sitting on the counter next to the microwave. She glances out to the garden before joining us at the long table. Once a month, a group of women horticulturists come to help the Babayagas grow crops in their 200-square-metre garden. The February soil is well thawed after winter, and they have planted bare-root strawberries in the ground. They should be ready by June.

We're in the common room (the room with the hole in the ceiling) with three other Babayagas: Carmen, Marie Christine and Catherine. Carmen can't stay long; a former dancer from Uruguay, she teaches tango and salsa in Room 1. This work also subsidises her pension, which is less than 300 euros a month due to her having freelanced and taken breaks to raise children. While they want to spend this stage of their life around women friends, some are keen to stress that they aren't men-haters.

'I like men,' Carmen emphasises. 'I don't like when women say they prefer women to men.'

'Because you have been lucky with men,' Flora tells her. There's a beat of silence before Carmen gets up to leave for her dance class.

There has been tension recently, the remaining group tells me. Just before I arrived, another Babayaga gave Flora a filthy look and called her a bitch in the shared laundry room.

Flora pushes a plate of crackers towards us and says, 'Gluten free,' before segueing into the topic at hand. 'The biggest disappointment is when we turn on each other.'

This tension started after a young mother moved into one of the studio apartments on the ground floor – one of the four reserved for those in need of social housing. When her partner also moved in, the building changed. The Babayagas heard a male voice yelling into the night, the children crying, furniture being thrown.

'Violence against women made its way inside a women's community,' Catherine says sadly.

The Babayagas made a decision. What was the point of a mission like theirs if they were going to ignore that a man was potentially dominating and harming a woman in their own home? What was the point in giving interviews about sisterhood and solidarity, and having a banner that spells out 'feminism', if they were going to ignore a raised male voice and crying children? So a group of Babayagas knocked on the door of the flat.

'We said to him, "We are a feminist building and this is a women-led community, you cannot behave this way",' Catherine recounts. 'We said, "While you're here, you will follow our values."'

I admire them for taking action. Here are women who are

united, mostly, in enforcing the values of their community. There was never any shouting after that, and the couple broke up and moved out.

This should have been good news, but one Babayaga – the one who called Flora a bitch – threw her support behind the alleged abuser, telling the other Babayagas that they were wrong to intervene in the couple's relationship.

For Flora, this revealed a type of internalised misogyny that she believes many women still hold. A woman should support other women, she insists.

'Is this Babayaga even a feminist?' she asks now, shaking her head.

Does it matter that she supported a man on one occasion, I ask?

'Yes,' Flora replies, pointing to the banner which reads 'Féminisme'. 'It's written in our values.'

Some of the newer residents who have moved into the flats are less involved. In 2012, all twenty-one Babayagas in the building were on the housing committee. Now there are only twelve. The newer residents rarely have coffee in the common room, or go for classes in Room 1, or join in with the gardening, Flora says. To them, the list of values and Thérèse's letter are just posters on the wall.

Flora is quiet for a few moments, then says she wants to show us a second letter from Thérèse. This one is not on the wall. Flora keeps a copy in a binder full of press coverage about the Babayagas. Thérèse addressed it to each of the twenty-one residents in their first year in the building. There had been a particularly explosive argument about whether they should build a communal jacuzzi, and if they did, who would clean it. The stress of the years of making a vision a reality had taken its toll on everyone.

The letter is dated 10 August 2013. In beautiful, cursive handwriting, Thérèse implores them to make peace: 'Isn't it time we all returned to a less passionate attitude (which has caused us all to suffer) and put all our energy into a political project that has united us for the last 10 years. A project which offers society a new model for old age until our final passage? This project, which is the envy of the world, could not exist without all of us, so we must make up.'

At the time of my visit in February 2024, six of the original twenty-one Babayagas have died, but they did not die alone. The group looked after each of them in illness, attending doctor's visits, making dinner for them, and later helping families organise the funerals.

'We are capable of caring for ourselves and each other,' Flora says.

A few years ago, a private firm approached the Babayagas to ask if they wanted a building manager to help manage the requests from visitors and deal with the administration and communication from the council. They would also be able to help with any maintenance issues, such as the hole in the common room ceiling.

The Babayagas declined.

'Whatever happens, we remain independent.'

'Des trous dans la raquette' is a phrase French politicians and journalists love to deploy as a metaphor. It translates to 'holes in the racquet' – meaning that even the best plan has flaws.

Flora, Marie Christine and Catherine are in floods of giggles as they tell Laure and me about a visit they will soon be having with a German co-housing board who would like to pick their brains. The Germans want to know how the French have built an affordable utopia for older women in Paris. It's the word 'utopia' that is inspiring the laughter.

'We will sit in this room with them and put a picture of a racquet over the hole in the ceiling!' Flora says.

An imperfect house of women, but one that is surviving – and that has plans for the future. They want to start a podcast, and a young journalist for Montreuil has offered to show them how.

As they laugh, I feel a surprise pang of jealousy over their natural camaraderie. It takes my friends and me months to organise going for lunch. I wish we still lived down the hall from each other, like we did at university. Like the Babayagas do, despite the natural disagreements that happen with strong women and friendship.

'They have had several issues and conflicts over the years,' Danielle Michel-Chic told me. 'And they continue.'

Maison Des Babayagas has never been a utopia.

'You can't have a utopia when you have strong women,' Thérèse Clerc constantly reminded her fellow Babayagas. 'We are not here to be perfect. We are here to show a new way for older women.'

On the Eurostar back home to London, I take a photo of my Montreuil Girl Gang badge and send it to my girls group chat. No one responds. I know it's a particularly busy week for them all. The last time we spoke they mentioned work trips and kids' illnesses and parents visiting. They'll probably mention it when we meet next.

But wouldn't it be great if I could drop round tonight and tell them about the Babayagas and New Ground? Maybe if I could show them examples, we'd be more serious about our plan to become neighbours in older age. I realise that whenever we've talked about this dream, we don't ever mention our male partners. Are we subconsciously planning for a time when we're alone? I think the reality is, if any woman is lucky to live to elderhood, she may well be alone. We all need a plan because it's rare that anyone else will make one for us. The women of New Ground and Maison des Babayagas made a plan.

The Babayagas and the residents of New Ground see each other almost every day for coffee, or in the laundry room, or a visit to the cinema or doctor, or a salsa class. The women argue. They don't all like each other. They garden. They welcome visitors from around the world. One year, a group of single mothers from Belgium came to ask the Babayagas how they could set up a community like theirs. The Babayagas made them delicious coffee and offered them gluten-free biscuits, looked out onto the garden, and told them.

On the garden wall, in front of the strawberries, there is a mural in shades of Prussian and baby blue with pockets of lawn green, by artist Anne Michelle Vrillet. Two beautiful women are climbing ladders as a third assists from the ground, and a wild forest threatens to devour them all.

'They're escaping loneliness,' Flora told me as Laure and I left Maison des Babayagas.

That's not how I interpreted the mural, however. I saw three Babayagas anticipating the obstacles that threaten to engulf them in their current environment, and choosing together to find a new way. When they're over that wall, they will build a world that will serve them. A world where they aren't ruled by the male gaze, they aren't peripheral members of society. They may have reclaimed the Baba Yaga trope, but they certainly aren't witches. Women like the Babayagas are vital, central solution-finders in communities that have expected them to shoulder a relentless cycle of unpaid and undervalued domestic work. The Babayagas, New Ground and Senior Women Living Together have secured their own futures.

On the Eurostar, as I look down at my Montreuil Girl Gang badge again, I feel a mixture of emotions. Each women-only society I have visited so far has been made up of several women who contribute so much to their communities, replenishing and enhancing them. They are each offering a blueprint on how we can improve our own communities. They are asking for nothing in exchange.

I get out my phone and open my photo gallery. I scroll to the favourites folder and tap on a photo of an older woman with high cheekbones and a chic grey bun (similar to Thérèse Clerc). This is the only photo I have of my great-grandmother Sreedevi. The woman whose story inspired me to write this book.

Paris has made me think of Palayil Tharavad.

10

The Nair Tharavad: Four Corners for Women

India, 1800s

I first heard about my ancestral matrilineal home, a house built for women – our tharavad – through an unplanned visitor one Christmas. It was a story I had never even thought to seek out.

I had always known that women were valued in my family. Unlike other families, who still overwhelmingly desire male children,[1] my mother's side was the opposite.

I remember my amuma, my mum's mum, writing to me when my eldest niece was born, to say that she was delighted that her first great-grandchild – like her first child and her first grandchild – was a girl. But she didn't explain the huge importance of the female line in our family's history. Perhaps my amuma was barely conscious of it, and was instead expressing something that came from deep within her, without grasping the reasons she was so happy to have a great-granddaughter. It fell to a family friend, a very distant relative, to become the narrator of this intriguing part of my family's story.

It all began one frosty December day, several years ago, when Geetha chechi (*chechi* means 'older sister') slipped on a sheet of ice on her driveway and injured her wrist. As her husband was away on an overseas trip, it made sense for

Geetha chechi to stay with my family in Yorkshire while she recovered.

I'd known Geetha chechi my whole life – her family in India had been connected to mine over several generations. She and her husband lived a few hours away. Yet visits to each other's homes had been limited to short lunches and dinners that ended before 10 p.m., and the conversation often circled around current life events such as careers and holidays.

This December, though, we had more time together. Curled up in our pyjamas, clutching mugs of steaming cocoa while festive songs played on the radio, Geetha chechi told me long descriptive stories about our families in central Kerala.

I already knew parts of Kerala. I was born in the populous and diverse western coastal city of Calicut, where my parents had attended university, and that's where we visited whenever we returned to India. But rural central Kerala, where my mother, grandmother and great-grandmother had all been born, was alien to me.

Geetha chechi described it enticingly. Peaceful roads that threaded through fields of rice, where congregations of egrets gathered at the edges. Hushed stone temples surrounded by jackfruit and tamarind trees, where village families would walk each evening to light the vilakku, a traditional brass lamp used for spiritual practices in the region. The large temple pond, where children bathed and splashed each other.

Geetha chechi also told me about communities led by women who lived together in a tharavad.

This was the first time I had heard the word 'tharavad' (also spelled taravad, tharawad). A tharavad, she explained, was an ancestral home shared by extended family members linked to one common female elder. It was a female-led ecosystem. Sometimes over fifty members of a joint family

THE NAIR THARAVAD: FOUR CORNERS FOR WOMEN

would have lived together on the grounds of a tharavad. In the seventeenth and eighteenth centuries, 'thara' was a unit of division to measure land, but in modern Malayalam – the official language of Kerala – the term means a foundation on a mound. A tharavad was, therefore, a house on a mound.

In most tharavads, women could enter all rooms, but some were not open to men. A tharavad was a communal microcosm, with childcare, finances and household chores split evenly between the occupants. Unlike ancestral homes in several other parts of India, where unmarried and widowed women were looked on with suspicion, the tharavad embraced all its women. If a woman married, she remained within the matrilineal tharavad, and her husband moved to her tharavad. He didn't often sleep there though, as it was for women – men slept in outhouses on the grounds.

I would learn later how much a woman's tharavad defined her identity and set the tone for her whole community. My own family belonged to an ancestral tharavad called Palayil. The last woman to live in our family tharavad was my amuma's mother, a woman named Palayil Sreedevi.

Sreedevi was her first name, used every day by people who knew her, and Palayil, of course, referred to her tharavad. Women of Sreedevi's social class and generation did not take the names of their fathers; instead they took the names of their homes – their multigenerational, women-led tharavads.

My great-grandmother Palayil Sreedevi was born sometime in the 1890s in Tholanur, a lush inland village in central Kerala. Tholanur sits within the district of Palakkad, which translates as 'the forest of milky pine trees'. Today Tholanur – enveloped by paddy fields, and consisting of houses built under dozens of coconut palms – is part of the state of Kerala, which was formed in 1956, almost a decade after India's emergence from

British colonial rule. But Palayil, Sreedevi's house of women, had by then stood for hundreds of years – the keys passed down from one female ancestor to the next, woman to woman.

Only one faded photograph exists of my great-grandmother, from sometime in the 1960s. It shows Palayil Sreedevi as a thin woman with pronounced cheekbones, her shoulders bent inward and covered by a sari, her mouth slightly downturned. One arm protectively clings to her body in a sort of half-hug. She is dressed in white, the colour of mourning in Kerala – a colour she had worn since one of her children passed away from a neurological disease. In the photograph Sreedevi sits next to her husband Guru Kunju Kurup, a man whose face I know well.

Unlike the one photograph of my great-grandmother, I have seen dozens and dozens of images of my great-grandfather. At one time, Guru Kunju Kurup was one of Kerala's most famous men. He was a celebrated Kathakali performer.

Part dance and part mime, Kathakali originated in south India in the sixteenth and seventeenth centuries, around the same time as Shakespeare. Kathakali literally translates as 'story play', and it combines drama, dance, elaborate costumes, jewellery and make-up, to tell the stories of the great Hindu epics the *Mahabharatha* and the *Ramayana*. Each performance is considered not just theatre, but an act of worship.

Having heard so much about my great-grandfather, I was desperate to learn more about my great-grandmother and her tharavad, but no living family members had been to the village of Tholanur, where Palayil Tharavad once stood. Before Geetha chechi, no one had even mentioned it.

And Palayil Sreedevi herself had left few leads.

There were no documents or diaries, and her children, including my mother's mother, my amuma, had by this time

THE NAIR THARAVAD: FOUR CORNERS FOR WOMEN

all passed away. Sreedevi's grandchildren – my mother and her siblings – had vague memories of her being elegant and kind-hearted. Unhelpfully, their most vivid description was that their grandmother had been a woman who said very little. It was her charismatic, famous husband who had commanded everyone's attention. And they didn't know anything about Palayil, our ancestral home.

So I did what I usually do when I get stuck during research. I went on social media. Logging on to then Twitter, I typed in the word 'Tholanur'. Within seconds, a tweet from a user called Raghu popped up from 2020, posted during the height of the coronavirus lockdown. Raghu had been messaging the local Tholanur police station in a public tweet, asking how he could pick up medication for his grandmother without breaking the lockdown rules. I sent Raghu a direct message and introduced myself as an Indian journalist living in the UK who wanted to learn about my great-grandmother.

I said that I knew it was unlikely that he could help, but by living in Tholanur he was the closest connection I had to my great-grandmother's past. Sreedevi had been married to a well-known man named Guru Kunju Kurup, I told him, and maybe that might make it easier to place her.

Raghu replied that same day.

'My grandmother Leela remembers your great-grandmother Palayil Sreedevi and her tharavad,' he wrote. 'My grandmother has a lot to tell you.'

The unique culture of Nair women

A few weeks after her stay with us, Geetha chechi sent several books to me to help me research kinship systems in southern India. Unsurprisingly, a matrilineal caste that prioritised women-led spaces in India had fascinated English-speaking historians and anthropologists, and there was plenty to read. My great-grandmother Palayil Sreedevi had belonged to the Nair caste (sometimes spelled Nayar), one of southern India's most enduring noble land-owning castes that can be traced to at least the ninth century CE. Anthropological books such as *The Nayars Today* (1976) and *Daughters of Independence* (1986) note that the Nairs were one of India's most distinct and unique communities, resisting several patriarchal norms.

When Nair boys reached the age of twelve, they were expected to leave their homes and train as soldiers in military gymnasiums, named kalaris, and then serve the royal families.[2] Not too dissimilar to Spartan society, men were sent off to fight while women ruled the community that was left behind.

As soldiers, Nair men went on to join troops like the Nair Brigade, defending the kingdom of Travancore, which existed from 1729 to 1949 and spread over most of the region of what is now Kerala and Tamil Nadu. The most elite Nair soldiers joined the Chavers, who were essentially suicide squads and sometimes described as similar to Japan's samurai warriors. With Nair men away serving the crown, their home and the land on which it stood became the domain of the Nair women – who designed these spaces for their own convenience.

Nair women therefore enjoyed a freedom that was unusual for largely patriarchal India. Unlike many other Indian women, who were expected to move into their husband's home after marriage, Nair women remained in the matrilineal tharavad in which they were born.

Although customs varied greatly from region to region, several Nair communities enjoyed a relaxed form of marriage,

THE NAIR THARAVAD: FOUR CORNERS FOR WOMEN

or sambadhanam, during the seventeenth and eighteenth centuries.[3] It's worth noting however that there are no first-hand testimonies of a sambadhanam, and Nair families I've spoken with, including my own, do not know who the last woman in their bloodline was to take part in one. Yet several people have told me they are certain the system existed, and women benefitted from it.

In these marriages, women were not expected to cater to the comforts of husbands or put their needs before their own. The term 'sambadhanam' most likely originates from the Sanskrit words *sama*, which means 'equal', and *bandham*, which translates as 'union'. There is debate amongst scholars as to whether sambadhanams required sexual fidelity, but several academics agree that it was an alliance that existed only when it suited both the man and the woman. A sambadhanam could easily be dissolved at the request of either party.

But instead of being looked on as a period where some women enjoyed a unique sense of security, Nair culture has been reimagined and subjected to shame by some parts of modern Indian society.

In 1989, Indian politician Shashi Tharoor wrote the following about Nair culture in his book *The Great Indian Novel*: 'In Kerala, the men of Nair community realise that their wives are free to receive them by seeing if another man's slippers aren't outside her door.' Although the quote is from a novel with fictional characters, and not a historic assessment, Tharoor's words went viral decades later when they were shared on Twitter. Commentators suggested that his description of the informal marriage – the sambadhanam – was a judgement of Nair women, insinuating that they were promiscuous.

Whether Tharoor meant this description as an insult or not, there definitely are men who are critical of the historic freedom enjoyed by Nair women. A female cousin of mine, who gently asked a male colleague she supervised to be more punctual to work, logged on to Facebook hours later to find that he had posted a long online rant about entitled and domineering Nair women. His post ended with a reference to the freedom of sambadhanam; 'Your ancestors were whores!' When my cousin recounted this story to me, she noted that it was funny that men of our generation seemed to have regressed from men of our great-grandmother's time.

I'm sure, like all systems of social organisation, the Nair culture was not perfect for women, but it did seem to grant most of its women some status and security. The tharavads, as mentioned earlier, were inherited through the female line, from mother to daughter. Family trees were recorded to include women and their female children. The system was even codified into law as Marumakkathayam (which translates as 'sister's child').

Researching the Nairs, I realised how little I knew about my own lineage. And the only way to learn more seemed to be to visit the village of Tholanur myself. I wanted to talk with people who had known my great-grandmother Sreedevi – the last woman in my immediate family to have lived in a tharavad. And I wanted to find out why she would choose to leave a system that seemed to benefit women.

Kolathil Leela and the women of Tholanur

By car, it takes over four hours to reach Tholanur from the international airport in Calicut, the seaside city where I was born. Calicut is an incredibly vibrant and diverse place, and has been for centuries, having served as a major port for the

THE NAIR THARAVAD: FOUR CORNERS FOR WOMEN

Indian Ocean trade route from the 1200s. Merchants there were said to manipulate the monsoon winds to transport spices, cotton and sugar to ports in Kenya, Egypt and Iraq.

As a journalist, I have filed several reports about Calicut. In a previous article, I wrote that Calicut looks like someone 'had cut roads into the middle of a lush forest'. I described towering trees lining the streets, providing shade for street vendors selling guavas and sugar cane juice, in this city where the Arabian Sea sparkles to the west and the Wayanad hills rise in the east.

The drive from coastal Calicut to inland Tholanur is not for someone who is sensitive to motion sickness, like me. The roads are narrow and squiggle-like. It is late May, on the cusp of monsoon season, and the weather swings unpredictably from sudden and heavy curtains of rain to unforgiving forty-five-degree Celsius heat at twenty-minute intervals. By the time we reach the home of Kolathil Leela, which sits behind a gate on Tholanur's quiet main road – just past a tailor and a banana chip stall – I am ready for the long and welcoming hug and sweet coffee she has brewing. It is over six months since I found her grandson on Twitter and learned that she knew my great-grandmother Sreedevi and Palayil Tharavad.

Leela, a small woman in her mid-eighties, with sharp eyes and masses of silvery-white hair, was born in Tholanur two decades before they built the first road through the village, and it is where she has remained. She says that she likes to refer to herself by her full tharavad name, so from now on we will call her Kolathil Leela. The air-conditioned single-storey home where she lives with her daughter and son-in-law is modern, with wheat-coloured walls and high ceilings. It has been built on the grounds where her family's tharavad,

Kolathil, once stood. This was a neighbouring tharavad of Palayil, and Kolathil Leela's son-in-law has promised to take me there after coffee.

The rain has subsided and the sun is once again beating down, a relentless heat absorbed slightly by the canopy of jackfruit, mango and papaya trees in Kolathil Leela's garden. Three wild peacocks walk past me, incurious at the visitor who has travelled hours to reach their village.

'This village is your village,' Kolathil Leela says, taking my hand as we sit next to each other on her couch.

Then she begins to tell me about her childhood, when Tholanur was arranged around three main families and their tharavads: Palayil, Kolathil, and another named Kuppathil.

In order to reach the three tharavads, before the roads were built, you had to negotiate acres and acres of grassland populated by vipers and cobras, and wet paddy fields. Ribbon-like uneven single-lane paths led to the tharavads, which were built on a foundation of brick and tile.

'Tholanur is your home, where your grandmothers are from. Let me tell you about it, mol.'

Mol. She has called me 'daughter'.

The gendered architecture of a tharavad

Kolathil Leela describes Palayil like she is telling me about a film she has watched that day, it is so clear in her memory.

To enter the tharavad, she says, you first had to climb steps to pass through a padippura, an arched gateway with lockable gates which led to the main house. As you walked towards the house, which was on a raised foundation to prevent monsoon flooding, you would see the poomukham, a large porch with several wooden chairs. This was where the men of the family sat, keeping a sort of watch, like sentries, over the grounds.

Palayil was constructed over two floors, with the upper level used to store produce tilled from the fields – large earthen vessels of rice and grain. The house was arranged in a rectangular structure called a nallukettu, meaning 'four corners', held up with bulbous pillars made from wild jackfruit wood and teak. Locally sourced materials – like clay, timber, stone and palm leaves – rejected foreign influence. The four sections were named according to the direction they faced: the vadakkini (northern block), kizhakkini (eastern block), thekkini (southern block) and padinjattini (western block). Much thought was put into the design of each section.[4]

The roof sloped close to the ground to ensure the beating monsoon rain would quickly run off it. The four sections of the nalukettu opened onto a central roofless courtyard, the nadumuttam. A corridor ran around the outside of the house – the chuttu verandah (the hallway that encircled the house). It was adorned with brass lamps that would have held oil and flammable thread, which could be lit to illuminate the halls. The verandah also gave the external walls robust protection from the unforgiving sun and heavy rains. The small windows were built at low heights, to invite in diffused light. Gabled windows ensured cross-ventilation, and hot air rose up through the nadumuttam, which also served as a kind of family town square, where the majority of the socialising and family festivities took place.

Kolathil Leela recalls the women of Palayil as being 'intellectual' and said that all Nair women living in Tholanur's tharavads knew how to read and write. At Palayil, the women would gather together each evening in the nalukettu courtyard with their books – mostly local literature and religious texts like the *Bhagavad Gita* and the *Mahabharata* – as the men sat talking on the porch outside. As of 2024, Kerala's female literacy rate was the highest in India, with 95 per cent of women in the state knowing how to read and write, according to the country's national census.[5]

The kitchen at Palayil was where the majority of women could be found from early morning until lunchtime, preparing lunch for the household as well as the farmworkers. 'As they served the food they would call out "Is anyone hungry?" into the fields and ensure that everyone was fed,' Kolathil Leela tells me. 'And in the evening, before they locked the gates, they would call it again, so no one in the community went to bed hungry. That's how it was.'

The main dishes made at Palayil were kanji, a soupy rice porridge and puzhukku, a curry made of boiled root vegetables, including elephant foot yam, and dahl flavoured with seasoned coconut paste. Around a hundred people were fed daily at Palayil Tharavad. The kitchen was located in the vadakkini, at the north-east corner.

'In tharavads, the kitchen is there specifically as Kerala's winds travel from the south-west to the north-east,' architect Benny Kuriakose, who has restored tharavads in the region, told me over Zoom. 'It prevents the carrying of hot air from the kitchen to the rest of the house.'

The least visited rooms were the bedrooms, which were situated in the western block, the padinjattini. As they were only used for a few hours every night, the direct western sun didn't cause discomfort. There were no designated bedrooms, and family members would change their roommates depending on conversation, convenience or visitors. There might be several women in the tharavad's sleeping chambers – maybe a grandmother, her daughter and her daughter's children, and a younger cousin or two sleeping in several large cots in the space.

Men – especially partners – were of course allowed to enter the bedrooms, especially for conjugal visits. However, they rarely stayed a whole night. Husbands and male relatives generally slept in bunk beds in pathayapura, which were converted storehouses.

This culture where women lived in the main house and men slept in satellite buildings was repeated in several (but not all) tharavads across the state.[6] Men and boys – generally visiting from military outposts – were given separate quarters in order to cause the least disruption to the women-led running of the tharavad and its task of feeding over a hundred people a day. Within the tharavad, women also cordoned off spaces that men were not allowed to enter.

I visited another tharavad around a twenty-minute drive away from Tholanur called Kandath, which had been converted into a homestay. It had two purathalams – raised areas against a wall, filled with cushions and designed for lounging. At the front of the house, in the first purathalam, the men would have congregated to chat. The purathalam at the back of the house was where women would have gathered.

'It has been designed so that acoustically no word spoken by the women can be heard by the men and vice versa, even if you should shout,' the custodian of Kandath Tharavad, Sudevan Bhagwaldas – whose family has lived there since 1723 – told me over ginger tea. 'The purathalams are diagonally opposite to each other, with the courtyard in between.'

Sudevan's statement made me think about the First Nations women's sites in Australia. Did the acoustically divided purathalams exist to allow women and men to discuss their respective matters – Women's Business and Men's

Business – without fear of being overheard by the other? Could these conversations also have centred around gendered rites of passage, birthing knowledge, the sharing of sacred stories and songs only known to women, and land-related knowledge? As I was daydreaming, I saw Sudevan point to a door. That was the entrance for women, he told me. There were specific entrances for women at most tharavads.

At my family home in Palayil, the two smaller rooms next to the main bedrooms were exclusively for women. One was a room where they slept during their periods, and a second – the prasava moori – was the delivery room for pregnant women.

There's considerable debate around the purpose of these period rooms. According to the Hindu practice of chaupadi (a practice that shares a name with the period tents of Nepal that I referred to in an earlier chapter), menstruating women are considered impure and unlucky during their periods. They therefore need to be separated from others.

However, a different school of thought, promoted by Indian menstrual health activists like author Sinu Joseph, insists that women are at their purest during their menstrual cycle – a belief held by several communities, including the Nairs. Their desire was not to isolate women during their menstrual cycles but to provide them with rest.

This is a theory my mother Usha shared with me. It was first told to her by her grandmother Palayil Sreedevi. A well-ventilated period room within a traditional Nair home, where they were brought food and drinks and were excused from any household chores, allowed a woman time to rest without guilt.

And in addition to gendered physical spaces, there were also some rituals that separated men and women.

Every morning, just after sunrise, the women of Palayil

THE NAIR THARAVAD: FOUR CORNERS FOR WOMEN

walked across the paddy fields to bathe together in the family pond, or kulam, washing their bodies with turmeric and fragrant spices. Then, in the evenings, they would gather in the courtyard to read and sing. Every year, festivals with women-only dances would be hosted in the grounds of the house. One example was Thiruvathira, a day on which the women of the tharavad would fast and dance, praying for true love and a kind and supportive partner in order to continue the family.

The birth of a girl was a moment of huge excitement for the tharavads and would have been celebrated with the ringing of bells and rattling of chains.

'The moment signified a continuation of the matrilineal line,' Kerala-based gender academic Lekha N.B., who has researched the history of tharavads, told me over Zoom. 'The birth of a girl child was more prized than a male child because of the role a woman has in physically carrying the progeny. This ensured the continuation of the tharavad legacy.'

A girl's first period was also celebrated for this reason. Although both men and women took part in the ceremonies, it was the women of neighbouring tharavads who arranged for gifts to be sent to the menstruating girl – to welcome her to womanhood.

Each tharavad in Tholanur housed more than thirty people; they were located a few kilometres apart and were surrounded by acres of farmland. The crops grown included grains like rice, little millet, sesame and horse gram, as well as fruits from the trees, such as jackfruit, banana, coconut and mango. These were sold to visiting tradespeople who would have travelled by bull-drawn carts, and they were the primary source of income for each tharavad.

'Women from the tharavad were in charge of negotiating

each sale,' Kolathil Leela tells me. 'Tharavad women had power.'

It's worth mentioning here that historians note that while the Nairs were undoubtedly a matrilineal society, and property was passed on from mother to daughter, the group still maintained some patriarchal structures. According to some researchers, it was the Karanavan – a male blood relation to the eldest woman – who had the ultimate say when it came to the welfare of the tharavad. As the oldest uncle, the Karanavan could orchestrate marital matches and had the right to expel members who disobeyed him.[7]

Kolathil Leela, however, says that this was not the case in Tholanur. In my great-grandmother's village, it was the oldest woman in the tharavad, called the Tharavad Amma – the tharavad mother – who held the most influence. The blessing of the Tharavad Amma had to be given before any business or romantic relationship could start or any child was given a name. She also held the keys to the main gate, and the storage room where any jewellery was kept.

'The Tharavad Amma's decision was final,' Kolathil Leela explains. 'The last Tharavad Amma at Palayail was your great-great-grandmother. Palayil Sreedevi's mother. Her name was Palayil Kalyani.'

Kalyani is 'beautiful' in Sanskrit.

'The name suited her!' Kolathil Leela adds, smiling.

Palayail Kalyani was responsible for the modernising of the tharavad. Before the First World War, she arranged for the dried coconut leaf roof to be replaced with clay tiles. She insisted that daughters of Palayil Tharavad should always live in a safe and secure home.

Tharavads, historically at least, were built to support and celebrate Nair women. There's no doubt that if you were a woman whose family owned a tharavad, you enjoyed a life that was not available to women of all classes and Indian castes. The freedom and status of tharavad women varied greatly from household to household and region to region, but the original make-up of a tharavad, before colonial interference in the nineteenth century, favoured women.

According to Keralite academics Antony Palackal and Lekha N.B. in their book *Unveiling the Gender Paradox: Dynamics of Power, Sexuality and Property in Kerala,* Nair women were safeguarded in their tharavads. 'Marriage was not at all compulsory and the [tharavad] protected women who remained single. In contemporary times . . . unmarried women [in Kerala] are looked on with stigma and suspicion . . . Protection of unmarried and single women young and old – was one of the most important functions [of the tharavad].'[8]

As I put down my coffee, Kolathil Leela nods to her son-in-law, who stands and fetches his car keys. It is time for me to see the grounds of Palayil.

We've been driving down Tholanur's main road for less than five minutes when Raman, Kolathil Leela's son-in-law, pulls over and tells me that we'll have to walk the rest of the way. A car won't be able to manage the uneven, narrow, unpaved grassy path that leads to Palayil.

As we walk, there are lush wild plants on either side of us – lime-green palm trees with six-foot-wide fan-shaped leaves, banana trees with bunches of arching elongated leaves, and rows and rows of towering coconut trees. Dozens of pale yellow butterflies fly across our path. In front of us is a rusted grey gate, designed with shapes that look like the diamonds from a deck of playing cards. The gate is open.

'This is Palayil,' Raman says, pointing ahead.

An acre of grassland slopes down to the surrounding paddy fields. Ahead of us stands a small white Sarpa Kavu, an area found in several Kerala Hindu houses, set aside as a shrine to the serpent gods.

When I was a child, I asked my amuma why we had a Sarpa Kavu in our backyard in Calicut.

'We thank the snakes for letting us live on their land,' she replied, as she continued reading her newspaper. That simple sentence has stayed with me. It was the first time I understood that we, as humans, hold no greater claim to the land than any other creature.

The land at Palayil is well kept, the grass cut short and piles of coconuts neatly arranged under trees. A grey hut-like building with a sloping tin roof stands in the middle – a tiny bungalow. The structure looks a couple of decades old, at most.

'That's where the current groundskeeper lives,' Raman says, following my gaze.

This is when I learn that Palayil Tharavad was pulled down decades ago. The land still belongs to our family, but the original house, abandoned as the large women-led Nair family broke up into several nuclear husband-wife units, slowly decayed and was eventually deconstructed.

My ancestral home, a tharavad designed for women, exists only in memory.

When I return to her house, Kolathil Leela's family feed me a vegetarian feast prepared from locally grown crops – creamy savoury mango curry, spicy okra, puffed matta rice, and black gram papads lightly fried with coconut oil.

They give me the contact details of other relatives, all of whom are daughters of Palayil. Relatives who remember my great-grandmother as a young woman and my grandmother as a toddler. They have since helped fill in the blanks of life in a tharavad, and provided me with valuable first-hand testimony and context for traditional Nair life.

They meet once a year on the grounds of Palayil, light a vilakku at the Sarpa Kavu shrine and honour our ancestors, thanking them for the foundation that has given us all the life we have today.

'The invitation is always open for you to join us any year you are available,' Santha Kumari, a daughter of Palayil Sreedevi's sister, said over the phone. 'You are a daughter of Palayil.'

Why Sreedevi left Palayil

Palayil was different from other tharavads. Its residents loved several types of artistic medium and used the house and its grounds as inspiration – and also as a stage on which to share their creations. Women in Palayil gave singing lessons to children in the local community, although they refused to accept money in return. This was a form of community service, like that conducted by the Babayagas of Paris.

Palayil men were experts in Kathakali, which was very much a male-led art form, and soon attracted students from all over the region. One student was Guru Kunju Kurup, a young man who was already making a name for himself as an expressive and talented Kathakali performer.

Prior to the First World War, Guru Kunju Kurup had travelled from village to city to perform for audiences and nobility, including the Travancore royal family. In between shows, he would seek tutelage from Kathakali masters all around the region. Hearing of a great teacher named Palayil

Menon in Tholanur village, he travelled there, hoping to bunk in the pathayapura outhouse for men on the grounds of the tharavad where Palayil Menon lived. He was in luck. Palayil Tharavad welcomed Guru Kunju Kurup with open arms, and he was immediately given a plate of food and a bed. It was there he met my great-grandmother, Palayil Sreedevi.

My mother told me that Palayil Sreedevi had seen my great-grandfather first, from a doorway inside the tharavad, through a curtain made of multicoloured glass beads. When they locked eyes, it was instant love.

But with this love, Palayil Sreedevi's life and identity were about to change. Up to this point, she had enjoyed a life of freedom and privilege within Palayil that was rarely experienced by women in any part of the world in the early twentieth century.

Were he not a famous man, Guru Kunju Kurup might have embraced Palayil Sreedevi's life. He might have moved to Palayil, and my great-grandmother could have remained in the family, and one day become the Tharavad Amma. But instead Palayil Sreedevi became the first woman to leave Palayil Tharavad following marriage.

From the several interviews I've watched of my great-grandfather, and after speaking to several people who knew him, it's clear that Guru Kunju Kurup was a man with an ego – and a man who couldn't live in a house ruled by women. It is likely that he wanted a base where he could be the patriarch – a more nuclear family set-up, which was becoming increasingly fashionable in the twentieth century.

'Palayil Sreedevi was a kind woman, a generous woman,' Kolathil Leela told me. 'My own mother used to say that she was one of the most generous women in Tholanur. She would give anyone anything they asked for.'

I can imagine that Palayil Sreedevi – a woman raised

to support the collective good of her community and household – chose to leave her tharavad in support of a man whose talent was evident to everyone who saw him perform, and in doing so allowed his identity and legacy to dominate the story of our family. Guru Kunju Kurup went on to win the Padma Bhushan and Padma Shri, two of India's highest civilian awards, for his performances and services to the arts. I've read and watched several reports about him, diligently stored in archives around the world, from the David Bolland Collection at Rose Bruford College in the UK to the India Ministry of Culture. In no interview I've read or watched does Guru Kunju Kurup mention his wife or the sacrifices she must have made for him – especially leaving a community that had kept women at its centre. Even his Wikipedia page includes the name of Palayil Sreedevi's relative who introduced them, the great Kathakali teacher Palayil Menon, but not his wife.

My mother told me that when Palayil Sreedevi left her tharavad, she took the curtain of multicoloured beads, unthreaded them, and kept them in a small box in their bedroom. Mum believed it to be a lovers' keepsake, a token from the first time Palayil Sreedevi saw the man who would become her husband. But I wondered whether the beads were actually a keepsake from a time when she'd lived in a world where her identity as a woman was valued and celebrated.

The complexity of a tharavad and women's rights

Yet while it's tempting to romanticise the tharavad, especially as a female storyteller imagining the life of her great-grandmother, there is evidence that – like all women-led spaces – life there had its challenges.

Nair women spent most of their time within the grounds of the tharavad; the streets outside, which were still a masculine domain, were not available for them to explore unchaperoned. A woman couldn't wander Tholanur without the supervision or companionship of several other women from her tharavad – unlike men, who would regularly go for solitary walks.

Also tharavads, like all societies built on hierarchy, took advantage of poorer women labourers in order to thrive. During the nineteenth century, tharavads comfortably supported a large number of dependants.[9] The Nair caste had enjoyed dominance in southern India for centuries; as part of this, they utilised the cheap labour of farming classes to tend to their crops and wetlands, and observed restrictive and severe caste-based discrimination – especially towards the female workers employed by tharavad families. Women from more marginalised social castes in the region were dominated and often humiliated.

On my father's side, I partly belong to the Ezhava caste. In the eighteenth century, when the Nair women of my mother's family were thriving, Ezhava women in the region now known as Kerala were made to pay mulakkaram, or a 'breast tax' – a fee of money or rice for the right to cover their chests. Historians have noted that forcing women and girls to show their chests from puberty is a means of maintaining hierarchy, by controlling and humiliating marginalised women. In the nineteenth century, it was a woman named Nangeli, from the Ezhava caste, who ended this oppressive system by refusing the tax, cutting off her own breasts and handing them to an inspector on a banana leaf. It was said that this defiant act shocked people in the region and put an end to the tax. But the oppression of lower-caste women continued.

The shunning of lower-caste women definitely occurred in my Nair family. While Palayil women were enjoying the freedoms of their tharavad during the nineteenth and early twentieth centuries, the women who laboured in the fields were not permitted inside the household. Understandably, there was a growing resentment towards this social set-up.

At the same time, British colonists, who presided over large parts of southern India, were openly hostile to Nair matriliny and keen to dismantle it.[10] The colonists, helped by the Travancore royal family, undermined the role of tharavad women by only liaising with the elder men in tharavad families. The eldest uncle – the Karanavar – then began to enjoy an inflated role, essentially acting as the tharavad's property manager.[11] Such was the rise of the Karanavar's control that a welfare committee, the Nair Service Society, voiced concerns about the autocratic nature of several Karanavars, claiming that they often had sole say over when girls were pulled out of education and that some women were oppressed within the home.[12]

Kerala-based artists have also raised critical questions about whether tharavads actually restricted women rather than liberated them. The 2021 Malayalam film *The Great Indian Kitchen* portrays life in a contemporary tharavad, where women are relegated to the back of the house, performing domestic labour out of sight, while men relax and gather leisurely in the front courtyard and veranda. This portrayal challenges the idealised image of the tharavad, recognising that it may not have always been a supportive or equitable environment for women.

A Malayalam novel titled *Indulekha*, published in 1889,

pointed to casteism in tharavad life as well as family interference and pressure to enter into sambadhanam. Indulekha tells the story of a beautiful Nair woman with a Western education, who is tired of the communal expectation of the tharavad and keen to experience a nuclear family life. Her love – a university-educated Indian man – is a fan of Western culture and the positives of a nuclear family set-up.

The book, written by author O. Chandu Menon – who received British schooling and campaigned to end matrilineal inheritance – held a mirror up to the changing socio-cultural climate of the time. Ideas of a modern family, where you owned your own property and only had to prepare meals for a handful of people, were seen as progressive. Additionally, modern jobs, outside the agrarian industry, were leading to migration away from the villages where tharavads had been built. Men like my great-grandfather Guru Kunju Kurup, who were the beneficiaries of most of these jobs, wanted their wives with them.

In the early twentieth century, a slew of laws aimed to undo the Nair matriliny, the Marumakkathayam. The Travancore Nair Act of 1912 and 1925 and the Cochin Nair Act of 1920 made the informal marriage, the sambadhanam, illegal, and as a result joint female-led set-ups dissipated, giving way to the heteronormative husband-and-wife home life we know now.

The matrilineal system was over.

There are still dozens of tharavads standing in Kerala, although today very few have large multigenerational families living in them. Some are in varying stages of decay, sitting in wild overgrown fields, covered in creeper vines. Others have been converted to homestays or become part of heritage trusts. A handful are occupied by nuclear families, who live in one part of the house, with wings of the nalukettu – and spaces just for women – unvisited and locked up.

Digital tharavad

Palayil Sreedevi's daughter line continues.

My mother and her older sister moved to Calicut in the 1970s to attend medical school, and that's where they met their future husbands. Their younger siblings and parents followed. Eventually we moved to the UK for my parents' work, and my mother's younger sister headed to the US and her brother to northern India, but Calicut still acts as a base for the family. My mother's oldest sister still lives there, as do her children and grandchildren, all within walking distance – a truly matrilocal Nair family.

We keep in touch through WhatsApp group chats with outposts over three continents. Our digital tharavad. It's a women-led set-up consisting of my mother, her sisters, their brother's wife and their children – my cousins. Women usually initiate the transglobal conversation, sharing memes, news articles, promotions, recipes, and photos of birthdays and anniversaries, holidays and school plays. It's also the women who organise visits and family holidays, and the women who act as publicists for shyer individuals – celebrating and advertising the wins of family members to the wider collective.

Our closeness most likely comes from the fact that, for the first few years of my life, we all lived together – my parents, my mother's sisters and their husbands. It was a modern house, not a tharavad, but it was communal living. Each nuclear family had their own bedroom and bathroom. My cousins and I were supervised by my grandmother, my mother's mother, when the adults went to work. We would play together, nap together, and wait for our parents to come home for lunch and dinner.

That house didn't have different spaces for women – the men didn't sleep in a shed outside – but women did still gather together. At 4 p.m., my grandmother, my mother, my aunts and my female cousin would all sit round the kitchen table, opening bags of banana chips, cutting a slice of plum cake, sipping stove-brewed tea, and talking and talking. A mini Palayil.

11

Lessons of Herlands

In a Nair family, cousins are as close as siblings. My first best friend, and cousin closest in age, was born just a month after me – though we couldn't be more different women. I crave experiences, to immerse myself in the worlds and lives of people from all backgrounds and beliefs. She has lived on the same street for most of her life, building her own beautiful house a few doors down from her mother. She met the man who would become her husband when we were still teenagers, and fast-tracked her way to building a family. She had her first daughter while I was backpacking and in between flatshares. She knows what she likes and my palate changes with the months. Yet we both still seem to follow certain protocols of the tharavad. We both see family as a collective, not as atomised nuclear groups.

My cousin's daughter, my niece, calls me Megha vellyamma – which translates as Megha Big Mother. I may only be a month older (and a lot less capable of handling a crisis) than her anchored mother, but I'm still an older woman, and so I deserve the respect.

In giving each woman relative an individual title after their name, my niece is continuing a long, tharavad-based tradition. There are no 'aunts' in our family – a generic title that could apply to a number of women. My mother's mother was of course my amuma. Amuma's older sister is a vellyachi (big aunt) and her younger sister is a cheriachi (small aunt). My mother's younger sister is a chitta. These titles also extend to my mother's female cousins – like 'chechi' for an older sister.

Male family members have their own titles, and each person enjoys an individualised identity – and therefore valued role – within a Nair communal-living family. These titles are one of the last remaining legacies of our once-tharavad-based family. In a generation or two I wonder what will remain of Palayil Sreedevi's women-led community.

A few years ago, we added my niece to our digital tharavad – the family WhatsApp group. She has never posted in it. She has no photos on her Instagram grid, whereas I post several times a month. I'm also quick to like her stories, whereas she watches mine with no response. My niece is part of Generation Z and she has no desire to document – let alone embellish – her life on digital platforms, unlike her elder millennial relatives, who use social media to maintain their family community.

Before I comfort myself that she's a teenager and still yet to be a proactive family plan-maker, I sometimes wonder if my generation will be the last to follow our matrilineal social organisation, where women who don't share the same mother are still connected like sisters. How long can our women-led space, our matrilineal Nair tharavad – even in its loose digital form – continue?

The need for Herlands

In a world that glorifies the Eternal War, celebrates dominant masculinity and takes women's unpaid labour for granted, it's no surprise that writers, artists, activists and organisers have turned to women-centred spaces as a form of resistance – an antidote to their environment.

The women-led communities we have visited together in this book emerged for this reason. The nation of South Africa's Rain Queen sprang up from a desire for peaceful unity after generations of warring male leaders. The same could be said for the Casa das Mulheres in the Maré favelas of Brazil, where women-only spaces act as a political stage – a place to organise infrastructure, and to challenge the machismo and male-dominated hierarchy of the wider community.

Similarly, a desire for security from male violence has motivated several single-gender spaces, including Kenya's Umoja and Unity villages. When governments don't provide, women make their own sanctuaries – whether that's Belmont Terrace for Chiswick Women's Aid or the Samburu manyattas of Umoja and Unity. Each is a sanctuary from the cycle of domestic abuse. But these spaces are more than locations where women gather together to identify patterns of abuse; they are environments that offer women the opportunity to define their identities outside these violent and abusive experiences.

This impulse – to challenge convention and carve out space beyond the limits of male-dominated structures – extends across the women's communities we have visited. The residents of New Ground in London and the Babayagas of Paris have built women-led havens that redefine a woman's status in elderhood. Most cultures in the world not only centre a woman's value on youth and fertility, but actively create circumstances that leave women vulnerable in the future. Years of unpaid labour caring for children and ageing parents have led women to financial insecurity in elderhood.

The women of Umoja, Unity, New Ground and the Babayagas, however, have rewritten a tired script and defined new identities for women let down by a world that has not been created for them.

A shared identity naturally fosters community. Some women craved and still crave what the US academic Eve Kosofsky Sedgwick called 'homosocial' companionship – or the desire to cultivate friendships, relationships, mentorship and bonds with people of your own gender.[1] The lesbian womyn's lands of North America were partly set up to give women who shared a sexual identity – one that has been historically ignored in cultures that prioritise male-led stories – a place to be visible. As my friend the writer Sophie Wilkinson says, you need to do some dexterous detective work to scour cultural history for the crumbs of lesbian existence. Misogyny even trumped homophobia. Laws that banned sexual contact between people of the same sex focused on men and didn't deem women worthy of mention. The feeling that the contributions of lesbians were being systemically erased and ignored within male-dominated LGBTQ activism, due to a male-centred lens, meant that some women wanted a space of their own.

Womyn's lands were a form of degrowth, a statement against unending capitalist expansion. They encouraged ecofeminism: building your homes from sustainable materials, and nurturing and growing your own food on the land.

Forming a reciprocal and nurturing relationship with the land on which you lived was, of course, a practice put into motion centuries ago by women from rural and Indigenous communities around the world, before colonialism and the feudal system of the ruling classes took over and taxed land. This system took hold in Europe and Japan in the Middle Ages. In England at least, the origins of land ownership can be traced back to the Norman Conquest of 1066, when

William the Conqueror claimed territories for the Crown. In the centuries that followed, land formally became a commodity to be possessed and extracted from.

Many women-led societies – such as the ones we have visited in this book – push back against the notion of pillaging the earth of its resources, by insisting on minimal disruption to land. This value is written out and pinned up in the common room of the Babayagas in Paris. They view the land on which they live as a sister in their community, one they are in a reciprocal relationship with. The land is a community member who needs nourishment in exchange for the bounty she provides. It is a radical notion – the idea that land should be protected from disturbance.

A world that demands disturbance, and the continuous, often unrecognised labour of women, has also led women in executive and corporate leadership positions to create places where they can claim space, rest, and rethink the boys' club structure of corporate leadership in places such as the Gaia club in Lagos, Nigeria. The 2010s ushered in the girlboss era but didn't remove the gendered demands placed on women, especially within the home. Women who wanted it all – a career and a family – were expected to sacrifice rest. Women's clubs have insisted on pushing back against this culture, inviting women to network with other women and reconfigure the values of the organisations they lead.

These spaces are not a monolith, of course, and women do not have a singular experience in them. And while the women in these communities share some values, they are far from being perfect societies free from disagreement. Every place I visited said they accept that conflict is part of community – they just have to work to ensure that it doesn't descend into violence. Conflict will always exist, as people have different approaches and thoughts on how to live. A community is a conglomerate of backstories.

Conflict has fragmented communities like Megalia. Others have fallen apart due to administration. SuperShe Island took a lot of time, energy and resources to operate, and the splattering of excited media coverage clearly didn't provide enough incentive to keep the ideological – and expensive – retreat going. That's the thing about women-led worlds: they need constant championing and a communal will in order to continue.

The trouble with Herlands

El-Samaha village for divorced and widowed women in Egypt was initially met with eager anticipation. Here was an opportunity for women to cultivate agency in a women-only sanctuary. An oasis for single Arabic-speaking women, promoted in English articles aimed at Western audiences. It was soon cut adrift. Women there told me that they would return to their husbands if they could. There is no specialist support, and little in the way of transport links. The women of El-Samaha do not have the means to create a sustainable and financially viable living for themselves. Their sons have become the patriarchs their former husbands once were. The male village supervisor speaks on their behalf. Feminist organisations find it difficult to get the funding to visit them. El-Samaha demonstrates the vulnerability of women's spaces when broader community support is absent and male-dominated structures close in around them.

The recognition that men ultimately have control over decision-making in several societies around the world has prompted women to demand environments of their own so they can work out how to push back. The Megalians in

South Korea created an online space to stage their rebellion and expose the issues affecting women – including the gender pay gap, harassment, spy-cam abuse and domestic violence. Yet they also mirrored the worst of the misogynistic corners of the internet, showing that women are just as capable of aggressive and controversial tactics such as body shaming and bullying. But Megalia's defenders argue that such a space was needed so that women could expose the ugliest aspects of gender discrimination, as well as giving women the power that comes from defiance. The power of saying *no* – a word that often signals the beginning of liberation.

Women-only spaces have been built on the borders of the mainstream. Megalia emerged from an internet forum in 2015 and was abandoned by 2017 – a short life cycle. Yet it provided women with a place in which to resist the practices that limited them. It created a powerful enough culture to punch through from the edges of online discourse into mainstream media. Megalians demanded that women be heard.

In *Feminist Theory: From Margin to Center*, a meditation on Black women's activism, bell hooks argues that the periphery – the margins – are incubators of possibility.[2] The women we have met in this book often come from the margins; divorce, abuse, and minority identities have pushed them to the edges, exposing them to further attacks. But not only do women-only spaces created in the margins secure and improve chances of survival, they also provide the possibility of upheaval and transformative change. The women-led spaces we've visited together are blueprints for a system update – a means to reset administrations conceived by male governance. When men are the default decision-makers, there is often oversight in the decision-making.

In the aftermath of the horrific 2012 Delhi gang rape, it became evident following surveys by organisations like UN

Women that city planning and transportation policies had largely excluded women's perspectives, contributing to systemic safety issues.[3] However, the immediate reaction from the authorities seemed to blame women. Some politicians even encouraged women to stay inside and wear modest clothing.[4]

But women didn't stay indoors. In the days that followed, they took to the streets in mass women-led protests that lasted weeks. The anger mushroomed to a global women-centred outrage. Indian victims of rape have a right to anonymity, and for years the media didn't name the twenty-three-year-old victim – instead referring to her as Nirbhaya ('fearless one'). Then, in 2015, her mother Asha Devi gave a public speech saying: 'My daughter was Jyoti Singh and I am not ashamed to name her. It is the offenders who should be ashamed and hide their name. I want to tell everyone that my daughter's name was Jyoti Singh. From today, everyone should know her as Jyoti Singh.'

The rape and murder of Jyoti Singh proved to be a watershed moment, with the public outcry prompting the creation of dedicated and specialist units to handle cases of sexual assault. There were some meaningful reforms – laws were amended to include broader, more nuanced definitions of violence against women, penalties were introduced for police negligence, and harsher punishments were established for perpetrators. It wasn't the end of the issue though.

Women in India continue to face threats that are so serious that in April 2025 the Supreme Court voiced a plea for the creation of more safe spaces. Justice Nagarathna specifically referenced the lack of women's toilets, especially for rural women – and named examples of women being assaulted while searching for a place to relieve themselves. Earlier in this book, we talked about how a century ago the lack of public restrooms limited the movements of women. Women are still fighting for the existence of these spaces today.

Indian women are taking action to tackle violence against women. The Honour for Women National Campaign, spearheaded by activist Manasi Pradhan, takes a multi-pronged and dynamic women-led approach to addressing violence against women, communicating the message to the women who need it the most, where they need it the most. Venues included women's community gatherings, exhibitions, and street theatre, all of which served to inform women about the legal and institutional resources available to them in cases of abuse.

At the same time, the Indian government has increased the recruitment of women police officers and expanded the number of women-only police stations across the country. Since the 2012 Delhi bus rape, the number of these stations has doubled – yet they still total only around 745 in a country of more than 1.4 billion people.[5] But this model is gaining ground, not just in India but internationally. Women's police stations (WPSs) have been established in various countries, particularly in Latin America and South Asia, as a targeted response to gender-based violence. A 2017 study found that municipalities in Brazil with women-only police stations had reported a 17 per cent reduction in female homicide rates.[6] These findings suggest that, while limited in scale, a women-led approach to law enforcement could help to create safer environments and more accessible justice pathways for *all* women.

Over the first two decades of the twenty-first century, women-only spaces have become more publicised and attracted worldwide media coverage. Some spaces are functional, centring safety; these include women-only taxis in the UK and women-only beaches in the UAE. Others are part of older traditions and rituals – including waulking circles in the Highlands of Scotland, a women-only tradition that transforms newly woven wool into a softer and more durable textile. Waulking circles have been revived in recent years, getting a boost from Instagram reels that have gone viral. There is also the Shout Sisters group in Australia, who meet in parks to scream and release their frustrations, and also release the expectation of women to be silent – a tradition inspired by the country's First Nations women.

There's been a rise in the number of commercial ventures including women-only holiday packages and women-only hotels. Yet these spaces still have to comply with local labour laws and employ men. One women-only hotel near Porto Cristo in Spain has male staff – and was in 2025 led by a male president. These spaces are not always rooted in a collective desire for an alternative lifestyle; at times, they are profit-driven opportunities rather than community-centred initiatives.

As several grassroots feminists have pointed out, spaces that appeal to a glossy girlboss version of feminism are inherently paternalistic. They are designed by executives and promoted by the media, rather than being places that maximise choice, autonomy and economic independence for women.

'Women's spaces appeal to development funders on paper but materially they don't always prioritise women's best interests,' says Janey Starling, who came to El-Samaha village with me and actively works in gendered justice programmes across the UK.

There are also vocal critics, especially in the West, who insist that women-led and women-only spaces are unnecessary and indulgent. When the London art gallery Tate Modern prioritised rooms with women artists in a 2016 installation,[7] some journalists argued that it was condescending – and a means to further make a spectacle of women instead of including them. The *Telegraph* published an article titled

'The Tate Modern "women's room" is patronising nonsense dressed up as gender equality'[8] Others are also uncomfortable with the term 'women-only', seeing it as provocative and exclusionary. The Danish Board of Equal Treatment ruled in 2014 that women-only floors in hotels were discriminatory.[9]

The inclusion of transgender women and those who don't conform to binary gender identities in women's spaces is a delicate and sensitive subject. There is no one law or uniform culture across towns and cities, let alone countries. One response, since 2010, has been a rise in gender-neutral spaces – like toilets and dormitories – in dozens of countries, especially in schools, universities, public buildings, and workplaces. I have reported on the rise of gender-neutral facilities in India, Japan, the US and several countries in Europe. These spaces felt like they might be more inclusive, and good for women too, but their use has become an increasingly polarised conversation. There has been pushback almost everywhere. In Singapore, a photograph of a gender-neutral toilet at the Suntec Singapore Convention and Exhibition Centre provoked a hostile reaction online, resulting in the centre's managers insisting that the spaces were temporary and would soon go back to binary designations. Similarly, in 2024, the UK's governing Conservative Party proposed legislation that new restaurants, public toilets, shopping centres and offices in England would be required to have separate male and female toilets. The party, and groups that advocated for sex-based rights, stated that it was part of a push to curb the growth of gender-neutral spaces.

In March 2023, women and equalities minister Kemi Badenoch said the announcement would 'create better provision for women so that our particular biological, health and sanitary needs are met'.[10] Badenoch is now the leader of the Conservative Party. The ruling Labour government has been vague on their position on gender-neutral spaces. Prime Minister Keir Starmer has stated that it is 'very important that we protect female-only spaces',[11] a remark that has been interpreted by some as a cautious approach to the inclusion of transgender women and gender-nonconforming people in such spaces.

Some cultural commentators – including Natalie Wynn, who speaks about gender and identity on her popular YouTube channel ContraPoints – argue that the anger towards including transgender women in women's spaces is a type of misdirected frustration at misogyny and long-established patriarchal social structures (both historical and current-day) that has resulted in the oppression of women around the world. These are structures that disempower all women, including transgender women.

A future for Herlands

If we're going by the data, there will be a greater need for facilities that cater to women.

For a start, women are outliving men in almost every country on earth,[12] and women's life expectancy is projected to increase in every region of the world between 2023 and 2050.[13] And while men outnumber women in eighty-six countries, that figure is expected to decline to sixty-seven countries by 2050 – demonstrating a rise in majority-female populations.[14]

Women are also choosing lives lived alone and independently. According to the Morgan Stanley analysts in their *Rise of the SHEconomy* report, 45 per cent of women in the US will be single (as in, not in a relationship) in 2030 (up from 41 per cent in 2018).[15] The cause for the shift, the authors say, is a desire for financial independence and personal fulfilment away from cohabitation or marriage. If this projection is accurate, it would be fair to predict that the single woman, a rapidly multiplying cohort, will be seeking community, solace and space amongst other women.

Women's communities and women's spaces will therefore multiply. We will likely see the rise of women-led feminist housing cooperatives like La Morada (the Dwelling), which opened in 2024 in Barcelona's Nou Barris district. The project is said to be an alternative to patriarchal living, which often relegates caregiving to women. 'The nuclear family model is outdated,' Míriam Solà, a member of La Morada, told *Catalan News*.[16]

The public sphere has been dominated by men, and women have been hidden away inside homes. Some societies around the world have vocally pledged to change this by creating more spaces for women in the public sphere.

In Saudi Arabia, a country which has a male-guardian system that restricts women's freedom of movement, some women have pushed for the creation of women-led cities. The idea was first proposed by a group of businesswomen in 2003, with the vision of creating a place for women-led businesses and boosting women's employment.

'The plan to create women-only industrial cities is a positive step that will mutually benefit Saudi women and the Kingdom,' Basmah Omair, the executive director of the Khadijah bint Khwailid Businesswomen's Center at the Jeddah Chamber of Commerce and Industry, told *Arab News*.[17] Although the plans were said to have the approval of the Saudi government in the eastern province city of Hofuf, progress has been slow.

Indian government bodies have also announced plans for women-led public spaces, with the Municipal Corporation of

Delhi stating an intention to build over 200 'pink parks',[18] but here as well we haven't yet seen what this will mean in practice.

Women's rights activists say that while women-spaces in public are essential, they cannot be driven and devised by male-led governments. These ventures may not benefit women if they are not designed by women for local communities. Some point to the work done by grassroots feminists as better examples for future models.[19] Feminists such Vinaya N.A., a retired police officer from my home state of Kerala. Vinaya was concerned that girls did not have the same kinds of outdoor spaces to play sports – to kick around a football or enjoy a volley of tennis. So she built a girls-only playground at her home in the rolling hills of Wayanad. It's called Penkalikkalam (Women's Playground), and it's floodlit and open all day and night. So far it has been used to host local girls' sports teams, but Vinaya's hope is that it will become a space women will use to relax – or even loiter. It'll be a space women can dip into for play.

In the twenty-first century, it's almost impossible to imagine a place like a beguinage, or a fictional Themyscira – a Herland where men are entirely forbidden. Even the Saudi industrial women's cities anticipate male visitors, while certain areas are to be for the exclusive use of women.[20]

Women's communities, including the ones I have visited, accept that within inclusive societies sometimes men will make an appearance. Even those who remain firm in excluding men – especially places for women escaping domestic abuse, or lesbian communities – welcome male children and employ men for certain services, like those employed to care for the cattle in Umoja and Unity.

None of the women's communities I have spent time in want to live permanently as a separatist society. They just want the option of a women-only space while also being able to fully engage with the wider world and all the people who live in it. First Nations women in Australia have perfected allowing time for women to gather in circles and deal with Women's Business on sacred women's land. Newer women's communities are also finding their rhythm as they seek to gather in a meaningful way without men.

Perhaps one future model we will all adopt will be similar to '际屿With' in China. The name roughly translates as 'Island With' – indicating that each woman is an enclave with an individual and personalised story, and they wish to be together 'with' other women.

My good friend, the brilliant documentary maker Natalia Zuo, who was born in China, sent me the story after finding it on the microblogging site Weibo. In 2023, a unique women's community group of forty-seven women – aged between twenty and thirty-five years old – decided to live together for one month in a multi-room mountain villa in Guizhou, an inland province in south-west China. It was a temporary cohabiting experiment with three rules:

- There is no leader
- Don't do anything to burn down the house
- There are no other rules

In February 2024, Natalia located the founders of the community – Tinto (who was twenty-eight years old) and Jennifer (who was twenty-seven) – and the four of us jumped on a call together. Tinto and Jennifer explained that the women of '际屿With' in Guizhou – who met online – had rented out the home as a temporary respite from their lives as wives, mothers, daughters and employees, in order to be in a women-only space for a few weeks. They shared bedrooms and housework and expenses, and set up workstations to connect remotely to the office. They could remain in their pyjamas all day.

Each evening they sat by a fire and discussed women's rights around the world – from abortion rights in the US to troll feminism in South Korea. Then they talked about women's rights in current-day China. How sexual harassment in their country demands 'smoking gun' evidence like video recordings of the alleged abuse in order to secure a conviction. They discussed the lack of representation in Chinese politics – less than 30 per cent of parliamentary positions are held by women [21]

They also talked about their sexual experiences – the enjoyable and terrifying ones. They talked about their fathers. They washed their clothes and hung out their bras in the garden that overlooked the valley. They cooked tofu and practised Nüshu, the women-only rebellious script of sisterhood that they knew had meant so much to the foremothers of China.

They decided that this one-month experiment would turn into something permanent. They would keep renting out dorm-like houses around China, where women could drop in and out, at any time. From days to weeks or longer. These would be women-only spaces, away from fathers, husbands, children and employers. The '际屿With' Guizhou experiment was a physical location, yes, but it was also a conversation about building a better world. They made no money from their meet-up.

'Ours is a subtle revolution,' Tinto told me. 'Instead of torpedoing society by loudly demanding our rights, we are quietly carving out our place through a space just for women.'

I can see the lower commitment model of '际屿With' being replicated around the world in a more fruitful way than some of the more fixed communities we have visited. There were tensions in Umoja and Megalia that resulted in women leaving to form their own offshoot spaces. This is to be expected. All communities – especially those who live in close proximity to each other – invariably experience tension from misunderstandings or the escalation of minor disputes. There's the irritation of neighbours dropping by uninvited, the fight for personal space, or the difficulty of deciding who is the spokesperson for the neighbourhood. This is a common type of community strain that the German philosopher Arthur Schopenhauer illustrated with the 'hedgehog's dilemma': a group of hedgehogs in winter are seeking the delicate balance of being close enough together to share enough body heat to stay alive, but not so close that their spikes poke into and harm each other. It's probably important to note here that this is a metaphor: in nature, hedgehogs often hibernate alone and apart from groups. But the complexities of intimacy are still worth considering. Consistent contact will invariably lead to conflict.

Communities like '际屿With' offer a good solution to the hedgehog's dilemma. They are a compromise – a fluid women-only space. They aren't an expensive and commercialised women's retreat, but nor are they a residence. They offer sisterhood without the inevitable conflict that comes from living with a sister. '际屿With' could well be the most popular future model of Herlands.

Spending the past few years exploring women-led spaces in depth has made me think deeply about the meaning of community, which is perhaps more pertinent now than ever before, as people feel increasingly distanced and disengaged from mainstream politics. A multi-country analysis from the Pew Research Center concluded that many people in over sixty countries with elections in 2024 felt disconnected from political leaders and institutions.[22] With this sense of distrust being present in a countrywide or worldwide political space, there is a strong likelihood that people will engage in local community-building in order to feel a sense of empowerment. A localised community space is an act of defiance. It helps to cultivate a sense of autonomy when the wider world feels out of control. These spaces aren't perfect ecosystems led by perfect people, of course, and it would be superficial to come to this conclusion. However, there's no denying that several of the women-led spaces we have explored have been ahead of their time when it comes to organising physical environments, finances and social support systems.

This is why a woman's space cannot be dismissed as a sidebar story. We should all be paying attention.

When my niece turned seventeen, I took her and her younger brother to Palakkad – the birthplace of her great-great-grandmother Palayil Sreedevi. We walked together on the grounds of Palayil, through the rusted grey gate, under the coconut trees. She'd been quiet for a lot of the drive, the pulsing summer heat making her slightly nauseous in the back seat. My nephew, walking alongside us, had taken my press card from my wallet and was holding its hologram up to the sun, his attention on its shimmer of authority.

The card had my name and title: *Megha Mohan, Senior Reporter*.

It could have read *Palayil Megha*.

'Imagine a world where women take on the name of the house and not the name of fathers or husbands,' I said out loud. 'That's what Palayil Sreedevi did.'

My niece linked arms with me.

'Pretty cool,' she said, looking around the land. I had told her about all my research on tharavads and the Nair matrilineal line, and she had listened intently, smiling, just like I had with Geetha chechi when she first told me about our tharavad. Now, here we were, on our land.

My niece squinted her eyes slightly and I wondered if it was the sun or if she, like me, was trying to imagine Palayil Tharavad, and our female ancestors living together here – eating what they farmed off the land, with an emphasis on organic processes, intuition and collaboration. Living together in a women-led house, bathing together in the family pond, thinking of the community as they cooked for dozens of people, singing together and reading together. Shouting 'Is anyone hungry?' every night to the fields, because no one in a community should go to bed hungry. Selling only enough farm crops to have financial solvency, not for profit. It seems a reversal of the world's current values – a time when care and cooperation were prioritised over aggressive and dominating capitalist tactics. For a time, Palayil Tharavad offered a sense of freedom to Nair women – a bubble where not all women had to marry, worry about their finances, or fear old age.

The idea attracted me, as someone living in the pulsing strain of a city like London, spending a lot of time alone on commutes or at work, furiously budgeting and planning, trying to find a time weeks in advance to connect with my friends and family. Producing work with the aim of changing the narrative of under-represented communities, but knowing that there would be a wall of personal, often misogynist and racist, criticism waiting in my DMs and inbox. Knowing that few people would publicly defend me, because so many have accepted the reality that women will be attacked, trolled, criticised and undermined whenever they have a voice.

Maybe I would have been happier living in a tharavad, I thought, living day-to-day with people, with women, who would protect me.

Then I looked over at my niece, who was taking photos of the paddy fields. She had plans to move to a new city – to start university. She'd be finding lifelong friends from all social and cultural backgrounds, unlike the very class-limited interactions she would have had living in a tharavad. I suddenly felt a wave of gratitude that my niece wasn't limited to this small world that had emerged to serve the needs of women at a particular time and place.

Thank goodness she can make decisions for herself, I thought, independent of the consensus of her sisters and cousins or the final approval of a Tharavad Amma. Thank goodness she has the option to dip into any community she wishes to be part of. Thank goodness women before her have not just asked for but demanded her freedom – and built, with their own hands, havens for her safety. If she needs a women-only space, it won't take her long to find one, wherever she is in this world. Or if there isn't one to hand, she can read of the Herlands imagined by several imperfect women writers. She's been given the gift of education. Her great-great-great-grandmother left the protected pocket of a small community so that the daughters of Palayil would have options. Maybe one day my niece will wish to create a space for her own community. One with its own identity and sense of solidarity. A place where she can talk to and share with other women. Or perhaps it will be more informal, more of a neighbourhood with some common values and its own parameters of identity. Palayil Sreedevi left us a blueprint of what is possible, with all its flaws and limitations. Our family tharavad may no longer exist in clay, timber and palm leaves, but the foundation for sisterhood has been laid for all the daughters of Palayil. From that, if my niece wishes, she can design her own Herland.

Acknowledgements

Thank you to my community. This book exists because of the meaningful and material encouragement I'm lucky to enjoy. This book exists because my family understands and cherishes the value of women.

I love you Tushanka, Ajoy mama, Vidya aunty, Rohan, Jenivia, Naomi, Geetha chechi, Murali ettan, Lathi vellyamma, Rajan vellyachen, Anju, Arun, Gauri, Gautum, Abishek, Winny, Bharat, Bhaumi, Sudha chitta, Gopi kochachen, Sushant, Susheel, Morgen, Jai, Eli, Priyanka, Danial, Rashmi, Anuja, Mangala aunty and Rosna aunty.

Books don't magic themselves into existence. I've had so many people share meaningful resources with me, including their own book proposals, advising me on contracts, sleep hygiene and accountants. Thank you to my friends Sian Norris, Sophia Smith Galer, Hanna Flint, Natalia Zuo, James Glynn, Philippa Stewart, Flora Gill, Rachel Thompson, Dhruti Shah, Roohi Hasan, Omar Mehtab, Fern Riddell, Sam Bright, Sarah-Jane Fenton, Deane DeMenezes, Rachel Savage, Farhad Dalal and Deirdre Finnerty. Thank you to those who helped me with access, research and translations, including Malesela Mubane, Thembi Siago, Federica Cocco, Richard Senra, Salma Khattab, Renata Peppl, Laure Cometti, Salma Halim, Michael Kaloki, Haein Shim, Kareem Abdo Elhafeez, Sri Lakshmi K M, Michaela Makusha and Iseult de Mallet

Burgess. Thank you to Diane Callahan, for continuously reading, coaching and offering encouragement for almost every version.

Thank you my pals, for the years of laughter, travel and counsel, especially Alex Collins, Yousef Eldin, Janey Starling, Fay Nurse, Abdirahim Saeed, Marko Zoric, Yannick Tona, Mark Sandell, Lauren McClean, Michelle McKenzie, Sarah Durham, Niki Durham, Liv Johnson, Hannah Owen, Eve Owen, Charlie Brinkhurst-Cuff, Beth Ryder, Reina Val, Fahima Abdulrahman, Vicky Spratt, Seren Jones, Runako Celina, Naomi Pallas, Lucy Hancock, Sharan Dhaliwal, Ce Benedict, Shivani Dave, Alvaro Alvarez, Jodi McNamara, Barbara Speed, Jessica Elgot, Sandra Glab, Stephanie Boland, all the women at Second Source, Kate Adair, Jess Brindle, Ugla Stefanía Kristjönudóttir Jónsdóttir, Rianna Croxford, Jeremy Walker and Billy Brazil. Thank you Nisha Rani for keeping my keys safe. Thank you to the women who have offered me healing when I needed it most: Surma Shah, Dee Marshall, Aarti Purohit, Connie Habash and Manju Singh. And a special mention for my oldest, closest friends, especially Claire Webster and Nicola Leighton, for your love and support all these decades. I can't even begin to imagine the years without the consistency of our sisterhood.

Throughout my career, I've been fortunate to receive guidance from those who reinforce my belief in public service journalism. I'm especially grateful to Stephen Mulvey, Sola Tayo, Ian Brimacombe, Jacky Martens, Fiona Crack, Peter Karlsen, Jess Brammar, Liliane Landor, Matthew Eltringham, Bethan Jinkinson, Jon Kelly, Alison Gee, Anuradha Awasthi, Katie Dahlstrom, Kirsty Reid, Joseph Winter, Thangavel Appachi, Rachel Akidi, Lucy Walker, Kevin Silverton, Claire Prosser, Peter Musembi, Miriam Quansah, Nick Eriksson and

ACKNOWLEDGEMENTS

Karen Peeks. Thank you to everyone in the Westwoodside village, including Adam, Deanna and the artists at the Hair Shop.

I appreciate the women who've shared and collaborated with me in professional spaces, including Afua Hirsch, Deborah Bonetti, Anne-Marie Tomchak, Georgina Pearce, Rand Khadir, Aina J. Khan, Yogita Limaye, Nomia Iqbal, Mishal Husain, Lagipoiva Cherelle Jackson, Jean Mackenzie, Mai Noman, Farhana Haider, Anisa Subedar, Julia Macfarlane, Reha Kansara, Naga Munchetty, Lyse Doucet, Razia Iqbal, Nessa Tierney, Sangita Myska, Wahiba Ahmed, Sodaba Haidare, Natasha Peach, Nuala McGovern, Victoria Richards, Amelia Butterly, Ashitha Nagesh, Karishma Patel, Samantha Haque, Ru A Kermani, Catherine Byaruhanga, Tala Halawa, Kinjal Pandya-Wagh, Sharanya Hrishikesh, Courtney Bembridge, Gabriela Pomeroy, Lebo Diseko, Jess Furst, Melissa Hogenboom, Sharmaine Lovegrove, Gemma Wain, Catrin Nye, Kavya and Radhika Dodiya, Shaunagh Connaire, Gloria Nlewedim Eichar, Becky Palmstrom, Storm Lawrence and Perri Lyons. I admire you most, Hanna Yusuf – I think of you often.

Herlands began as doodles on Post-it notes and materialised through multiple versions thanks to the unwavering support of incredible colleagues at Curtis Brown and Harvill. They believed in it – and in me. Their kindness and encouragement gave me confidence when I needed it, and that is what most people need to achieve anything. I'm especially grateful to my brilliant, diligent agent Sabhbh Curran, and my fantastic, clear-sighted editor Ellie Steel. Collaborating with you has been a beautiful experience.

And finally, this is for Usha, who creates community wherever she goes. For your values, your intelligence, your kindness, your achievements, your creativity, your independence, your self-sufficiency, your desire to share and bring comfort

ACKNOWLEDGEMENTS

to everyone you know. Thank you for being such a role model of a woman. Thank you for our travels together and all the worlds you have shown me. How lucky I am that you are also my mum.

Notes

INTRODUCTION

1. Charlotte Perkins Gilman, *Herland* (1915; repr., New York: Pantheon Books, 1979).
2. Charlotte Perkins Gilman, 'A Suggestion on the Negro Problem', *American Journal of Sociology* 14/1 (July 1908): 78–85, https://www.jstor.org/stable/2762762?seq=1.
3. Cynthia Davis, *Charlotte Perkins Gilman: A Biography* (Stanford: Stanford University Press, 2010), chapter 8.
4. United Nations Development Programme, 'One Killing Every 11 Minutes', https://stories.undp.org/one-killing-every-11-minutes.
5. Stop Street Harassment, 'Statistics', https://stopstreetharassment.org/our-work/nationalstudy/2018-national-sexual-abuse-report/.
6. UCLA Williams Institute, 'Transgender people over four times more likely than cisgender people to be victims of violent crime', 23 March 2021, https://williamsinstitute.law.ucla.edu/press/ncvs-trans-press-release/.
7. BBC World Service, 'Obama, Clooney and French Gates tackle child marriage', https://www.youtube.com/watch?v=5smEoYI9lAw.
8. Jonas Helth Lønborg, '134 years to go? The data behind achieving gender equality this International Women's Day', World Bank Blogs 8 March 2025, https://blogs.worldbank.org/en/opendata/134-years-to-go--the-data-behind-achieving-gender-equality-this-.
9. UN Women, *Progress on the Sustainable Development Goals: The Gender Snapshot 2022* (2022), https://unstats.un.org/sdgs/gender-snapshot/2022/.
10. Laura Swan, *The Wisdom of the Beguines: The Forgotten Story of a Medieval Women's Movement* (Katonah: Blue Bridge, 2014).

11. Saskia Murk-Jansen, *Brides in the Desert: The Spirituality of the Beguines* (New York: Orbis Books, 1998).
12. UNESCO World Heritage Centre, 'Flemish Béguinages', https://whc.unesco.org/en/list/855/.
13. Jennifer Read-Dominguez, 'Best Women-Only Hotels in the World,' *The Women's Journal*, 13 March 2023, https://www.thewomensjournal.co.uk/womens-travel/female-solo-travel/best-women-only-hotels-worldwide/.
14. Jessica Gardiner, 'Female-Only Gyms: Is This Trend Gaining Momentum?' HerSport, 11 February 2024, https://hersport.ie/2024/02/11/female-only-gyms-is-this-trend-gaining-momentum/.
15. 'Are Yarning Circles the New Decal?', *Architecture Australia*, November 2023, https://architectureau.com/articles/are-yarning-circles-the-new-decal/.
16. Samantha Lock, 'All the Rage: The Women Who Meet to Scream into the Night', *Guardian*, November 19, 2022, https://www.theguardian.com/society/2022/nov/19/all-the-rage-the-women-who-meet-to-scream-into-the-night.
17. United Nations Conference on Trade and Development (UNCTAD), *The Least Developed Countries Report 2021* (United Nations, 2021), https://unctad.org/publication/least-developed-countries-report-2021.
18. Emily Tomasik and Jeffrey Gottfried, 'U.S. Journalists' Beats Vary Widely by Gender and Other Factors,' Pew Research Center, 4 April 2023, https://www.pewresearch.org/short-reads/2023/04/04/us-journalists-beats-vary-widely-by-gender-and-other-factors/.
19. Mark Spilsbury, 'Diversity in Journalism', in *NCTJ Launches Landmark Journalists at Work 2024 Report* (National Council for the Training of Journalists, May 2023), https://www.nctj.com/wp-content/uploads/2023/05/Diversity-in-journalism-2023-4WEB.pdf.
20. United Nations Development Programme (UNDP), '2020 Gender Social Norms Index (GSNI)', 5 March 2020, https://hdr.undp.org/content/2020-gender-social-norms-index-gsni.
21. Nieman Lab, 'The Passive News Consumer Is on the Rise', June 2023, https://www.niemanlab.org/2023/06/the-passive-news-consumer-is-on-the-rise/.
22. Charlotte Tobitt, 'News Avoidance at Record Levels as Four

NOTES

in Ten Worn Out by News,' *Press Gazette*, 9 July 2024, https://pressgazette.co.uk/media-audience-and-business-data/news-avoidance-at-record-levels-as-four-in-ten-worn-out-by-news/.

23. Mingxiao Sui, 'Is News for Men?: Effects of Women's Participation in News-Making on Audience Perceptions and Behaviors,' *Journalism* 25/1 (2022), https://journals.sagepub.com/doi/10.1177/14648849221125412.

24. Mary Rose O'Reilley, *Radical Presence: Teaching as Contemplative Practice* (Portsmouth: Boynton/Cook, 1998).

I HERSTORY

1. UN Women, 'Facts and Figures: Women's Leadership and Political Participation,' accessed 5 May 2025, https://social.desa.un.org/sdn/facts-and-figures-womens-leadership-and-political-participation.

2. Claudia Elphick, 'History of Women's Public Toilets in Britain', Historic UK, https://www.historic-uk.com/CultureUK/History-of-Womens-Public-Toilets-in-Britain/.

3. Silvia Federici, *Witches, Witch-Hunting, and Women* (San Francisco: PM Press, 2018).

4. Sasha Cohen, 'No Unescorted Ladies Will Be Served,' *JSTOR Daily*, 20 March 2019, https://daily.jstor.org/no-unescorted-ladies-will-be-served/.

5. University of Kent, 'The Opening of the First Refuge (1971)', Women's Legal Landmarks, 8 August 2017, https://womenslegallandmarks.com/2017/08/08/first-womens-refuge-opens-1971/.

6. Giorgia Tolfo, 'How the First Women's Refuge Enacted Change in the UK', National Archives, https://beta.nationalarchives.gov.uk/explore-the-collection/stories/how-the-first-women-refuge-enacted-change/.

7. Carol Dix, 'Hell from Home', *Guardian*, 16 October 1975, https://www.theguardian.com/world/1975/oct/16/gender.uk.

8. Government Equalities Office, 'Equality Act 2010: guidance', https://www.gov.uk/guidance/equality-act-2010-guidance.

9. 'What Is a Woman?,' *Prospect*, 12 May 2022, https://www.prospectmagazine.co.uk/society/38626/what-is-a-woman.

10. Angus Cochrane, 'Supreme Court Backs "Biological" Definition of Woman', BBC News, 15 April 2025, https://www.bbc.co.uk/news/articles/cvg7pqzk47zo.
11. Susan Stryker, 'What Does It Mean to Be a Woman? It's Complicated', *Time*, 5 March 2020, https://time.com/5795626/what-womanhood-means/.
12. Isabella Thurston, 'The History of Two Spirit Folks', Indigenous Foundation, https://www.theindigenousfoundation.org/articles/the-history-of-two-spirit-folks.
13. Stephanie Pappas, 'Is the Alpha Wolf Idea a Myth?', *Scientific American*, 21 October 2022, https://www.scientificamerican.com/article/is-the-alpha-wolf-idea-a-myth/.
14. Heide Goettner-Abendroth, *Matriarchal Societies of the Past and the Rise of Patriarchy: West Asia and Europe* (New York: Peter Lang, 2023), p. 16.
15. Alison George, 'In Search of the Very First Coded Symbols', *New Scientist*, 9 November 2016, https://www.newscientist.com/article/mg23230990-700-in-search-of-the-very-first-coded-symbols/.
16. Francisco Javier Murcia, 'Wine, Women, and Wisdom: The Symposia of Ancient Greece', *National Geographic*, Jan/Feb 2017, https://www.nationalgeographic.com/history/history-magazine/article/ancient-greece-symposium-dinner-party.
17. Claude Calame, *Choruses of Young Women in Ancient Greece: Their Morphology, Religious Role, and Social Function* (Lanham: Rowman & Littlefield, 1997), https://archive.org/details/chorusesofyoungwooocala/page/292/mode/2up.
18. *Poems of Sappho*, trans. Julia Dubnoff, University of Houston https://uh.edu/~cldue/texts/sappho.html.
19. Alessandra Battistelli, 'Introduction to Nüshu: The Secret Identity of Chinese Women,' Leiden University working paper (March 2016), https://www.researchgate.net/publication/317932693_Introduction_to_Nushu_The_Secret_Identity_of_Chinese_Women.
20. Chen Xiaorong, 'Nüshu: From Tears to Sunshine', UNESCO, 24 January 2018, https://www.unesco.org/en/articles/nushu-tears-sunshine-0.

NOTES

21. Ariadna Mañé, 'Nüshu, The Women-Only Language that Recorded a Hidden Perspective of History', European Guanxi, 8 Februrary 2023, https://www.europeanguanxi.com/post/nüshu-the-women-only-language-that-recorded-a-hidden-perspective-of-history.
22. Amjai Singh, 'Gold Ownership: Indian Women Hold 24,000 Tons, Representing 11% of the World's Gold', *Daily Guardian*, 29 December 2024, https://thedailyguardian.com/business/gold-ownership-indian-women-hold-24000-tons-representing-11-of-the-worlds-gold/.

2 THE QUEEN AND HER WIVES

1. Liz McGregor, 'Rain Queen's Heir Is Pawn in a Battle Royal,' *Guardian*, 14 October 2007, https://www.theguardian.com/world/2007/oct/14/southafrica.theobserver.
2. Paula Akpan, *When We Ruled: The Rise and Fall of Twelve African Queens and Warriors* (London: Trapeze, 2025).
3. Beth Greene, 'The Institution of Woman-Marriage in Africa: A Cross-Cultural Analysis', *Journal of African Cultural Studies* 11/1 (1998): 13–32, https://doi.org/10.2307/3773789.
4. Todd Sanders, 'Reflections on Two Sticks: Gender, Sexuality and Rainmaking,' *Cahiers d'Études Africaines* 42/166 (2002): 285–313, https://www.jstor.org/stable/4393208.
5. 'The Mandela Diaries: 25 May 1999', SABC News, https://www.youtube.com/watch?v=EpvQjAitrF8.
6. Department of Cooperative Governance and Traditional Affairs (CoGTA), Republic of South Africa, 'The Balobedu Queenship Recognised and Dignity Restored', 27 July 2016, https://www.cogta.gov.za/index.php/2016/07/27/the-balobedu-queenship-recognised-and-dignity-restored/.
7. The Presidency of the Republic of South Africa, 'President Ramaphosa Legally Recognises Her Majesty Queen Masalanabo Modjadji VII of the Balobedu Queenship', 13 December 2024, https://www.thepresidency.gov.za/president-ramaphosa-legally-recognises-her-majesty-queen-masalanabo-modjadji-vii-balobedu-queenship.

NOTES

8. 'Rain Queen Laid to Rest', News24, 20 June 2005. https://mg.co.za/article/2005-06-20-rain-queen-laid-to-rest/.
9. Kabelo O. Motasa and Lilly (S. J.) Nortjé-Meyer, 'Patriarchal Usurpation of the Modjadji Dynasty: A Gender-Critical Reading of the History and Reign of the Modjadji Rain Queens', Department of Religion Studies, University of Johannesburg (2021), https://ujcontent.uj.ac.za/esploro/outputs/journalArticle/Patriarchal-usurpation-of-the-Modjadji-dynasty/9912567407691.
10. Richard Bell, *Understanding African Philosophy: A Cross-Cultural Approach to Classic and Contemporary Issues* (New York and London: Routledge, 2002), p. 40.

3 HOUSE OF WOMEN

1. Edu Carvalho, 'Sobrinha-neta de primeira moradora da Maré faz vaquinha para ter casa própria', Maré Online, 18 February 2021, https://mareonline.com.br/sobrinha-neta-de-primeira-moradora-da-mare-faz-vaquinha-para-ter-casa-propria/.
2. Enrique Desmond Arias and Nicholas Barnes, 'The Logic of Criminal Territorial Control: Military Intervention in Rio de Janeiro', *Comparative Political Studies* 55/9 (August 2021), https://doi.org/ 0.1177/00104140211036035.
3. César Muñoz, 'Brazil Suffers Its Own Scourge of Police Brutality', Human Rights Watch, 3 June 2020, https://www.hrw.org/news/2020/06/03/brazil-suffers-its-own-scourge-police-brutality.
4. Oscar Williams, 'British Journalism Is 94% White and 55% Male, Survey Finds', *Guardian*, 24 March 2016, https://www.theguardian.com/media-network/2016/mar/24/british-journalism-diversity-white-female-male-survey.
5. Marcus Ryder, 'The Problem of Watching World News Through White Eyes Only', EachOther, 26 August 2020, https://eachother.org.uk/the-problem-of-watching-world-news-through-white-eyes-only/.
6. Nadine Terasa and Pauline Beaumont, '2019 Report Shows Rising Armed Violence in Complexo da Maré, Continued State Impunity', RioOnWatch, 19 February 2020, https://rioonwatch.org/?p=57860.

NOTES

7. Office of the High Commissioner for Human Rights, 'Brazil: UN Experts Urge New Government to Target Violence Against Women and Girls, Repeal Parental Alienation Law', 4 November 2022, https://www.ohchr.org/en/statements-and-speeches/2022/11/brazil-un-experts-urge-new-government-target-violence-against-women.
8. Daniel Mello, 'Brazil Records 10,600 Femicides in Eight Years', Agência Brasil, 8 March 2024, https://agenciabrasil.ebc.com.br/en/direitos-humanos/noticia/2024-03/brazil-records-10600-femicides-eight-years.
9. Leo Rodrigues, 'Homicides Rise Among Black Women and Drop Among Non-Black Women', *Brasil de Fato*, 11 December 2023, https://www.brasildefato.com.br/2023/12/11/homicides-rise-among-black-women-and-drop-among-non-black-women.
10. 'Half of Brazilian Women Living in London Have Experienced Gender-Based Violence', Queen Mary University of London, 15 March 2018, https://www.qmul.ac.uk/media/news/2018/pr/half-of-brazilian-women-living-in-london-have-experienced-gender-based-violence.html.

4 THE EVOLUTION OF WOMYN'S LANDS

1. Ashley Mateo and Kaitlin Menza, 'The Results of a 1976 Survey of Women About Sexual Harassment At Work Remain Virtually Unchanged In 2017', *Redbook*, 27 March 2017, https://www.redbookmag.com/life/money-career/a49220/sexual-harassment-in-the-workplace/.
2. Jaden Loo, 'Marriage: More Than a Century of Change, 1900–2022', National Center for Family & Marriage Research, Bowling Green State University, 2024, https://www.bgsu.edu/ncfmr/resources/data/family-profiles/FP-24-10.html.
3. Gabrielle Juteau, 'Marriage Rate in the U.S.: Geographic Variation, 2021', Bowling Green State University, 2022, https://www.bgsu.edu/ncfmr/resources/data/family-profiles/juteau-marriage-rate-US-geographic-variation-2021-fp-22-25.html.

4. 'Mrs. America: Women's Roles in the 1950s', PBS, https://www.pbs.org/wgbh/americanexperience/features/pill-mrs-america-womens-roles-1950s/.
5. Bethany Kaylor, 'Who Wants to Live on Women's Land?', *The Sunday Long Read*, 2 December 2023, https://sundaylongread.com/2023/12/02/who-wants-to-live-on-womens-land/.
6. Roy Reed, 'Back-to-Land Movement Seeks Self-Sufficiency,' *New York Times*, 9 June 1975, https://www.nytimes.com/1975/06/09/archives/backtoland-movement-seeks-selfsufficiency-the-growing-backtotheland.html.
7. Heather Jo Burmeister, 'Rural Revolution: Documenting the Lesbian Land Communities of Southern Oregon', Portland State University, Department of History, 6 December 2013, https://pdxscholar.library.pdx.edu/open_access_etds/1080/.
8. Sasha Archibald, 'On Wimmin's Land', *Places Journal*, February 2021, https://placesjournal.org/article/on-wimmins-land-the-heartland-of-lesbian-separatism/.
9. Cedar Heartwood, at Shewolf's memorial in 2020, https://www.youtube.com/watch?v=MJyx1IHkIcU&t=1584s.
10. Cedar Heartwood, 'Finding Women's Lands and Lesbian Communities', Southern Lesbian Feminist Activist Herstory Project, https://slfaherstoryproject.org/finding-womens-lands-and-lesbian-communities/.
11. 'The Combahee River Collective Statement', 1977, https://www.blackpast.org/african-american-history/combahee-river-collective-statement-1977/.
12. Michael T. Light, Jingying He, and Jason P. Robey, 'Comparing Crime Rates between Undocumented Immigrants, Legal Immigrants, and Native-Born US Citizens in Texas', Proc. Natl. Acad. Sci. U.S.A. 117/51 (2020): 32340-32347, https://doi.org/10.1073/pnas.2014704117.
13. Alex Nowrasteh, 'Illegal Immigrant Murderers in Texas, 2013–2022', Cato Institute, June 2026, https://www.cato.org/policy-analysis/illegal-immigrant-murderers-texas-2013-2022.
14. Larry Buchanan et al., 'Black Lives Matter May Be the Largest Movement in U.S. History', *New York Times*, 3 July 2020, https://

www.nytimes.com/interactive/2020/07/03/us/george-floyd-protests-crowd-size.html.
15. 'Redfin Reports Only 16% of Home Listings Were Affordable for the Typical Household in 2023', 21 December 2023, https://investors.redfin.com/news-events/press-releases/detail/1024/redfin-reports-only-16-of-home-listings-were-affordable; Veronika Bondarenko, 'The Housing Market Just Hit Its Most Grim Milestone Yet', The Street, 3 March 2023, https://www.thestreet.com/real-estate/how-many-affordable-houses-up-for-sale.
16. Abigail Johnson Hess, 'Here's How Much College Cost the Year You Were Born', CNBC, 4 September 2019, https://www.cnbc.com/2019/09/04/heres-how-much-college-cost-the-year-you-were-born.html.
17. Monique Villa, 'Women Own Less Than 20% of the World's Land. It's Time to Give Them Equal Property Rights', World Economic Forum, January 2017, https://www.weforum.org/stories/2017/01/women-own-less-than-20-of-the-worlds-land-its-time-to-give-them-equal-property-rights/.
18. Bina Agarwal, *A Field of One's Own: Gender and Land Rights in South Asia* (Cambridge: Cambridge University Press, 1994).
19. Economic Research Service, US Department of Agriculture, 'Population & Migration', 6 December 2025, https://www.ers.usda.gov/topics/rural-economy-population/population-migration.

5 OASIS OF FORGIVENESS

1. Youssra el-Sharkawy and Menna A. Farouk, 'Modern Amazons: The Egyptian Village Run by Women', *The New Humanitarian*, 3 October 2017, https://deeply.thenewhumanitarian.org/womensadvancement/articles/2017/10/03/modern-amazons-the-egyptian-village-run-by-women.
2. 'It Takes a Village in Egypt to Show Women's Heroism', *Arab Weekly*, 29 July 2018, https://thearabweekly.com/it-takes-village-egypt-show-womens-heroism.

3. 'Breaking Barriers: Boosting Women's Labor Force Participation in Egypt', World Bank, 12 March 2025, https://www.worldbank.org/en/news/feature/2025/03/12/breaking-barriers-boosting-women-s-labor-force-participation-in-egypt.
4. 'UK has the fastest fall in divorce rates across Europe', Marriage Foundation, 2 January 2020, https://marriagefoundation.org.uk/research/divorce-rates-are-falling-across-europe-and-the-uk-is-leading-the-way/.
5. 'Arabs Are Divorcing More Often', *The Economist*, 15 September 2022, https://www.economist.com/middle-east-and-africa/2022/09/15/arabs-are-divorcing-more-often.
6. Debbie Mohnblatt, 'Divorce Rates in the Arab World Are Increasing – Here's Why', The Media Line, 31 July 2021, https://themedialine.org/life-lines/divorce-rates-in-the-arab-world-are-increasing-heres-why/.
7. Mahmoud Hassan, 'Outrageously High Prices Raise Divorce and Violence Rates in Egypt', Middle East Monitor, 29 August 2023, https://www.middleeastmonitor.com/20230829-outrageously-high-prices-raise-divorce-and-violence-rates-in-egypt.
8. Simon Kemp, 'Digital 2025: Egypt', DataReportal, 3 March 2025, https://datareportal.com/reports/digital-2025-egypt; 'Egypt', Trading Economics, https://tradingeconomics.com/egypt/individuals-using-the-internet-percent-of-population-wb-data.html.
9. 'Divorced, but Not Free: Egypt's Personal Status Laws', Human Rights Watch, December 2004, https://www.hrw.org/reports/2004/egypt1204/5.htm.
10. 'Nubians – Marriage and Family', Everyculture.com, www.everyculture.com/Africa-Middle-East/Nubians-Marriage-and-Family.html.

6 VILLAGES FOR SINGLE WOMEN

1. Monique Villa, 'Women Own Less Than 20% of the World's Land. It's Time to Give Them Equal Property Rights', World Economic Forum, 11 January 2017, https://www.weforum.org/stories/2017/01/women-own-less-than-20-of-the-worlds-land-its-time-to-give-them-equal-property-rights/.

NOTES

2. Vincent Ng'ethe, 'Who owns land in Kenya? Unpacking what the KDHS 2022 data tells us about men and women's land ownership', Africa Data Hub, 11 September 2023, https://www.africadatahub.org/blog/gender-differences-in-land-ownership-kenya.
3. Kenya National Bureau of Statistics, *Kenya Demographic and Health Survey (KDHS) 2022: Key Indicators Report* (Nairobi, Kenya, and Rockville, MA: KNBS and ICF 2023), https://www.dhsprogram.com/pubs/pdf/PR143/PR143.pdf; UK Visas and Immigration, 'Country Policy and Information Note: Female Genital Mutilation (FGM), Kenya', April 2025 https://www.gov.uk/government/publications/kenya-country-policy-and-information-notes/country-policy-and-information-note-female-genital-mutilation-fgm-kenya-april-2025-accessible.
4. Kamau Maichuhie, 'Rebecca Lolosoli: Why I Ran Against My Husband for a Political Seat', *Daily Nation*, 18 September 2024, https://nation.africa/kenya/news/gender/rebecca-lolosoli-why-i-ran-against-my-husband-for-a-political-seat-4765468.
5. 'These Tablets Bring Information and Empowerment to Women in Rural Kenya', ONE.org, 15 December 2016, https://www.one.org/us/stories/these-tablets-bring-information-and-empowerment-to-women-in-rural-kenya/.
6. 'Kenya – Literacy Rate', Country Economy, https://countryeconomy.com/demography/literacy-rate/kenya.
7. Emmanuel Asher Ikwara et al., 'Prevalence and Factors Influencing Sexual Violence against Women Aged 15–49 in Kenya: Findings from the 2022 Kenya Demographic and Health Survey', *BMC Womens Health* 25/74 (February 2025), https://doi.org/10.1186/s12905-025-03593-7.
8. 'Kenya's growing call for more GBV shelters', UN Women, 21 June 2023, https://africa.unwomen.org/en/stories/feature-story/2023/06/kenyas-growing-call-for-more-gbv-shelters.
9. Generation Equality Forum, *Kenya's Roadmap for Advancing Gender Equality and Ending All Forms of Gender Based Violence and Female Genital Mutilation by 2026*, https://gender.go.ke/sites/default/files/publications/Generation-Equality-Forum_Kenya-Roadmap_Policy-Brief-COMMITMENTS.pdf.

NOTES

7 GIRLBOSS ISLAND – AND A CLUB FOR AFRICA'S ELITE

1. Anne Doquet, *Les masques dogon: ethnologie savante et ethnologie autochtone* (Paris: Karthala Editions, 1999).
2. '*Toguna*, Youssouf Dara, Paweł Althamer', 2011, https://park.artmuseum.pl/en/rzezby/toguna.
3. Amelia Gentleman, 'Garrick Club's Men-Only Members List a "Roll Call of British Establishment"', *Guardian*, 18 March 2024, https://www.theguardian.com/society/2024/mar/18/garrick-club-men-only-members-list-roll-call-british-establishment.
4. Amelia Gentleman, 'Judi Dench and Siân Phillips Become First Female Members of Garrick Club', *Guardian*, 1 July 2024, https://www.theguardian.com/uk-news/article/2024/jul/01/judi-dench-and-sian-phillips-become-first-female-members-of-garrick-club.
5. Finbar O'Mallon, '"Beyond belief": Elite Men's Club Votes No to Letting Women In', *Financial Review*, 15 June 2021, https://www.afr.com/politics/beyond-belief-elite-men-s-club-votes-no-to-letting-women-in-20210615-p5819n.
6. Nigel Jones, 'In Defence of Private Members' Clubs', *Spectator*, 19 March 2024, https://www.spectator.co.uk/article/in-defence-of-private-members-clubs/.
7. Stephanie Merritt, '*The Authority Gap* by Mary Ann Sieghart review – Mocked, Patronised and Still Paid Less Than Men', *Guardian*, 5 July 2021, https://www.theguardian.com/books/2021/jul/05/the-authority-gap-by-mary-ann-sicghart-review-why-women-are-still-taken-less-seriously-than-men-and-what-we-can-do-about-it.
8. European Commission, 'Which EU Regions Employ More Women in High-Tech?', *Eurostat*, 30 October 2023, https://ec.europa.eu/eurostat/web/products-eurostat-news/w/ddn-20231030-1.
9. 'Which EU Regions Employ More Women in High-Tech?', *Forbes*, 30 October 2023, https://www.forbes.com/pictures/mkl45elekd/8-kristina-roth-ceo-m/.
10. 'Jenni Murray, 'What Did Margaret Thatcher Do for Women?', *Guardian*, 9 April 2013, https://www.theguardian.com/politics/2013/apr/09/margaret-thatcher-women.

NOTES

11. Catherine A. Rottenberg, *The Rise of Neoliberal Feminism* (Oxford: Oxford University Press, 2018).
12. 'Amy Schumer & the Plague of White Feminism', *A Bit Fruity with Matt Bernstein* (podcast), 21 May 2024, https://open.spotify.com/episode/6Cakz0Le4ayh6bA1lAbCQy.
13. Ruth Wilkinson, 'International Women's Day: Seven Ways Women Changed the Face of the Last Decade', Global Justice Now, 5 March 2020, https://www.globaljustice.org.uk/blog/2020/03/international-womens-day-seven-ways-women-changed-face-last-decade/.
14. 'Jobs and Recovery Monitor – Gender and Pay', TUC, 8 March 2023, https://www.tuc.org.uk/research-analysis/reports/jobs-and-recovery-monitor-gender-and-pay.
15. Emily Field et al., *Women in the Workplace 2023* (McKinsey, 2023), https://www.mckinsey.com/featured-insights/diversity-and-inclusion/women-in-the-workplace-2023.
16. Rachel Thomas et al., *Women in the Workplace 2022* (McKinsey, 2022), https://www.mckinsey.com/~/media/mckinsey/featured%20insights/diversity%20and%20inclusion/women%20in%20the%20workplace%202022/women-in-the-workplace-2022.pdf.
17. Judith Woods, 'Jacinda Ardern Has Shown How Hard It Is Being a Woman in a World Built for Men by Men', *Telegraph*, 19 January 2023, https://www.telegraph.co.uk/columnists/2023/01/19/new-zealand-prime-minister-jacinda-ardern-has-helped-women-honest/.
18. Frenchie Ferenczi, 'I Was a Director at The Wing. I Made Some Big Mistakes', *Independent*, September 2, 2022, https://www.independent.co.uk/voices/the-wing-startup-director-mistakes-b2158714.html.
19. Julie Gerstein, 'Gone Girl(boss)', *Business Insider*, 31 August 2022, https://www.businessinsider.nl/gone-girlboss-troubled-co-working-space-the-wing-announced-its-shutting-down-but-all-anybody-cares-about-is-what-will-happen-to-its-furniture/.
20. Liam Bailey and Patrick Gower, *The Knight Frank Guide to Private Members' Clubs* (Knight Frank, 2024), https://content.knightfrank.com/research/2894/documents/en/a-guide-to-private-members-clubs-2024-11541.pdf.
21. RLA Global, 'Profiting from the Rise of Private Members' Clubs', November 2023, https://rlaglobal.com/en/insights/profiting-from-the-rise-of-private-members-clubs.

22. 'Minimum Wage – Nigeria', WageIndicator.org, https://wageindicator.org/salary/minimum-wage/Nigeria.
23. University of California Los Angeles, 'UCLA Researchers Identify Key Biobehavioral Pattern Used By Women To Manage Stress', *Science Daily*, 22 May 2000, https://www.sciencedaily.com/releases/2000/05/000522082151.htm.
24. Jennifer Watling Neal, 'Exploring Empowerment in Settings: Mapping Distributions of Network Power', *American Journal of Community Psychology* 53/3–4 (9 November 2013): 394–406, https://doi.org/10.1007/s10464-013-9609-z.
25. Mayra Guerrero et al., 'Women's Friendships: A Basis for Individual-Level Resources and Their Connection to Power and Optimism', *Humanist Psychology* 50/3 (September 2022): 360–375, https://doi.org/ 10.1037/hum0000295.
26. Dr Kerryn Baker and Dr Theresa Meki, 'One Step Forward, Two Steps Back: Women's Political Representation in the Pacific', *Australian Institute of International Affairs*, 17 October 2023, https://www.internationalaffairs.org.au/australianoutlook/one-step-forward-two-steps-back-womens-political-representation-in-the-pacific/.
27. Megha Mohan, 'The "Gals" Behind Samoa's First Woman PM', BBC News, 8 December 2021, https://www.bbc.co.uk/news/world-asia-59569649.

8 THE TROLL FEMINISM OF MEGALIA

1. Chulwoo Park, 'MERS-CoV Infection in South Korea and Strategies for Possible Future Outbreak: Narrative Review', *Journal of Global Health Reports* 3 (March 2022), https://doi.org/10.29392/joghr.3.e2019088.
2. Yong-Shik Park et al., 'The First Case of the 2015 Korean Middle East Respiratory Syndrome Outbreak', *Epidemiology and Health* 37 (14 November 2015), https://doi.org/10.4178/epih/e2015049.
3. Danny Lee and Jennifer Ngo, 'Punish Travellers Who Lie About Their Health, SARS Expert Urges', *South China Morning Post*, 30 May 2015, https://www.scmp.com/news/hong-kong/health-environment/article/1813158/two-south-koreans-who-refused-mers-quarantine.

NOTES

4. Victoria Kim, 'What's Size Got to Do with It? Mocking a Man's Manhood Spurs a Reverse #MeToo in South Korea', *Los Angeles Times*, 11 June 2021, https://www.latimes.com/world-nation/story/2021-06-11/whats-size-got-to-do-with-it-the-pinching-hand-anti-feminist-backlash-drive-up-the-fever-pitch-of-south-koreas-gender-wars.
5. 'Escaping Gender-Based Violence', World Bank, 18 December 2022, https://genderdata.worldbank.org/en/data-stories/seeking-help-for-gender-based-violence#.
6. Yae Ahn Park, 'The Overdue Abolishment of Hojuje', Columbia Law paper, https://moglen.law.columbia.edu/twiki/bin/view/LawContempSoc/YaeAhnPark-SecondPaper.
7. Vik Jaitly, 'The Legality of "Kye" Loans in Korean Immigrant Communities', *National Law Review*, 17 October 2014, https://natlawreview.com/article/legality-kye-loans-korean-immigrant-communities.
8. Lee Hyo-jin, 'No Men Allowed: Women-Only Spaces Increasing in Korea', *Korea Times*, 22 September 2022, https://www.koreatimes.co.kr/amp/learningenglish/national/20220922/no-men-allowed-women-only-spaces-increasing-in-korea.
9. Jung-yoon Choi, 'Seoul to Bring Back Women-Only Subway Cars', *Los Angeles Times*, 17 August 2011, https://www.latimes.com/nation/la-xpm-2011-aug-17-la-fg-south-korea-subway-20110817-story.html.
10. Bae Ji-sook, 'Groping Rises on Metro', *Korea Times*, 2 August 2009, https://www.koreatimes.co.kr/southkorea/20090802/groping-rises-on-metro.
11. Laura Bicker, '"I Was Humiliated": The Continuing Trauma of South Korea's Spy Cam Victims', BBC News, 16 June 2021, https://www.bbc.co.uk/news/world-asia-57493020.
12. Sonal Shah, 'Women-Only Transport: A "Solution" To What End?', *Sustainable Transport Journal* 30 (December 2018), https://itdp.org/wp-content/uploads/2019/01/Women-only-Transport.pdf.
13. Justin McCurry. 'Women-Only Carriages Halt Tokyo Gropers', *Guardian*, 10 May 2005, https://www.theguardian.com/world/2005/may/10/japan.justinmccurry.

14. Emma Graham-Harrison, 'Women-Only Carriages Around the World: Do They Work?' *Guardian*, 26 August 2015, https://www.theguardian.com/world/2015/aug/26/women-only-train-carriages-around-the-world-jeremy-corbyn.
15. Jean Mackenzie, 'Seoul Removes Women-Only Parking Spaces in Gender Policy Reversal', BBC News, 16 February 2023, https://www.bbc.co.uk/news/world-asia-64659861.
16. Owen Galea, 'Seoul: Authorities to Remove Parking Spaces Reserved Solely for Women', TVM News, 16 February 2023, https://tvmnews.mt/en/news/seoul-authorities-to-remove-parking-spaces-reserved-solely-for-women/.
17. Whan-woo Yi, 'Women-Only Library Violates Human Rights', *Korea Times*, 7 February 2012, https://www.koreatimes.co.kr/www/nation/2025/02/113_104351.html.
18. International Monetary Fund, 'Press Information Notice: IMF Concludes Article IV Consultation with Korea', 19 June 1998 https://www.imf.org/en/News/Articles/2015/09/28/04/53/pn9839.
19. Se-IL Park, 'The Labor Market Policy and Social Safety Net in Korea: After the 1997 Crisis', Brookings Institute, 1 September 1999, https://www.brookings.edu/articles/the-labor-market-policy-and-social-safety-net-in-korea-after-the-1997-crisis.
20. Charlie Turner and Elizabeth Monk-Turner, 'Earnings Differences in the South Korean Labor Market: Decomposing the Gender Wage Gap, 1988–98', 2006, https://www.researchgate.net/publication/277773325_Earnings_Differences_in_the_South_Korean_Labor_Market_Decomposing_the_Gender_Wage_Gap_1988-98.
21. Jae-Ho Keum and Jayoung Yoon, *Changes in the Female Labor Market After the Financial Crisis and Policy Issues* (Korea Labor Institute, 31 March 2011).
22. Choi In-hyuk, 'Korea Achieved the Impossible Within 20 Years', *Korea Times*, 18 August 2010, https://www.koreatimes.co.kr/economy/others/20100818/korea-achieved-the-impossible-within-20-years.

23. Nina Jobst, 'South Korea: Internet Penetration 2000-2023', Statista, 6 November 2024, https://www.statista.com/statistics/255859/internet-penetration-in-south-korea/.
24. Claire Lee, 'Misogyny in Korean Online Communities a Serious Concern: Report', *Korea Herald*, 31 July 2018, https://m.koreaherald.com/article/1739355.
25. Kelly Kasulis, 'Inside Ilbe: How South Korea's Angry Young Men Formed a Powerful New Alt-Right Movement', *Mic*, 18 September 2017, https://www.mic.com/articles/184477/inside-ilbe-how-south-koreas-angry-young-men-formed-a-powerful-new-alt-right-movement.
26. 4chan.org, https://www.4chan.org/advertise.
27. Jinsook Kim, 'Misogyny for Male Solidarity: Online Hate Discourse Against Women in South Korea', in J. Vickery and T. Everbach (eds), *Mediating Misogyny* (New York: Palgrave Macmillan, 2018), https://doi.org/10.1007/978-3-319-72917-6_8.
28. Claire Lee, 'Misogyny in Korean Online Communities a Serious Concern: Report', *Korea Herald*, 31 July 2008, https://www.koreaherald.com/article/1739355.
29. Euisol Jeong, 'Troll Feminism: The Rise of Popular Feminism in South Korea', University of York PhD thesis, 2020, https://etheses.whiterose.ac.uk/id/eprint/28959/.
30. 'South Korea Porn: Co-Founder of the Soranet Site Jailed', BBC News, 9 January 2019, https://www.bbc.com/news/world-asia-46810775.
31. '"Because I Want to Eat Clean X . . .": Controversy Over Pedophile Writings by Former Kindergarten Teacher', Naver News, 29 December 2015, https://n.news.naver.com/mnews/article/119/0002112413.
32. 'Megalian Kindergarten Teacher "I Want to Work with Children" Controversy', *Financial News*, 28 December 2015, https://www.fnnews.com/news/201512281443223082.
33. 'Given Courage Through "MeToo". . . : 23% Increase in Sexual Violence Consultations with Korea Women's Hotline', *Yonhap News*, 8 March 2018, https://www.yna.co.kr/view/AKR20180308041600005.

NOTES

34. Farz Edraki, 'Escape the Corset: The Simmering Feminist Revolution in South Korea', ABC Radio National, 19 December 2019, https://www.abc.net.au/news/2019-12-20/south-korean-women-escape-the-corset/11611180.
35. Jean Mackenzie, 'As South Korea Abolishes Its Gender Ministry, Women Fight Back', BBC News, 14 December 2022, https://www.bbc.co.uk/news/world-asia-63905490.
36. Yoon Ja-young, 'One in Three Seoulites Have Sexless Life: Study', *Korea Times*, 6 July 2021, https://www.koreatimes.co.kr/southkorea/health/20210706/one-in-three-seoulites-have-sexless-life-study.
37. Yoonjung Seo and Julia Hollingsworth, 'How Feminism Became a Hot Topic in South Korea's Presidential Election', CNN, 8 March 2022, https://edition.cnn.com/2022/03/08/asia/south-korea-election-young-people-intl-hnk-dst.
38. Park So-eun, 'Limbus Company Feminism Controversy, Star Rating Terror . . . Illustrator Fired', 27 July 2023, https://www.news1.kr/it-science/game-review/5121577.
39. L. Yoon, 'Share of Women in the National Assembly South Korea 2005–2025', Statista, 29 April 2025, https://www.statista.com/statistics/641688/south-korea-female-national-assembly-member/.

9 THE BABAYAGAS AND NEW GROUND: CO-LIVING IN ELDERHOOD

1. 'Unleashing the Economic Potential of Older Women', AARP International, October 2022, https://www.aarpinternational.org/resources/unleashing-the-economic-potential-of-older-women.
2. Saloni Dattani and Lucas Rodés-Guirao, 'Why Do Women Live Longer Than Men?' 27 November 2023, https://ourworldindata.org/why-do-women-live-longer-than-men.
3. International Labour Organization, *Global Wage Report 2018/19: What Lies Behind Gender Pay Gaps* (Geneva: ILO, 2019), https://www.ilo.org/sites/default/files/wcmsp5/groups/public/@dgreports/@dcomm/@publ/documents/publication/wcms_650553.pdf.

NOTES

4. The Geneva Association, *The Pension Gap Epidemic*, October 2016, https://www.genevaassociation.org/sites/default/files/research-topics-document-type/pdf_public/pensions_epidemic_summary_final.pdf.
5. Miguel Requena, David Reher, Mojgan Padyab, and Glenn Sandström, 'Women Living Alone in Later Life: A Multicountry Comparative Analysis', *Population, Space and Place* 25/7 (October 2019), https://doi.org/10.1002/psp.2269.
6. Dr Vivek H. Murthy, *Our Epidemic of Loneliness and Isolation: The US Surgeon General's Advisory on the Healing Effects of Social Connection and Community* (US Department of Health and Human Services, 2023), https://www.hhs.gov/sites/default/files/surgeon-general-social-connection-advisory.pdf.
7. 'Cohousing in the UK and Worldwide', UK Cohousing, https://cohousing.org.uk/cohousing-in-the-uk-and-worldwide/.
8. Washington Commons, 'What Is Cohousing?', https://www.washington-commons.org/what-is-cohousing.html.
9. Peter Burke, 'Living in Intentional Communities: Exploring Cohousing', A Fairer Society, 29 June 2023, https://afairersociety.com/living-in-intentional-communities-cohousing.
10. Anne Solaz, 'More Frequent Separation and Repartnering among People Aged 50 and Over', *Population & Societies* 586 (February 2021), https://www.ined.fr/fichier/s_rubrique/31128/586.couple.50years.population.societies.february.2021.en.pdf.
11. Edith M. Lederer, 'UN Report: By 2030 Two-Thirds of World Will Live in Cities', AP News, 18 May 2016, https://apnews.com/general-news-40b530ac84ab4931874e1f7efb4f1a22; OECD, *Ageing in Cities* (Paris: OECD Publishing, 2015), https://www.oecd.org/content/dam/oecd/en/publications/reports/2015/04/ageing-in-cities_g1g51d27/9789264231160-en.pdf.
12. Office of the Surgeon General, *Our Epidemic of Loneliness and Isolation: The U.S. Surgeon General's Advisory on the Healing Effects of Social Connection and Community* (Office of the Surgeon General, 2023), https://www.hhs.gov/sites/default/files/surgeon-general-social-connection-advisory.pdf.

13. Pascal Mannaerts, 'The Widows Who Can't Return Home', BBC Travel, 13 September 2016, https://www.bbc.co.uk/travel/article/20160907-the-widows-who-cant-return-home.

10 THE NAIR THARAVAD: FOUR CORNERS FOR WOMEN

1. Shadab Nazmi, 'NFHS-5: India's Preference for Sons Over Daughters Remains', BBC News, 17 May 2022, https://www.bbc.co.uk/news/world-asia-india-61462052.
2. K. M. Panikkar, 'Some Aspects of Nayar Life', *Journal of the Royal Anthropological Institute of Great Britain and Ireland* 48 (July 1918): 254–293, https://ia902905.us.archive.org/28/items/SomeAspectsOfNayarLife/SomeAspectsOfNayarLifeCopy.pdf.
3. Akshay Shankar, 'On the Nair Community of Kerala and Their Sambandham System', 21 August 2020, https://www.indiafacts.org.in/on-the-nair-community-of-kerala-and-their-sambandham-system/.
4. 'Nalukettu – The Heart of a Tharavad', *Archipasta*, 2 September 2020, https://archipasta.com/archipasta/.
5. Inderjeet Singh, 'High Literacy Rate States in India', 14 April 2024, India Inputs, https://www.indiainputs.com/high-literacy-rate-states-in-india/1297/.
6. Benny Kuriakose, 'Paliam Nalukettu: A Glimpse into a Matrilineal Society', 20 April 2023, https://www.bennykuriakose.com/post/paliam-nalukettu-a-glimpse-into-a-matrilineal-society.
7. Sivakumar Narayana Kurup, *Know the Nairs More* (Kindle edition, December 2021).
8. Lekha N.B. and Antony Palackal, *Unveiling the Gender Paradox: Dynamics of Power, Sexuality and Property in Kerala* (Springer Nature, 2022).
9. Praveena Kodoth, *Framing Custom, Directing Practices: Authority, Property and Matriliny under Colonial Law in Nineteenth Century Malabar*, working paper 338 (Thiruvananthapuram: Centre for Development Studies, January 2002), https://www.researchgate.net/publication/5127074_Framing_custom_directing_practices_Authority_property_and_matriliny_under_colonial_law_in_nineteenth_century_Malabar.

10. E. Kathleen Gough, 'The Nayars and the Definition of Marriage', *Journal of the Royal Anthropological Institute of Great Britain and Ireland* 89/1 (1959): 23–34, https://www.jstor.org/stable/2844434.
11. P. V. Balakrishnan, *Matrilineal System in Malabar* (CBH Publications, 1981).
12. S. R. Saumya Raj, 'Nair Service Society and the Emancipation of Taravad Women', January 2016, https://doi.org/10.5281/zenodo.179040.

11 LESSONS OF HERLANDS

1. Eve Kosofsky Sedgwick, *Between Men: English Literature and Male Homosocial Desire* (New York: Columbia University Press, 1985).
2. bell hooks, 'Choosing the Margin as a Space of Radical Openness', *Framework: The Journal of Cinema and Media* 36 (1989): 15–23, https://www.jstor.org/stable/44111660.
3. UN Women, 'UN Women Supported Survey in Delhi Shows 95 Per Cent of Women and Girls Feel Unsafe in Public Spaces', 20 February 2013, https://www.unwomen.org/en/news/stories/2013/2/un-women-supported-survey-in-delhi.
4. 'India Outrage After Woman Politician Blames Women for Rape', BBC News, 29 January 2014, https://www.bbc.co.uk/news/world-asia-india-25940583.
5. 'Just 11.75% Women in Police Forces in Country: Govt Informs Parliament', *Business Standard*, 5 December 2023, https://www.business-standard.com/india-news/just-11-75-women-in-police-forces-in-country-govt-informs-parliament-123120500793_1.html.
6. Elizaveta Perova and Sarah Anne Reynolds, 'Women's Police Stations and Intimate Partner Violence: Evidence from Brazil', *Social Science & Medicine* 174 (February 2017): 188–196, https://doi.org/10.1016/j.socscimed.2016.12.008.
7. Mark Brown, 'New Tate Modern Switch House: More Women and International Macaws', *Guardian*, 14 June 2016, https://www.theguardian.com/artanddesign/2016/jun/14/new-tate-modern-switch-house-more-women-international-macaws.
8. Celia Walden, 'The Tate Modern "Women's Room" Is Patronising Nonsense Dressed Up As Gender Equality', *Telegraph*, 15 January

2016, https://www.telegraph.co.uk/women/life/the-tate-modern-womens-room-is-patronising-nonsense-dressed-up-a/.
9. Harriet Baskas, 'Women-Only Hotel Floor Ruled Illegal and Discriminatory', CNBC, 30 April 2014, https://www.cnbc.com/2014/04/30/women-only-hotel-floor-ruled-illegal-discriminatory.html.
10. Lee Rowley and The Rt Hon Kemi Badenoch MP, 'Government to lay new law to halt the march of gender-neutral toilets in buildings', Department for Levelling Up, Housing and Communities, 6 May 2024, https://www.gov.uk/government/news/government-to-lay-new-law-to-halt-the-march-of-gender-neutral-toilets-in-buildings.
11. Eleanor Lawrie, 'What Are the Parties Saying About Women's Rights and Gender Identity?', BBC News, 29 June 2024, https://www.bbc.co.uk/news/articles/c4nng2j42xro.
12. PRB, 'Around the Globe, Women Outlive Men', Population Reference Bureau, 1 September 2001, https://www.prb.org/resources/around-the-globe-women-outlive-men/.
13. S. Galan, 'Global Female Life Expectancy in 2023 with a Forecast for 2050, by Region', Statista, 23 January 2025, https://www.statista.com/statistics/1359994/projected-global-life-expectancy-female/.
14. Isabel Webb Carey and Conrad Hackett, 'Global Population Skews Male, but UN Projects Parity Between Sexes by 2050', Pew Research Center, 31 August 2022, https://www.pewresearch.org/global/2022/08/31/global-population-skews-male-but-un-projects-parity-between-sexes-by-2050/.
15. 'Rise of the SHEconomy', Morgan Stanley, 23 September 2019, https://www.morganstanley.com/ideas/womens-impact-on-the-economy.
16. 'Catalonia's First Feminist Housing Cooperative Opens in Barcelona', *Catalan News*, 29 October 2024, https://www.catalannews.com/society-science/item/catalonias-first-feminist-housing-cooperative-opens-in-barcelona.
17. 'Saudi Arabia plans string of women-only industrial cities', *Global Construction Review*, 13 August 2014, https://

www.globalconstructionreview.com/saudi-arabia-plans-string-women-only73635355353333.
18. Sushmita Pathak, '"Pink parks": Delhi's Bid to Build Safer City for Women Sparks Debate', *Christian Science Monitor*, 27 September 2023, https://www.csmonitor.com/World/Asia-South-Central/2023/0725/Pink-parks-Delhi-s-bid-to-build-safer-city-for-women-sparks-debate.
19. Amritha Mohan, 'A Ground of Her Own: How a Retired Policewoman Built a Playground for Women in Kerala', *The News Minute*, 3 January 2025, https://www.thenewsminute.com/kerala/a-ground-of-her-own-how-a-retired-policewoman-built-a-playground-for-women-in-kerala.
20. Rea Savla, 'The Fake Liberation: Dissecting the Impact of Saudi Arabia's All-Women Cities', *Berkeley Political Review*, 12 January 2016, https://bpr.studentorg.berkeley.edu/2016/01/12/the-fake-liberation-dissecting-the-impact-of-saudi-arabias-all-women-cities/.
21. Minglu Chen, 'Where Are the Women in Chinese Politics?', East Asia Forum, 25 May 2023, https://eastasiaforum.org/2023/05/25/where-are-the-women-in-chinese-politics/.
22. Richard Wike, Moira Fagan and Laura Clancy, 'Global Elections in 2024: What We Learned in a Year of Political Disruption', Pew Research Center, 11 December 2024, https://www.pewresearch.org/global/2024/12/11/global-elections-in-2024-what-we-learned-in-a-year-of-political-disruption/.

About the Author

Megha Mohan became the BBC's first global gender and identity correspondent in 2018, covering women's rights, LGBT communities, race and ethnicity for the BBC's language services worldwide. She has investigated the black market for abortion pills in Honduras, the multi-billion dollar global love-coaching industry, and gender roles in North Korea's army – a report that ranked among Chartbeat's 100 most-read articles in the world. Mohan was named in Progress 1000's list of most influential storytellers, and she consulted on Level Up's media guidelines on how to sensitively report on domestic violence. She is also the co-founder of Second Source, a network of women journalists from underrepresented backgrounds.